The Moundbuilders

George R. Milner

The Moundbuilders: Ancient Societies of Eastern North America

2nd Edition

158 illustrations

Contents

The Moundbuilders © 2004 and © 2021
Thames & Hudson Ltd, London

Text and original illustrations © 2021
George R. Milner

Designed by Mark Bracey

First published in 2004 in the United States
of America as *The Moundbuilders* by
Thames & Hudson Inc., 500 Fifth Avenue,
New York, New York 10110

This Second Edition 2021

Library of Congress Control Number
2020932027

ISBN 978-0-500-29511-3

Printed in China by Shanghai Offset
Printing Products Limited

Preface

Who built the numerous earthen mounds in eastern North America? Two centuries ago, many thought they were the work of a mysterious people who had nothing to do with Native Americans, who were then being pushed ever westward by inexorable waves of immigrants, mainly from Europe. The reality is, however, that the mounds dotting the land were built by Native American ancestors, whose descendants remain in the United States and Canada.

This book examines the deep history of eastern North America. Its focus is, for the most part, on the two millennia preceding the arrival of Europeans and on the places where mounds are most abundant. The Midwest as far south as Kentucky receives the greatest attention simply because that is where I have conducted field-work. While there is much more about eastern North America's past that could be covered, the mound-building societies serve as a fine introduction to the remarkable achievements and rich cultural heritage of the land's original inhabitants.

This edition of *The Moundbuilders* has been revised to reflect new findings about the people who once occupied eastern North America. It includes, in Chapter 2, updated research on the peopling of the Americas, which is increasingly being supplemented

Cahokia-Temple Mound, near East St. Louis, Ill.
The largest pyramid in the world, 1080 feet long, 780 feet wide. 102 feet high. Erected by hand over 2,000 years ago, at a time when all appliances were crude and by a class of people whose life was dedicated to the most rigorous religious observances and pursuits.

Figure 1 Monks Mound at Cahokia, Illinois, is shown on this early twentieth-century postcard. Today the mound is preserved in a park.

by the findings of studies of ancient and modern DNA. More detail, including recent discoveries, has been added to the coverage of Middle and Late Archaic societies up to those of the sixteenth century CE when Europeans first established a permanent presence in North America (Chapter 3 onward). Among the topics that receive greater attention are long-occupied Middle to Late Archaic sites, the transition to agriculture, variation over time in the intensity of warfare, and Mississippian beliefs. Chapter 8, which covers post-contact-period Native Americans who were facing a time of great change, including population decline and movement, has been expanded. The effects of being swept up into the political and economic aims of European powers get a lengthier treatment, as does the introduction of new plants, animals, and pathogens.

The broad geographical coverage and temporal scope of this book mean that emphasis must be placed on the general characteristics of life at different points in time. Where the evidence is available, however, certain individuals are discussed to put a human face on what might otherwise simply be a dry account of archaeological materials. Because the focus is on life in the past, the multitude of names for, for example, various kinds of pottery and projectile points are avoided, as are those for the local cultural units that, taken together, make up lengthy regional sequences.[1]

Evidence Gathering

The chronological ordering of sites has advanced greatly since the mid-twentieth century when radiocarbon dating was developed. Conventional radiocarbon dates are not the same as calendar years estimated by calibrated radiocarbon dates. Adjustments to radiocarbon dates are needed because changes have occurred over time in the isotopic composition of atmospheric carbon. Discrepancies between radiocarbon and calendar dates are generally greater the further one goes back in time. In this book, dates for the early occupation of eastern North America, from Paleoindian through the Early Archaic period, are given in approximate calendar years after radiocarbon dates were calibrated using the OxCal 3.4 program. Calibrated dates facilitate comparisons with climatic events that are an especially important part of the story for the initial occupation of the Americas. Dates for later culture periods—from the Middle Archaic onward—come from a bewildering array of radiocarbon dates adjusted in various ways, or not at all. They are the ones customarily used by archaeologists. That is not a great problem in this book because the beginning and ending of these cultural periods are reasonably close approximations of calendar years. There is, in fact, variation from one place to the next in the timing of the cultural developments discussed here, often on the order of centuries. The objective here is to provide an overall feel for cultural change that occurred across a vast area over an immense period of time, so dates finely tuned to local cultural developments are unnecessary.

Artifacts and architectural remnants do not speak for themselves. Interpretations of archaeological materials that have the strongest evidentiary support from regional surveys, site excavations, and laboratory analyses are emphasized in this book. Assessments of these archaeological data are augmented by a comparative

Conventional Dates	Calendar Dates	Cultural Periods	Sites
		Various Late Prehistoric [Chap. 7]	*Spiro*
			Moundville
1000 CE	1000 CE		*Cahokia*
		Mississippian [Chap. 6]	*Toltec*
1 CE		Late Woodland [Chap. 5]	*Mound City, Hopewell*
			Robbins
		Middle Woodland [Chap. 4]	
1000 BCE	1000 BCE	Early Woodland [Chap. 4]	*Poverty Point*
2000 BCE			
	3000 BCE	Late Archaic [Chap. 3]	
3000 BCE			*Watson Brake*
			Read, Black Earth
4000 BCE	5000 BCE		
		Middle Archaic [Chap. 3]	
5000 BCE			
6000 BCE	7000 BCE		
7000 BCE		Early Archaic [Chap. 2]	
	9000 BCE		
8000 BCE			
		Paleoindian [Chap. 2]	
9000 BCE	11,000 BCE		*Kimmswick*
		The solid lines indicate dates used in this book.	
		●●●●●● The dotted lines show some of the variation in dating cultural periods that exists in the archaeological literature.	
10,000 BCE			

perspective based on an eclectic mix of ethnographic and historical information about roughly comparable societies from around the world. They include groups that faced similar opportunities and constraints related to their environmental settings, demographic footprint, and capacity to produce, store, and distribute food along with the other necessities of life. In short, I present in this book what I regard as being the most valid inferences from available evidence.

Acknowledgments

The two editions of this book could not have been completed without the help of many people. Several colleagues—David G. Anderson, Rebecca Ferrell, Richard W. Jefferies, Claire McHale Milner, Lee A. Newsom, Michael Shott, Dean R. Snow, and Michael D. Wiant—provided insightful comments on some, or all, of the first edition. Scott W. Hammerstedt and Timothy M. Murtha prepared maps, and Judy Cooper and Megaera Lorenz drew several figures specifically for this book.

I should also like to thank the scholars who reviewed this new edition of *The Moundbuilders* for their many helpful observations. These are: Constance Arzigian, David Carballo, Gabriel Hrynick, Christopher Moore, Brian Redmond, and Victor Thompson.

Many people answered questions and directed me to source material; provided illustrations, including their own photographs; or looked through museum collections and archives for potential illustrations. They include, among others, David G. Anderson, Jennifer Barber, Robin Beck, Scott Beld, Robert L. Brooks, James A. Brown, Brian M. Butler, Christopher Carr, Robert A. Cook, Frank Cowan, George M. Crothers, Claudia Cummings, Richard A. Diehl, Ann M. Early, Kenneth B. Farnsworth, Shannon Fie, Russell Graham, N'omi Greber, William Green, David Hally, Judy Hamilton, Scott W. Hammerstedt, Nancy Hawkins, A. Gwynn Henderson, Keith P. Jacobi, Richard W. Jefferies, Duryea Kemp, William H. Marquardt, Nicolette Meister, Jerald T. Milanich, Jeffrey M. Mitchem, Steven Nash, Lee A. Newsom, David Pollack, Robert Riordan, Michael Russo, Martha A. Rolingson, Joe Saunders, Sissel Schroeder, Bruce D. Smith, Dean R. Snow, Vincas P. Steponaitis, Lynne P. Sullivan, David H. Thomas, Michael D. Wiant, and Randolph J. Widmer. I could not use all of the material and insights they so generously provided, but the resulting book is richer for it. An immense debt of gratitude is also owed to the innumerable people, extending back to the nineteenth century, who took part in field projects and have maintained museum collections. The guidance of my Thames & Hudson editors, first Colin Ridler and later Mark Sapwell, as well as George Maudsley, helped immeasurably to transform academic writing into something more readable.

Left Chronological Table: Precisely when major cultural periods began and ended is debated, and new means of calibrating radiocarbon dates will continue to result in revisions of our understanding of when particular cultural developments took place.

My late parents, George R. and Norah L. Milner Jr., long ago encouraged me to pursue my dream of learning about the past and, more recently, inspired me to write the first edition. I cannot thank my wife, Claire, and son, Hugh, enough for putting up with the inconveniences in life that writing a book brings about. Their understanding and support made this project possible.

George R. Milner
2020

Chapter 1

A Heavily Forested and Thinly Peopled Land

It is hard to imagine eastern North America thickly blanketed by old-growth forest when today plowed fields and urban sprawl cover much of the land. It is equally difficult to envision what life was like at that time. To do so, we must turn to archaeology as the primary source of information for most of the lengthy human occupation of the continent.

The Eastern Woodlands

Several hundred years ago, a dense forest was broken only by the highest peaks of the Appalachian Mountains, grasslands of various sizes, and impermanent clearings for villages and gardens. The forest extended from the Gulf Coast northward to the arctic tundra, and from the Atlantic Ocean westward until it met vast rolling prairies [**Figure 2**, see p. 12]. Its western border extended from western Minnesota southeastward into the once-glaciated part of Illinois north of the Shawnee Hills. Here a tall-grass prairie pushed deep into the Eastern Woodlands, forming the Prairie Peninsula. This prairie—grasses and herbaceous plants maintained by frequent fires, some caused by humans—was itself laced by narrow woodlands flanking streams of various sizes. Its southern margin extended westward from southern Illinois into central Missouri. From there, the forest and prairie transition headed southward, passing through eastern Oklahoma into Texas.

The forest and the animals that lived in it varied greatly from one place to another. Woods rich in pines covered the Gulf and south Atlantic coastal plains where winters were mild, summers hot, and rainfall plentiful. To the north was a vast deciduous forest that differed in composition depending on temperature and moisture, although several types of oaks were dominant. Eventually, it gave way to a mix of deciduous and coniferous trees that stretched from the northern Great Lakes through Ontario, New York, and into New England. Even farther north, boreal forest conifers were replaced by barren tundra. Latitude, however, was not the entire story. The high peaks and plateaus of the Appalachians influenced plant and animal distributions, as did proximity to large bodies of water, notably the Great Lakes and Atlantic Ocean.

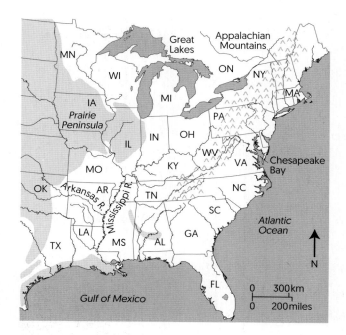

Figure 2 Eastern North America showing state boundaries along with some of the principal rivers, mountains, and prairies.

No matter how untamed the forest might have seemed to the first European explorers, it was no pristine wilderness untouched by human hands.[1] For millennia, land had been cleared for settlements and gardens by girdling trees and lighting fires. So much underbrush was consumed by fires that early European travelers could easily make their way through forests that in later centuries were all but impassable, such as the thick tangle that so impeded troops during the Civil War's Wilderness campaign in Virginia. Burning, intentional or not, increased browse for deer and created settings suitable for many other animals and edible plants.

Even the very composition of the eastern forest was changed by many centuries of settlement.[2] Eighteenth- and nineteenth-century CE land records show that several tree species were more common near long-abandoned Native American villages than they were elsewhere, but the reverse was true for other trees. Such differences were related to the tolerance of different tree species to clearing activities that included burning large areas, as well as the selection or avoidance of certain trees when acquiring wood for building and cooking purposes. Valuable trees included hickories, an important source of nuts, which were overrepresented near former Susquehanna settlements in southeastern Pennsylvania.

Living in a Heavily Forested Land

The mix of useful plants and animals varied from one place to another, as did their number and reliability. During the last half millennium before the arrival of Europeans, many native groups relied heavily on maize and, later, beans, both originally from Mesoamerica. Maize, an especially important crop, could be depended upon where there were more than about 140 frost-free days during the growing season.[3]

The northern limits of this area extended through southern Minnesota, Wisconsin, Michigan, and Ontario, and then into New England.

In the continental interior, the best places to live tended to be river valleys [**Figure 3**]. Many different plants and animals could be found as one went from river margins, through wet floodplains, to the surrounding drier uplands. People everywhere sought out white-tailed deer for their meat and hides, although the dietary contribution of venison lessened late in prehistory when human population densities rose, hunting increased, and large game became scarce locally.[4]

Wetlands, such as oxbow lakes from cut-off river channels, were especially good places to find food. Abandoned channels had long shorelines relative to their surface areas and were often shallow and choked with vegetation. They were ideal fishing spots. Annual floods [**Figure 4**] spread broadly across river bottomlands. When the

Figure 3 The Mississippi River valley in southern Illinois is often quite wet in the spring. Former swamps or lakes still fill with water, despite herculean efforts to drain this low-lying land. The western bluff in Missouri can be seen in the distance. The abundance of edible plants and animals, along with fertile soils, made river valleys especially good places to settle.

Figure 4 The great Mississippi River flood of 1927 was a wake-up call for the nation to improve its flood control, especially levee, system. The Winterville mounds in Mississippi were completely surrounded by water.

water receded, fish were trapped in ever-shrinking pools where they were easily caught with nets, yielding a huge return for little effort.[5] (Even today, innumerable dorsal fins creasing the surface of an almost dry Mississippi valley slough are a memorable sight. By mucking around in stagnant and foul-smelling water it is possible to grab large fish by hand, although it is a good idea to keep a sharp eye out for snapping turtles and snakes when doing so.)

Receding floodwaters left extensive mudflats soon covered by thick stands of pioneering vegetation. They included goosefoot and other weedy plants with edible greens and seeds, which were part of prehistoric diets, especially in the midcontinent.[6] New sediments deposited by annual floods maintained soil fertility, and the silty sands of river bottomland ridges and natural levees were easily worked with hand-held tools, often hoes with stone blades.

Coastal areas were also rich in edible plants and animals, especially in and around the shallow, brackish waters of estuaries, bays, and marshes [**Figure 5**]. Immense piles of shells grew where generations of people discarded the remains of their meals. Fish were particularly abundant where they swam upstream to spawn, with many captured in nets and weirs extending from shorelines. In early eighteenth-century CE tidewater Virginia, fish could fill streams to the point where it was said to be "almost impossible to ride through [the water], without treading on them."[7]

Figure 5 Shell heaps dot the Gulf and Atlantic coasts. This low mound, designated 3Mb°5 and excavated in 1941, was located in an Alabama marsh. Coastal wetlands were favorite places to settle throughout much of prehistory because they were exceedingly rich in natural resources.

Doing Archaeology

Early colonial writing about the native groups of eastern North America naturally focused on the customs and activities that were seen firsthand. After all, some of this information was immediately useful for the new arrivals who found themselves in an unfamiliar land where their very survival hung in the balance. But a deeper history was recognized as well. One early eighteenth-century traveler in the Carolinas wrote about "Earthen Pots that are often found under Ground, and at the Foot of the Banks where the Water has wash'd them away."[8] The pottery vessels were "for the most part broken in pieces; but we find them of a different sort, in Comparison of those the Indians use at this day." He went on to say that the "Bowels of the Earth cannot have alter'd them, since they are thicker, of another Shape, and Composition." A lengthy period of burial for the potsherds (broken pieces of ceramic vessels) was implied, but being able to measure how much time had passed had to wait until radiocarbon dating came into use in the late twentieth century.

Builders of Mounds

The earliest recording and excavation efforts focused on mounds and graves [**Figure 6**]. This work is usually said to have begun in the eighteenth century when Thomas Jefferson dug into a mound near his home in Virginia, although he was not the only one to do so at that time.[9] He wanted to know whether the mounds were monuments containing battlefield deaths, repositories of bones originally buried elsewhere, or common cemeteries. After looking at the soil and bones, Jefferson decided that the disarticulated remains of many people, the old and young alike, had been buried at different times. He also said that the ancestors of these

Figure 6 Visiting the Grave Creek mound in aptly named Moundsville, West Virginia, is much easier today than it was for Meriwether Lewis in September 1803, early in a journey that would eventually take him to the Pacific Ocean. When Lewis saw the mound, it was surrounded by forest, and there were only about a half-dozen houses nearby in what was then called Elizabethtown.

mound-building people had originated in Asia and come to the Americas across the Bering Strait, a remarkably sensible and prescient comment.

Public opinion instead latched onto a singularly strange idea: the existence of a separate race of moundbuilders. Fantastic stories flourished in the near absence of solid evidence, which was slow in coming. The moundbuilders were thought to have originated in distant corners of the world, perhaps even from Atlantis, according to some. Others held that they were indeed Native Americans, although they were part of much earlier and culturally advanced groups. These people had been pushed out by warlike tribes who were, in turn, displaced by the westward expansion of Euroamerican settlers. Here was convenient justification, for those concerned about such niceties, to seize land that was only thinly populated and scarcely used.

Direct connections were drawn between big piles of earth, enormous populations, and societies likened to the world's largest ancient civilizations: "a people capable of works requiring so much labor, must be numerous, and if numerous, somewhat advanced in the arts."[10] The Mississippi River valley must have supported "a population as numerous as that which once animated the borders of the Nile, or of the Euphrates, or of Mexico and Peru." Such wildly enthusiastic, but thoroughly uninformed, claims fueled speculation that the moundbuilders were entirely different from the people who were then being displaced from their homes and forced to live in squalid conditions on the worst possible land.

At the end of the nineteenth century, archaeologist Gerard Fowke specifically addressed the problems inherent in making conclusions about population size and societal complexity based on these mounds. He rightly saw it as one of the "many absurd theories and notions promulgated by authors ignorant of their subject and writing only to strike the popular mind and pocket."[11] Yet he, and others like him, could do little to put an end to fanciful notions of life in the past.

The ill-founded belief that the builders of mounds were people other than Native American ancestors was finally laid to rest just over a century ago, notably through work by the Bureau of Ethnology.[12] Surveys and excavations were undertaken to describe the mounds, determine how they were constructed, classify them by shape, and obtain artifacts from them. Cyrus Thomas directed this effort, and he relied heavily on correspondence with his field workers. In fact, their descriptions were often quoted verbatim in Thomas's lengthy report, published in 1894, which was chock-full of site and excavation details.

Fieldwork

Excavations during the nineteenth century CE were crude, since little in the way of even rudimentary training was available. Digging proceeded as quickly as possible, sometimes by tunneling towards the center of a mound to unearth artifacts [**Figure** 7]. As a result, much information about construction histories and how mounds were used was lost. Some objects were destined for museums or special exhibitions, including the World's Columbian Exposition in Chicago in 1893. Most of them, however, were left behind in the field because the excavators took only the items they thought worthwhile.

Figure 7 In a search for artifacts, tunnels were sometimes dug deep into mounds, as in this excavation in 1897 of the Carriage Factory mound in southern Ohio. Tunneling yielded little information on mound construction.

Through the 1920s, inadequately funded excavations were carried out by small crews that dug for short periods of time [**Figure 8**]. Better excavation and recording procedures were eventually introduced, haltingly and incrementally, most notably through the efforts of archaeologists from the University of Chicago, beginning in the mid-1920s.[13] Much of the Chicago archaeologists' work was undertaken in the central Illinois River valley near Dickson Mounds. There, starting in the late 1920s, local chiropractor Don Dickson dug into several overlapping mounds on his family farm. His exhibit of excavated skeletons soon attracted public attention. At that time, better roads along with more dependable and affordable automobiles were encouraging ever-greater numbers of sightseers. Archaeological roadside attractions soon sprang up elsewhere as well, such as western Kentucky's Ancient Buried City (Wickliffe Mounds), which was once a heavily advertised tourist trap.

Figure 8 This lantern slide shows an aerial view of excavations in a Kentucky rockshelter in the 1920s. Enthusiastic digging might produce many artifacts but little in the way of contextual control, diminishing the significance of the finds.

Innumerable archaeological sites—including impressive mounds—have fallen victim to the necessities and conveniences of modern life, as well as the curiosity and greed of looters, or "pot hunters" [**Plate 1**]. In fact, site destruction was one of the reasons Cyrus Thomas considered the late nineteenth-century Bureau of Ethnology's mound survey so important.[14] The situation today is no different, except there are even fewer intact sites, and land modification has greatly accelerated.

The means of protecting sites were quite limited before the last few decades. Appeals made to public pride were rarely effective. St. Louis, for example, once deserved the nickname Mound City, but that did nothing to stop the destruction of its mounds. One civic-minded person found it surprising that "individual taste and public spirit do not unite to preserve these beautiful eminences in their exact forms, and connect them by an enclosure, with shrubbery and walks, thus forming a promenade that might be the pride of St. Louis."[15] Sadly that was not done—land was too valuable and greed too great. By the mid-nineteenth century CE, the main group of mounds had vanished. When the biggest one was being leveled, a newspaper reported that "curiosity hunters flock there daily by the hundreds, armed with all sorts of vessels, hoping to secure and carry off some relic of the past ages"[16] [**Figure 9**]. Quick to capitalize on the excitement, a local business announced that "a curious two-wheeled vehicle, supposed to be an ancient velocipede" from the Big Mound was on display.[17] At that time, velocipedes (bicycles with pedals on the front wheel) were causing quite a stir in St. Louis, as they were elsewhere in the country. One said to be from the Big Mound was sure to excite gullible onlookers.

Fortunately, in some places mounds were afforded protection by being incorporated into city cemeteries or public parks. One such example is a tall conical mound in the Mound Cemetery in Marietta, Ohio.[18] Marietta's several mounds were so highly regarded that they were dignified with Latinized names, with the cemetery mound being called the Conus because of its shape. The Serpent Mound, also in Ohio, is another

Figure 9 The Big Mound at St. Louis was flattened in 1869. Other mounds in the rapidly growing city were also destroyed, despite the outcries of concerned citizens.

well-known site that was saved.[19] A group of prominent Boston women gathered the necessary funds to purchase it in the 1880s, and the earthwork was then handed over to Harvard University's Peabody Museum. In 1900, the Serpent Mound was deeded to the Ohio Historical Society, which still maintains it as a park.

Surviving mounds and villages are mostly located in rural areas, but such settings do not fully protect them. Plowing reduces mounds to low domes, obscuring their original shapes while removing the uppermost burials and building remnants. This destruction has a long history. As early as the eighteenth century, Thomas Jefferson reported that the height of the mound he excavated had already been diminished by plowing.[20]

Sites are also destroyed by pot hunters. The most notorious excavation for profit took place in the 1930s during the height of the Great Depression. Men who called themselves the Pocola Mining Company tunneled deep into a large mound at Spiro in eastern Oklahoma.[21] The artifacts they unearthed, including impressive engraved marine-shell cups, were sold for a tidy profit. Public outrage fanned by newspaper articles prompted efforts to halt the looting and to conduct proper excavations to make sense of what had been discovered. Today the site is preserved as Oklahoma's sole archaeological park.

Laws are now in place that protect many archaeological sites, especially those on public land. Pot hunters can be prosecuted for looting sites.

Archaeological fieldwork changed suddenly and dramatically in the 1930s and early 1940s during the Great Depression.[22] Several archaeologists—notably William S. Webb, whose nickname Bull Neck suited a forceful personality—realized that Roosevelt's initiatives to put people back to work were an ideal opportunity to excavate on a far greater scale than had ever before been imaginable. Projects undertaken through New Deal relief programs, notably the Works Progress Administration (WPA) and the Civilian Conservation Corps (CCC), revolutionized fieldwork [**Figure 10**].

Figure 10 During the Great Depression, federal work-relief programs put large numbers of unemployed people, mostly men, to work excavating archaeological sites, especially in the Southeast. A flat-topped Mississippian-period mound at the Bessemer site in Alabama can be seen behind laborers in 1939.

For the first time, big crews worked for long periods to expose large amounts of many sites, identifying the layouts of entire communities as they did so. In the best projects, the challenge of organizing untrained laborers led to a sorely needed improvement, including standardization, of field techniques.

Southeastern states were the primary beneficiaries of New Deal funding for excavations. Mild winters permitted long field seasons, and there was an abundance of labor as unemployment was high in desperately poor rural areas. Numerous villages and mounds would shortly be covered by huge reservoirs that were then being developed by the Tennessee Valley Authority (TVA). But major excavations were conducted elsewhere as well, including those that exposed complete late prehistoric villages in Pennsylvania.

Since World War II, archaeologists have increasingly focused their attention on sites threatened by the construction of dams, highways, buildings, and the like. Once referred to as "salvage archaeology," it is now called Cultural Resource Management (CRM). This work started as surveys and excavations along rivers that the U.S. Army Corps of Engineers were turning into enormous reservoirs.[23] It was inspired by the success of the New Deal excavations, especially those undertaken through TVA projects.

Vastly better funding since the mid-1970s has permitted more comprehensive surveys and excavations than ever before, as well as thorough analyses of the materials from them. In fact, the current CRM work represents the second, and most generous, period of major public funding for archaeology—the New Deal being the first.[24]

From Data to People

By the early twentieth century CE, enough information had been assembled from fieldwork to make some sense of the distributions of certain kinds of prehistoric remains, particularly pottery and mounds. But it remained difficult to grasp the significance of what had been found because well-described sites and materials were scarce. Groupings of seemingly associated artifacts and architectural features were known by a hodgepodge of locally and inconsistently applied names.

In the 1930s, the need to impose order on a chaotic situation came to a head. Something had to be done to make sense of what had been found, including the vast increase in discoveries that came about through the big New Deal excavations. Attempts to come to grips with this abundance of newly available information led to classifications of artifacts, especially pottery, and cultural time-and-space units that, with considerable refinement, are still used today.

Eventually, an emphasis on mere description gave way to a concern over how societies were organized and functioned, including their place in the natural environment. Those interests, however, came to dominate archaeological work only following World War II, during the so-called New Archaeology of the 1960s.

During the post-war period, these changes in research emphases were accompanied by a shift from individual sites to the distributions of settlements across large areas, notably segments of river valleys. Studies of the patterning of sites relative to each other and to landscape features got off to a fine start with a late-1940s survey of the lower Mississippi River valley.[25] It was followed by a considerable amount of fieldwork focusing on specific areas, often prompted by major construction projects, such as those associated with reservoirs and highways.

Current understandings of life in the past are not only a result of larger areas being surveyed and more sites being excavated [**Figure 11**]. Today archaeologists investigate a broader range of site types than they did in the early to mid-twentieth century. This shift stems from the CRM emphasis on project areas chosen because of modern land-use needs, not because of a search for sites that might yield the most artifacts or architectural remnants. Small sites, and those that were only briefly occupied, are finally getting the attention they so richly deserve. Nevertheless, the overall archaeological coverage of eastern North America remains patchy. That is because opportunities for, and constraints on, fieldwork differ from one place to the next, as do the emphases of archaeological research programs.

Today, many more materials are saved for later detailed study than ever before. This practice began with the New Deal projects, where specialists were occasionally hired to describe human skeletons, animal bones, mollusks, and pottery. It was recognized that skeletons, for example, could provide information about the health, particularly the nutritional status, of past groups.[26] That kind of specialized skeletal analysis was not begun in earnest, however, until the late 1960s.

Studies of plant and animal remains have been greatly enhanced in recent decades through the widespread adoption of flotation. It is a simple procedure, introduced by midwestern archaeologists in the 1960s, for separating small items from soil.

Figure 11 Stone tools, chips of stone, and pottery (small fragment on the right), such as these items from Kentucky, are usually found when walking over plowed fields. They indicate places where people once lived.

Dirt is washed through fine mesh with plenty of water in order to catch even the smallest animal bones and carbonized seeds. These tiny items provide a fuller picture of diets than the objects excavators can handpick out of soil. Late prehistoric people, for example, were once thought to have eaten mostly maize and deer—cobs and large bones are easy to spot while digging. But people are now known to have consumed a much broader array of plants and animals. Indeed, our fixation on deer as their principal quarry has more to do with Western views of ideal game animals, which date back to the Middle Ages, than it does with solid archaeological evidence. Stable carbon and nitrogen isotopes in human bones also provide direct measures of general dietary composition, especially maize consumption.

If the past several decades serve as a guide to the future, we can expect many breakthroughs in our ability to extract more information from old objects. Of course, doing so depends on finding and excavating sites before looters, construction projects, and modern agricultural practices destroy them [**Figure 12**]. Still, our greatest challenge today is not unlike what our Depression-era predecessors faced. How do we make the fullest use of the unprecedented amount of information that is being amassed through so much effort?

Figure 12 A mound at Cahokia in Illinois is shown here, hemmed in by buildings and roads. Many archaeological sites, including mounds, have been damaged or destroyed by modern construction.

Chapter 2

Mobile Hunter-Gatherers: Paleoindian and Early Archaic

People first arrived in the Americas toward the end of the last Ice Age (or Pleistocene), when massive ice sheets covered much of what is today Canada. No one knows precisely when or how they made their way southward, but it might have been around 15,000 years ago. For thousands of years thereafter, these mobile hunter-gatherers were thin on the ground, leaving few traces of their existence. They reached eastern North America by the Pleistocene's end, but most of the occupation of this part of the present-day United States and Canada dates to the Holocene, which began about 11,700 years ago [**Figure 13**, see page 24].

Beringia

To get to the Americas, people journeyed across dry land where the Bering Strait is now located. Here, the shallow ocean floor was exposed for thousands of years before and after the last glacial maximum around 26,500 to 19,000 years ago.[1] When the sea was at its lowest point, as much as 930 miles (1,500 kilometers) of land separated the Arctic and Pacific oceans.

This land bridge, known as Beringia, was cold and dry, but unglaciated. It was the eastern end of a vast grassland, the Mammoth Steppe, that extended mostly unbroken westward across Siberia and into Europe.[2] Large grazers, notably bison, horses, and woolly mammoths, along with many smaller ones, roamed this grassy plain and took refuge in sheltered stream valleys filled with shrubby growth. Hunter-gatherers who ventured into this region might have been particularly attracted to the range of potential food, including marine mammals, along now-submerged coastal margins.

Eastern Beringia was bordered by two immense masses of ice in what is now Alaska and the Yukon Territory. The largest was the Laurentide Ice Sheet, which covered most of Canada and extended southward into the United States. The other was the Cordilleran Ice Sheet, a complex of glaciers along the mountainous spine of western Canada.

Genetic evidence indicates that the ancestors of the very first Americans probably diverged from Asian populations when they were still living somewhere in northeastern Asia, perhaps in Beringia itself.[3] These people were isolated from other Asian

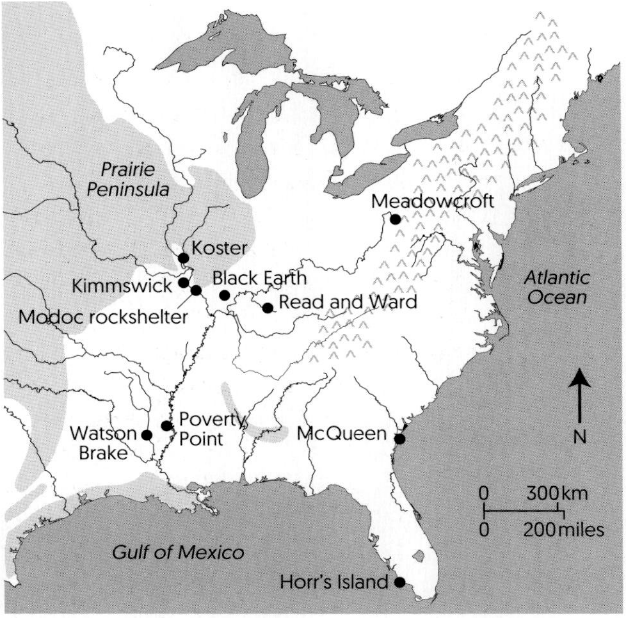

Figure 13 Selected sites mentioned in Chapters 2 and 3.

populations for thousands of years before moving on to colonize the Americas south of the ice sheets. Their isolation can be attributed to a sparse human occupation of high latitudes during unforgivingly harsh full glacial conditions. Interestingly, the little information available on early Holocene North American skeletons, specifically estimates of body breadth, is consistent with their distant ancestors having spent a prolonged period living in cold conditions. Therefore, separate sources of information—genetic and morphological—point in the same direction: a lengthy period was spent somewhere in northeast Asia or Beringia before people made it past the ice sheets.

Once south of the ice sheets, people dispersed quickly, soon reaching as far as South America. There are few early Holocene North American skeletons, but enough of them to suggest that craniofacial variation was just as great as in more recent skeletons. Some geographical patterning is also detectable.[4] Considerable variation existed in the rest of the skeleton as well. Although these individuals date to a period thousands of years after the first people arrived in the Americas, they provide us with a window on what life was like for the earliest inhabitants who were, if anything, even more thinly distributed. Differences among early Holocene skeletons correspond with what might be expected of people who lived in small foraging bands in a sparsely populated, and sometimes inhospitable, land. Local groups would have gone through periods of expansion and contraction. Population growth inevitably led to large bands breaking into smaller ones structured along kin lines. Local declines could have reached the point of extinction, perhaps when already hard-pressed bands experienced the bad luck of several key adults dying simultaneously on foraging trips. For individual groups, it must have been a precarious existence, although on the whole they persevered and overall population inched upward accordingly.

By Land or by Sea

From Beringia, there were two possible routes southward beyond the ice sheets, neither of which were easy going until the glacial retreat was well underway.[5] One of them was between the massive Laurentide and Cordilleran ice sheets just east of western Canada's rugged mountains. It is unlikely that humans passed through it until well after the ice sheets had begun their retreat. Much of this so-called Ice-Free Corridor must have been a forbidding landscape of frigid lakes and newly exposed ground with only light vegetation. Yet by 13,000 years ago, if not somewhat earlier, the corridor was open, with game to hunt.

The other route south involved hugging the rocky Pacific coast, almost certainly aided by watercraft, skirting glaciers that filled valleys between mountains. Unglaciated headlands during the glacial maximum, and for some time thereafter, must have been cold and sparsely vegetated places. But the glacial retreat, once it started, appears to have been relatively rapid. There soon followed plants and animals that made the shoreline more attractive. The coastline is thought to have been passable for humans by 16,000 years ago, if not before. People coming this way were presumably drawn forward by plentiful and vulnerable marine animals, such as seals, as well as other food available in coastal settings. It was probably a southward extension of a way of life structured around skills that had been honed for generations on Beringian shorelines.

Both migration routes have ardent supporters, and preferences for one or the other have shifted over time. Unfortunately, there is no direct evidence that backs up either position.[6] All we know for sure is that people moved south, colonizing what was, for them, a resource-rich new world.

It is in this context that Thomas Dillehay's excavation of Monte Verde, far to the south in Chile, is so important. His work shows that people had reached South America almost 15,000 years ago.[7] That was before the Ice-Free Corridor had opened, or at least had developed into a sufficiently hospitable landscape that people would have willingly entered and, in due course, traveled through. While some archaeologists dispute the dating of Monte Verde, it has gained widespread acceptance as a truly old site. Furthermore, other sites have come to light that support a human presence beyond the ice sheets consistent with an early occupation of Monte Verde.

The time that elapsed between when it was possible to get beyond the ice sheets, several thousand years after the last glacial maximum, and the occupation of Monte Verde tilts the balance toward the Pacific Coast as being the initial route southward from Beringia. If there was indeed a vigorous expansion down the coast, successive generations of people would have encountered different kinds of marine mammals, fish, and shellfish on their way to Chile. But despite challenges posed by having to deal with different species, their food acquisition strategies would not have had to change nearly as much as those of people who depended entirely on terrestrial plants and animals from distinctly different environmental settings. By focusing on the coast, people opted to stick with what they already knew, a conservative decision that took into account the risk of failure that trying something new involved. Although it seems likely that people followed the shoreline to get past the ice sheets, secure dating of sites along the Alaskan and Canadian coasts, proving them older than Monte Verde, is needed to demonstrate that this was indeed the initial route south.

Just because some people, including the earliest arrivals, might have bypassed glacial ice by traveling down the Pacific Coast does not mean that others did not later take the inland route through the Ice-Free Corridor. There is no reason why both routes, at different times, would not have been used by groups moving into a vast land that was initially unoccupied or, later, only sparsely populated.

It is not known how people made it to land east of the Mississippi River. To get there, they could have skirted the southern margin of the continental glacier, spreading out across tundra settings; followed eastward flowing rivers, such as the Missouri, and then moved their way up the Mississippi's eastern tributaries; or crossed to the Gulf of Mexico and continued a mainly coastal expansion, eventually reaching the Atlantic Coast.

Regardless of precisely when and how the earliest arrivals reached eastern North America, they faced environmental settings unlike those experienced by their distant descendants [**Figure 14**]. The overall trend was toward a warmer climate, but the transition from full glacial to modern conditions—from the late Pleistocene to Holocene—did not always proceed in the same direction and at the same rate.[8] Perhaps most notably, 12,900 years ago, and for about the next 1,200 years, there was an abrupt return to frigid conditions known as the Younger Dryas. Vegetation changed accordingly, as shown by pollen cores from the Midwest through the Great Lakes into New England.

Figure 14 The late Pleistocene landscape in Illinois was unlike that of more recent times.

Eventually, a late Pleistocene mosaic of forests and grasslands—a patchy environment by today's standards—gave way to the more homogeneous vegetation cover of recent times that is mainly patterned according to latitude and elevation.[9] The distributions of animal and plant species changed according to their individual temperature and moisture requirements. Some animals with ranges that overlapped in the late Pleistocene were no longer found together once the Holocene vegetation pattern had emerged.

The shift to modern conditions, therefore, was not a simple, slow northward movement and expansion of fixed plant and animal communities that remained intact from glacial to modern times. The change in vegetation patterns placed new pressures on animals, especially those with narrow feeding requirements. Many animals went extinct, from huge mastodons and mammoths down to tiny mice and bats.

Early Hunter-Gatherers

Pre-Clovis Occupation

The early occupation of Monte Verde means people were widely dispersed well before the first generally recognized evidence of their presence in North America south of the ice sheets: the distinctive Clovis projectile points. These projectile points, which date to no more than about 13,400 years ago (estimates based directly on radiocarbon dates are somewhere around 11,500 years ago), are the earliest sure sign of humans in eastern North America.[10] They are referred to as "fluted points" because long flakes were removed from their bases, producing shallow channels that extended up their sides.

Evidence for a pre-Clovis occupation of eastern North America is slowly coming to light, but the true ages of these sites are presently disputed.[11] The finds include a tortoise from Florida that appears to have been killed about 14,000 years ago by a wooden spear (radiocarbon date of 12,030 years ago). The best-known site for evidence of an early human presence is Meadowcroft rock shelter in southwestern Pennsylvania. This deeply stratified site has yielded a rich assemblage of artifacts, with the oldest supposedly preceding Clovis sites. Items in the lowest artifact-bearing deposits include stone flakes and tools, as well as burned basketry. But despite the quality of the excavation and the number of radiocarbon dates, skepticism remains about Meadowcroft's early occupation.

Sites thought to be pre-Clovis continue to be discovered, though they remain difficult to demonstrate to everyone's satisfaction. There were few people at that time, so sites are correspondingly scarce. Perhaps more importantly, they did not use highly distinctive stone tools that can be easily distinguished from those of later periods, unlike the fluted points. But if people made it all the way south to Monte Verde, there is no compelling reason why there would not have been a pre-Clovis presence in eastern North America.

Figure 15 Many Paleoindian fluted points have been found throughout the eastern United States, including Clovis points such as this one from Virginia. Length 2.2 in. (5.5 cm).

The Paleoindians

The first people to have left behind widespread and unambiguous evidence of their presence are called Paleoindians. They are known for several varieties of fluted points made at different times and places, as well as lanceolate points without the flake scars that thinned them [**Figure 15**].

Some places in eastern North America have far more than their share of Paleoindian points.[12] Early points are concentrated in several parts of the midcontinent, especially the middle Tennessee River valley, and along the Atlantic Seaboard. The overall distribution of known points, of course, is influenced by modern land use and the archaeological attention devoted to certain places. Both affect the probability that old projectile points might be found. While fully aware of these problems, David Anderson has argued that the hot spots reflect, however crudely, places favored by Paleoindians. Whatever its cause, the uneven distribution of sites continues throughout the Paleoindian period.

It is not known if Paleoindians lived along the coastlines, although there is no reason why they would not have done so.[13] Modern sea levels were reached only several thousand years ago, submerging the Paleoindian coastline through the melting of massive ice sheets. The bones and teeth of large mammals, including mastodons, have been dredged up far offshore from present beaches. One can only assume that early hunter-gatherers were attracted to the rich plant and animal life in these places. For example, Paleoindian points have been found in the shallow water of Tampa Bay on the Gulf Coast of Florida.

It is unusual for more than a handful of these early projectile points to be found at any single site. Furthermore, very little cultural material accompanies the great majority of the points. Most were probably left behind by small and highly mobile bands, each consisting of a few tens of people. Their tools are scattered across both river valleys and the intervening uplands, indicating that people foraged widely in different settings as various foods became available throughout the year.[14]

Relatively few Paleoindian sites yield many points and other artifacts.[15] Some of these Paleoindian camps were located near quarries, where good stone for making tools was readily available. Others were presumably close to places that were especially rich in edible plants and animals. These spots were repeatedly occupied and might have been periodically visited by somewhat larger groups of people. Perhaps they even mark places where people congregated to take part in communal hunts because herd animals, notably caribou, were abundant. For the members of normally widely distributed bands, such occasions would have facilitated finding marriage partners and renewing ties with kinsfolk and friends.

Much of what we would like to know about Paleoindians—including how mobile they were, and the size and distribution of cooperating groups—is wrapped up in questions about how they fed themselves. Rugged and brave hunters stalking dangerous big game dominate popular views of life in these distant times. Some researchers believe intrepid hunters drove a number of large herbivores, collectively known as megafauna, to extinction.[16] People are said to have increased rapidly and spread across a landscape chock-full of animals that were behaviorally susceptible to the new and insatiable human predator. Hunting soon outstripped the animals' reproductive capacities, and they died out.

As David Meltzer, among others, has noted, there is a resounding absence of support for the idea that eastern Paleoindians specialized in hunting megafauna.[17] Hunters killed mastodons and other large animals, but it probably took place when the animals were vulnerable, such as when the young, old, or lame became mired in a watering hole. Opportunistic hunting of that sort is much different from tracking down specially targeted prey, while largely ignoring other animals. Perhaps early hunters tipped the balance for animals already on the brink of extinction. But there is no reason to think that people were the primary reason for the disappearance of many species that differed widely in size and habitat preference.

In eastern North America, the best example of tools found alongside the bones of extinct animals comes from Kimmswick in Missouri.[18] The site is in a hollow, near its opening onto the Mississippi River floodplain [**Figure 16**]. Here the bones of Pleistocene animals, including mastodons, and two intact Clovis points were discovered in pond sediments sandwiched between other deposits of soil that had washed in from the adjacent bluff and stream. The context of the bones and artifacts, therefore, is especially good. Several other stone tools or broken pieces of them, numerous chert flakes, and other animal bones were found nearby. Taken together, the evidence indicates that the Kimmswick hunters occasionally killed situationally vulnerable megafauna.

Figure 16 Mastodon bones and Paleoindian points were found at Kimmswick, Missouri. The site's location indicates that situationally vulnerable animals fell victim to human hunters.

There is little additional direct evidence from the eastern United States for humans having hunted megafauna or scavenged their carcasses.[19] The skull of a late Pleistocene bison with a stone point fragment lodged in it has been found in a river in Florida. Other wet sites in Florida have yielded tools made from the bones and ivory of now-extinct megafauna. Humans presumably killed some of these animals, but bones and ivory fashioned into tools—and not all claims of purposefully worked objects are equally convincing—could also have been scavenged from animals that had died from natural causes.

Because Paleoindians lived in different natural settings that changed as the climate warmed, they cannot have all had the same diet.[20] People inhabited places ranging from periglacial tundra and spruce parklands to a more southerly mosaic of boreal and deciduous forests and grasslands. Species diversity was undoubtedly low in the bleak landscape immediately south of retreating ice sheets. But some animals were presumably present in large numbers, such as caribou, which travel in herds. If specialized hunters lived anywhere, they would have been in such settings. But evidence for what people ate is so thin that the only thing we know is that northern Paleoindians hunted caribou along with smaller animals that included hares. Farther away from the ice sheets, a wider array of potential food in diverse late Pleistocene landscapes favored generalized, and typically more reliable, hunting-and-gathering strategies. Fish bones, as well as fruit and weed seeds, from Shawnee-Minisink in eastern Pennsylvania are indicative of this dietary breadth. So too are the bones of deer and other animals at Meadowcroft. As mentioned previously, a now-extinct tortoise was hunted in Florida. Such creatures were easy prey, precisely the sort—slow, defenseless against spears, and edible—that people could have pushed to extinction. Yet, even here, climate change cannot be eliminated as the principal reason for the tortoise's demise.

Paleoindians routinely traveled across long distances, as shown by widely scattered sites, most of which were only briefly occupied. In addition to locally occurring stone that had been used to fashion projectile points and other tools, it is not at all uncommon to find high-quality material, usually chert, from outcrops as much as a few hundred miles away from where the artifacts were thrown away or lost.[21] Apparently people visited sources of good stone, made their tools, and took away only what was of most use. Carrying large amounts of heavy rock across long distances made no sense if much of it would later be discarded when fashioning tools. Usually, it is assumed that entire bands of people visited sources of good stone during their wide-ranging travel in search of food. It is also possible that certain individuals occasionally set off on journeys to obtain material of great practical, and perhaps symbolic, value. At least some of the tools made from non-local, and often attractive, stone might have been exchanged as gifts to solidify social relations among the members of separate bands when they happened to meet. It is difficult to tease apart these different possibilities with existing information. But no matter what happened, people of this time horizon moved a lot when compared to their distant descendants.

Tools made from quality stone were reworked to maintain sharp cutting edges.[22] Spear points and knives were resharpened when dull, and in so doing were often turned into scrapers, awls, and other tools. Clovis points from Kimmswick and other sites show wear indicative of their use as knives, as well as projectile points. People were thrifty with their use of high-quality stone when camped far from where it outcropped, and often used tools for multiple purposes to meet their immediate needs.

As time wore on, the amount of stone from distant sources decreased, consistent with people usually moving across shorter distances.[23] Regional traditions marked by different projectile point styles also became more apparent. Both changes in late Paleoindian stone tool assemblages were a natural outcome of an increase in population that inevitably restricted the distances over which people freely traveled.

Population Trends

We only have a crude notion of population change based on counts of sites, although it appears that throughout the entirety of the human occupation of eastern North America, periods of early and late growth were separated by a time of relative stasis (see box pp. 32–33). With a 0.06 percent annual increase in sites, Paleoindian population growth fails to support arguments that attribute megafaunal extinction to a rapid expansion in the number and distribution of people.

The site data are not good enough to detect changes in overall population size during periods that span mere centuries, although tallies of sites over the long run will probably capture general trends. Estimates of relative population change generated from summed radiocarbon probabilities, which can provide better temporal resolution, indicate a more irregular pattern of change over time.[24] That is precisely what one might expect, so minor wiggles in the site-count curves are of no great importance with respect to the general pattern that spans many thousands of years. Radiocarbon frequency distributions have their own share of problems, although the greater precision they can potentially provide is promising for future research. Radiocarbon data, for example, indicate a population decline, especially in the Southeast, that coincided with the sudden return to cold conditions at the onset of the Younger Dryas about 12,900 years ago. Several centuries later, the population rebounded. It is debated whether this downturn in human numbers actually occurred; it could be a result of poor sampling or the analytical procedure. If supported through additional work, the decline underscores the difficulties small groups of widely scattered hunter-gatherers faced during times of resource uncertainty. It would not be the only time in eastern North America when a large area experienced a reduction in population severe enough to be observed archaeologically (Chapters 6 and 7).

Interestingly, the rate of increase in Paleoindian sites over several millennia is similar to what took place during the last few thousand years of prehistory. Early hunter-gatherers accommodated their greater numbers by spreading out to a wider range of environmental settings and switching to a broader array of foods. But they still managed to maintain a highly mobile foraging way of life. Their distant descendants, in contrast, solved the dilemma of too many mouths to feed by intensifying food production through the cultivation of plants. But that is a story for later chapters.

Population Growth

By 1500 CE, there were many more people in eastern North America than there could ever have been in Paleoindian times. But we would like to be able to say more than simply that the population grew over time. Minimally, we want to know if the rate of increase remained fixed, or whether population growth was faster in some broadly defined periods of time compared to others. The only way to answer such a question is to look at data from areas ranging from present-day states up to regions as large as the Midwest or even the entire Eastern Woodlands. That is because population histories for smaller areas—intensively studied areas are rarely larger than a few hundred square miles—are quite varied, sometimes differing greatly between neighboring river valleys.

An initial stab at dealing with this issue is made here using site files from Alabama, Arkansas, Illinois, Kentucky, Mississippi, New York, Tennessee, and Wisconsin [**Figure 17**]. Different environmental settings are encompassed by these states, so it is probable that trends detected in the site records are broadly indicative of changes that occurred across much of the Eastern Woodlands, certainly the Midwest and Southeast.

There are many problems with estimating the numbers of people from tallies of sites. Artifact classifications and cultural phase designations can be inconsistent, vague, or inaccurate. Equal attention is not given to all time periods, and research emphases vary from one state to the next. Settlements differed in size and duration, mobile people produced more sites than sedentary ones, and it is harder to detect short-term hunter-gatherer camps than permanent agricultural villages. The age and location of sites influence whether they might have been eroded away or covered by thick sediments. Some of these problems will increase the number of known late sites relative to those of earlier times, while others have the opposite effect. Nevertheless, counts of sites must bear some relation to how many people were present, so they have value as a first approximation of population growth.

When considering the data, it is best not to become overly concerned with minor peaks and valleys in the distribution of sites. General trends, however, are a different story, and here we must be content with what happened over big chunks of time and huge areas. There appear to have been three general population growth stages: an early increase of about 0.06 percent per year; a middle stationary period; and a late growth period, again at 0.06 percent per year. It should be kept in mind that long-term trends across a large region mask periods of population increase, stagnation, or decline that might have taken place over several centuries in part or all of the eight-state area.

Whatever caused these changes in population growth across the Eastern Woodlands had to involve increasing fertility, decreasing mortality, or both. The area examined is sufficiently large to rule out migration—that is, movement in or out of the region—as a major contributor to the observed pattern.

Much attention has been directed toward population growth as it relates to the transition to agriculture and the capacity to feed more people. But it is difficult to tease apart what eventually resulted in greater numbers of people. The range of fertility rates for modern hunter-gatherers overlaps with that of agriculturalists who rely on simple tools and frequently shift their fields.[25] As far as mortality is concerned, death from starvation was surely never too distant for local social groups, up to entire communities, that relied on their own efforts to feed themselves in inherently risky environments. With the greater control over food acquisition and storage that came with a move toward agricultural economies, the frequency or severity of local mortality crises perhaps decreased ever so slightly. Over many millennia, populations and new means of food production ratcheted upward together.

No matter what took place, only slight shifts in fertility or mortality were needed to produce the patterning in population growth shown by the site data. The changes would have been imperceptible from the limited perspective of a human lifetime.

POPULATION GROWTH

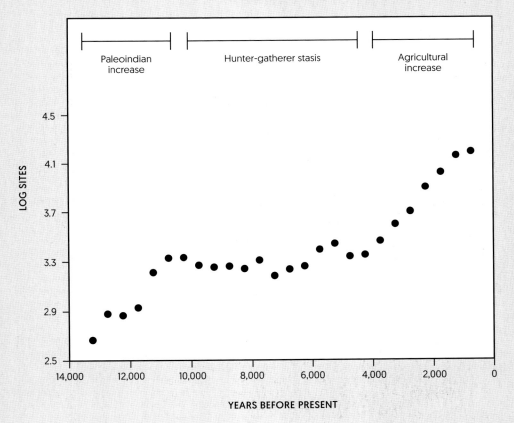

Figure 17 Sites from eight states—Alabama, Arkansas, Illinois, Kentucky, Mississippi, New York, Tennessee, and Wisconsin—indicate three main stages of population growth. Separate occupations of sites are often referred to as "components," and what is actually shown here are separate components, not sites. Periods of increase were separated by a long period of stasis. A log scale makes it easier to see different phases of growth.

Mobile Early Archaic Foragers

The following period, the Early Archaic, is thought to have lasted 2,000 or more years and to have ended about 8,900 years ago (the customarily used figure based on uncalibrated radiocarbon dates is 8,000 years ago). New kinds of projectile points have long been used by archaeologists as markers of this period, but precisely where a line between Paleoindian and Early Archaic should be drawn and when that shift took place are by no means settled to everyone's satisfaction. That is not of great concern here because it is always hard to divide a cultural continuum into discrete parts. Furthermore, the Early Archaic represented a continuation of a well-established mobile way of life. People remained few and their groups were well spread out. Population growth had slowed, presumably because the land supported about all the people it could, at least as long as they continued to move often and widely when foraging for food.

Early Archaic camps were distributed across both river valleys and the intervening uplands, with the largest tending to be near rivers [**Figure 18**].[26] In the midcontinent, for example, people made a greater use of uplands than later hunter-gatherers. Many Early Archaic sites were visited on one or more occasions by people whose stay must have been short, perhaps no more than a few days. Artifact diversity is low, consistent with a narrow range of tasks, such as killing and butchering an animal. Yet there are sites that show evidence of a broader array of activities and longer occupations. Shallow pits, piles of rock, hearths, shelters or drying racks indicated by postmolds (soil stains where wooden posts were planted in the ground), dog burials, and even debris-filled deposits (or middens) have been discovered. These sites yield many chipped stone tools, including points and scrapers, as well as hammerstones and grinding slabs fashioned from cobbles. Some blocks of stone had shallow depressions pecked into them to hold nuts when they were being cracked open with rocks in order to be eaten. Perishable materials were certainly used by these people, as shown by impressions of woven objects, both mats and bags, in clay hearths found at sites in Illinois and Tennessee. Human skeletons are rarely found, although people were occasionally interred near their camps.

Dogs were intentionally buried at two Early Archaic sites in the Illinois River valley.[27] They were presumably useful on foraging trips and provided company for the members of small mobile groups. The sample of measurable skeletons is small, but it is sufficient to show that the dogs varied in size and appearance, consistent with what is known from bones found elsewhere. Recent genetic analyses indicate that dogs originated in the Old World. Exactly when they were introduced to the Americas is unknown, but it happened relatively early, as indicated by these skeletons.

Based on what is known about recent hunter-gatherers, Early Archaic people probably lived in small bands consisting of only a few dozen men, women, and children. Contacts among these groups were absolutely essential for gaining access to neighbors' territories during times of hardship and ensuring there were a sufficient number of eligible marriage partners. There is little direct evidence of such contacts, although marine shell beads have been found at Modoc rock shelter [**Figure 19**] and

Figure 18 Deep archaeological deposits have been uncovered at several sites in eastern Tennessee, including Icehouse Bottom, shown here, where they date back to Early Archaic times.

Figure 19 In the early 1950s, deeply buried deposits extending back to the Early Archaic period were discovered beneath a limestone overhang, the Modoc rock shelter, in southwestern Illinois. The sequence of soil layers helped archaeologists work out the long history of hunter-gatherer occupation in this part of the Midwest.

Jerger in southwestern Illinois and Indiana, respectively.[28] Seashells from sites located almost 620 miles (1,000 kilometers) from the nearest coastline must have been passed from one person to the next, eventually ending up far from their points of origin.

Food remains indicate people relied on a broad spectrum of animals and plants from closed-canopy forests to places where trees were scarce, as well as streams.[29] Brushy edge zones, the borders between deep woods and open areas that ranged from small clearings to immense prairies, were particularly good locations to search for food. Hickory nuts and, to a lesser extent, acorns occur in archaeological deposits, as do the bones of white-tailed deer, rabbits, squirrels, raccoons, and other animals. Little is known about regional and temporal differences in what was eaten, but diets must have varied according to what was locally available. The use of plants—a reliable and expandable source of food—set the stage for what took place in the millennia that followed, when larger populations put greater pressures on local environmental settings.

Chapter 3

Sedentary Hunter-Gatherers: Middle to Late Archaic

At some point during the next several thousand years, many people began to live for longer periods in repeatedly occupied camps. Great deposits of debris, including bones and shells from innumerable meals, and chips of stone discarded when making tools, gradually accumulated in these frequently visited places. The "involuntary builders of such refuse heaps"—as New Deal archaeologist William S. Webb called them—left behind middens that yield many artifacts, features including shallow pits and piles of fire-cracked rocks, and burials of people and dogs.[1]

Discoveries at these sites give us a much fuller view of life than is available for earlier times. Perhaps most importantly, the first halting steps toward agriculture were being taken, a process that had great consequences many generations later. Growing crops was related to a more sedentary existence, although more or less permanent camps existed long before people got to the point where they depended heavily on cultivated plants. In some places, mounds were built for ceremonial purposes. That too would become more common later in time.

The period 6000 to 3000 BCE is customarily referred to as the Middle Archaic. Such time intervals are now being revised by calibrated radiocarbon dates that more closely approximate calendar years, in this instance pushing the beginning of the Middle Archaic back to about 900 years earlier. From this chapter onward, the dates for sites and culture periods usually correspond to those that, for better or worse, are deeply embedded in the archaeological literature. Rather predictably, the period that follows the Middle Archaic is called the Late Archaic, and it extends into the early part of the first millennium BCE.

Much of this time interval coincided with the warmest part of the Holocene, the Climatic Optimum, which ran from about 8,000 to 4,000 calendar years ago.[2] Pollen, where conditions favor its preservation, indicates that warmer and more arid conditions in the midcontinent led to an expansion of tall-grass prairie or a shift to drier woodlands. Drought-tolerant plants became more common in both upland and floodplain settings. By this time, river valley productivity had been enhanced by stream regime changes, beginning in the late Pleistocene, that contributed to the development of meandering rivers, which, during the course of channel movement, left behind narrow oxbow lakes.[3] Abandoned channels were ideal habitats for fish, waterfowl, and mammals, such as beaver and muskrat.

Figure 20 Many coastal shell heaps have been destroyed. This century-old postcard shows shell being carted off from a thick deposit at New Smyrna, Florida.

An inland movement of the sea, which had started in the terminal Pleistocene (after the glacial maximum), was essentially completed early in the Late Archaic period.[4] Up to modern times, fluctuations in sea level affecting shorelines, saltwater marshes, and tidal flats have influenced how and where people lived [**Figure 20**]. Today's coastlines are dotted with shell heaps marking camps used for many generations from the Late Archaic onward. Earlier people must have also frequented such resource-rich settings, but it is not known exactly how now-drowned shorelines were used. What is clear is that a settled existence indicated by coastal shell heaps was roughly contemporaneous with a shift to a more sedentary way of life in the continental interior, where deep middens developed alongside rivers and wetlands.

Tools and Containers

Stone points that were once part of spears and knives are among the most distinctive Middle and Late Archaic artifacts.[5] Their shapes varied somewhat across the Eastern Woodlands, indicating that regional traditions were well established by this time. Tools made by a combination of striking and grinding stone—instead of by chipping off flakes—had also become relatively common. They included axes, net weights, and atlatl weights fashioned from banded slate, basalt, quartz, and hematite, among other rocks. Atlatls were short sticks used to hurl spears more forcefully [**Figure 21**]. The butt ends of spears were held in place by hooks often made of antler. The stone weights (or bannerstones) were regularly polished, and each one was perforated by a hole laboriously drilled through it. When found alongside skeletons, the weights and hooks are frequently positioned as if they had once been attached to wooden shafts [**Figures 22 and 23**]. Tools and ornaments made of materials that tend not to survive well, such as bone awls and shell beads, were also used, much like they were during other times in prehistory.

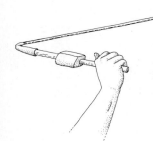

Figure 21 Spear-throwers, or atlatls, were commonly used by Middle and Late Archaic hunters. They often had stone weights and antler hooks attached to them.

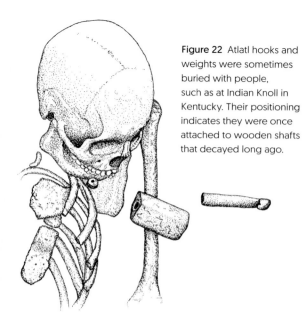

Figure 22 Atlatl hooks and weights were sometimes buried with people, such as at Indian Knoll in Kentucky. Their positioning indicates they were once attached to wooden shafts that decayed long ago.

Figure 23 Atlatl weights, or bannerstones, were frequently made from colorful stone, such as this one from Kentucky. Height 4.5 in. (11.4 cm).

Clues about how tools were used occasionally come from where they were originally lost. Many net weights, or plummets [**Figure 24**], in the Mississippi and Illinois River valleys of west-central Illinois have been found near backwater lakes.[6] They were probably tied to casting nets for hunting waterfowl. Migratory birds were especially abundant in the spring and fall because these rivers are located along the Mississippi Flyway. The bottomland distribution of plummets is consistent with numerous bones of migratory waterfowl being found in Middle Archaic deposits at the lower Illinois River valley Koster site.

One of the most important innovations to occur in the Middle and Late Archaic periods was the development of new kinds of containers for storing and cooking food.[7] They ultimately had such profound consequences on ways of life that Bruce Smith has dubbed this development the "Container Revolution." The cucurbits—squash and gourd—came first, and at the outset they were quite possibly more valued as containers or net floats than as food. They date back as early as 5000 BCE in the midcontinent, and an equally old gourd has been found with a burial in Florida. Recent genetic analyses of modern and ancient specimens show that the bottle gourd originated in Africa, floated across the Atlantic, and was subsequently grown and used in various ways by people. This research underscores the complexities, and frequent surprises, that come about when unraveling the deep histories of agriculture.

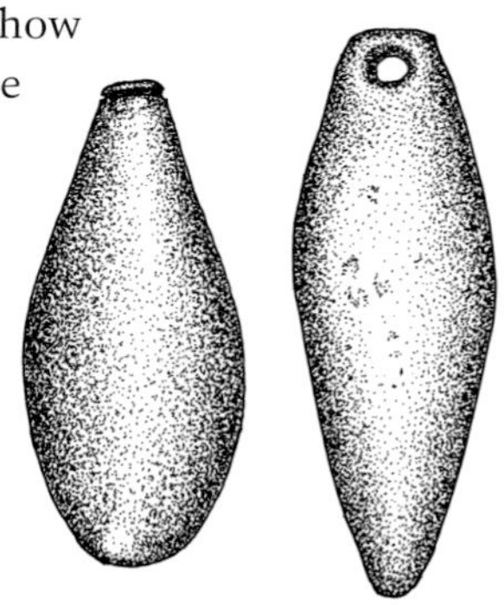

Figure 24 Stone plummets, such as these two found in the lower Illinois River valley, were used as net weights by Middle and Late Archaic people. The longest plummet is 3.3 in. (8.3 cm).

Figure 25 This steatite bowl, with handles on either side, is from southeastern Pennsylvania. The orifice is about 8.9 in. (22.5 cm) in diameter.

Starting around 2000 BCE, in the Late Archaic, people began to carve tub-like vessels out of steatite [**Figure 25**], or soapstone, outcrops of which occur in the Appalachians.[8] These vessels, along with some made from other kinds of relatively soft stone, are mostly found at sites in the Appalachians, to the east of the mountains, and in the Deep South. Soot on their exteriors indicates that they were often nestled amongst campfire coals. Presumably the steatite vessels were used for stone boiling, where water is heated by dropping hot rocks into a container.

The earliest pottery was made in the southern Atlantic coastal plain around 2500 BCE. More than a thousand years passed, however, before people west of the Appalachians began to use ceramic vessels.[9] It is not known why pottery-making spread so slowly and irregularly. Perhaps it was related to the availability of other suitable containers, such as light and durable baskets that in many situations are better than heavy and fragile pots. Only early in the first millennium BCE did pottery become common in many places, making it a convenient marker for the subsequent Early Woodland period.

Camps and Middens

Around 4500 BCE, midway through the Middle Archaic, mobile ways of life began to give way to the repeated use of camps occupied for lengthy periods of time, probably by larger numbers of people.[10] This shift toward a more sedentary existence, which occurred earlier in some places than in others, is perhaps most easily recognized in the development of large shell and midden heaps near rivers and wetlands in the southern Midwest and Southeast. What is found at these sites, intermittently occupied for as much as a few millennia, is an accumulation of innumerable individual events. Pits, usually shallow basins, as well as hearths, postmolds, human and dog burials, and house floors are encountered in these heaps of debris, as are piles of rock. The rocks, often scorched and badly cracked, came from earth ovens or had been used for stone boiling.

The Middle to Late Archaic Read site overlooking the Green River in western Kentucky is a good example of one of these debris heaps [**Figure 26**].[11] It was not particularly large when compared to the biggest middens, but when excavated it still consisted of about 130,000 cubic feet (3,700 cubic meters) of debris-laden soil and shell, in equal measures. This site, typical of others along the Green and Tennessee rivers, was located where stream conditions were such that mussels were plentiful and easy to collect. The people who occupied these camps focused much of their effort on foraging for nearby plants and animals that, during the right time of year, were reliable and abundant. Single individuals or small groups would also travel some distance from these sites to obtain food that was more widely dispersed, less predictable, or both.

People were frequently buried in the midcontinental midden and shell heaps.[12] Judging from their skeletons, the groups that visited these places included individuals of all ages and both sexes. Graves were dug close to where people camped, with burials occasionally near one another, but there was no formal cemetery structure. At Read, for example, there was no obvious arrangement of graves other than their placement in the part of the low, sprawling midden that faced the river.

Dogs were also carefully laid in pits dug into the middens, indicating that some of them were held in high regard.[13] They must have accompanied people on foraging trips, raised an alarm when strangers and dangerous animals approached camps, and gobbled up refuse that would otherwise rot and smell.

Camps were often located near wetlands, although the precise characteristics of these resource-rich settings varied from one place to the next.[14] For example, at Koster and at Modoc rock shelter, both in Illinois, thick deposits loaded with artifacts accumulated at the foot of bluffs bordering the Illinois and Mississippi River

Figure 26 Shell heaps along the Green River in western Kentucky, such as the Carlston Annis site, were excavated by WPA crews during the Great Depression.

Figure 27 Excavations at Koster, Illinois, at the base of a bluff bordering the Illinois River floodplain, exposed deeply buried deposits, which provided a rich record of life in the Archaic period.

floodplains [**Figure 27**]. Animal bones indicate the use of the river and, especially, backwater lakes and swamps. Farther south in Illinois, deep middens at Black Earth developed alongside a shallow lake and swamp, all that remained of a much larger late Pleistocene lake [**Figure 28**]. In western Kentucky, a midden known as the Ward site was perched on the edge of a steep bluff overlooking a broad bottomland, where a sluggish creek disappeared into an extensive swamp. All of these sites were in places where edible plants and small animals were abundant, dependable, and easily obtained. The concentrated nature of these resources and the high reproductive potential of heavily harvested species made it possible to visit the same place repeatedly without exhausting nearby sources of food.

Being close to sources of food was not the only reason people kept coming back to the middens. These places should not be thought of as massive and unsightly mounds of trash. Instead, somewhat raised and irregular ground was covered by thick vegetation, except for still-visible deposits of shells and rocks near patches of heavily trampled earth where people lived. The vegetation included weeds that soon invaded disturbed areas, with some of these plants being useful to humans, as is discussed later.

Midden sites were well known to the people that frequented them, and this familiarity undoubtedly added to their appeal.[15] It would only be natural to feel some affinity for old campsites associated with long histories. They were places where events had taken place that were of great significance to individuals, families, and entire groups. Graves are the most archaeologically noticeable markers of those occasions. But people frequenting these sites presumably also had memories of, for example, favorite but long-buried dogs or celebratory feasts. For generations on end, the simple act of coming back to the same place must have satisfied a desire for something familiar, while it simultaneously instilled a sense of shared experience and membership in a group with deep local roots.

Yet not all of the attention directed toward resource-rich places resulted in deep piles of discarded material. Several Late Archaic sites in the Mississippi River floodplain in southwestern Illinois consist of numerous features, primarily shallow pits often clustered together, beside long, shallow, vegetation-choked backwater lakes.[16] Many shallow pits have been found at these bottomland sites, which must have been occupied by small groups of closely related people.[17] Although the lake shores were repeatedly visited, people did not return to precisely the same spots often enough to produce deep middens. That was presumably because people could take advantage of many choices of potential campsites along the banks of long oxbow lakes and swamps that criss-crossed a broad floodplain.

While large shell and midden heaps have received the most archaeological attention, they are not the only sites that have been excavated in the midcontinent.[18] Briefly occupied camps, many in upland settings between river valleys, are indicated by widely scattered debris. They would have been used by people attracted to groves of nut trees, dense stands of berry- and seed-producing plants, and good hunting spots.

People elsewhere also naturally settled in especially favorable places. Far to the south, Middle to Late Archaic hunter-gatherers living along the lower Mississippi River and its tributaries were attracted to wetlands teeming with edible fish, waterfowl, and mammals.[19]

The Atlantic and Gulf coasts are dotted with deposits of shell that date from the third millennium BCE onward.[20] Many of these formed crescents or even complete rings, suggesting that when people settled down for lengthy periods they often arranged themselves in a circle. Old shell heaps were obvious landmarks in rather flat, wet, and heavily vegetated places—they still are today. It is not at all surprising that people intent on keeping their feet dry settled down in exactly the same places for years on end. Shell heaps increased in size over time, with some reaching enormous proportions. Radiocarbon dates from shell rings indicate the sites were used, at least intermittently, for centuries. There is no agreement over what the arcs and rings represent. But they grew through the accumulation of vast quantities of waste from daily living, seemingly interspersed with debris from occasional feasts. Establishing the significance of feast-related remains requires estimating how many individuals

Figure 28 Middens in plowed fields at Black Earth in southern Illinois are easily visible from the air. In the upper part of this photograph, they can be seen as dark spots in the light soil. The area in the lower part of the photograph was once a swamp.

took part in these events, the relationships among those people, the distances over which they traveled, and why they gathered together in the first place.

It is within this context that excavations at McQueen on a Georgia barrier island are so important.[21] A pit was found in the center of a shell ring, and it held the cremated and intentionally crushed bones of several people, along with a big piece of copper from the upper Great Lakes. Copper rarely occurs in Late Archaic contexts (after 3000 BCE) in that part of the Southeast, and the same can be said about cremation as a way of handling the dead. These finds indicate a connection, however indirect it might have been, with distant places, as well as the performance of a ritually significant act that was not typical of the area. Together, they underscore the fact that the shell deposits represent much more than piles of debris from long occupations.

Because various events took place at the shell heaps, their depositional histories can be complex, as shown by the St. Catherines shell ring, located on the same barrier island as McQueen.[22] Shells, mostly from oysters, had been piled up, but they also occur in thin layers interspersed with soil. Many were intact. But there were also places where they were broken and tightly compacted. Presumably these shells were trampled underfoot where people lived for extended periods.

Along this part of the Atlantic coast, and elsewhere as well, shell heaps were located on islands and within tidal marshes. Those in marshes were high enough to provide plants and animals with somewhat dryer settings, increasing local habitat diversity that, in turn, benefited people.[23] So through their actions—even if it was merely dumping trash—people had an impact on their immediate surroundings.

Accumulations of shells are not the only signs of a heavy use of coastal settings. At the Boylston Street Fishweir in Boston, Massachusetts, many weirs were constructed of closely spaced stakes.[24] The Late Archaic weirs, designed to trap fish as the tide receded, were built and replaced over 1,500 or more years. Collectively they covered an area that exceeded 5 acres (2 ha).

Despite the deep middens and other evidence for at least seasonally intensive occupations of specific places, there was not a unidirectional and steady progression toward increasingly sedentary ways of life during the Middle and Late Archaic periods. In some areas, people never really settled down in long-occupied camps. The Black Earth site in Illinois is a fine example of how mobility shifted to accommodate alterations in food availability brought about by climatic change.[25] Late Archaic people in that area were not as tightly tethered to wetland camps as their predecessors. They were able to disperse to take advantage of a wider distribution of reliable sources of food, as forests were expanding at the expense of grasslands following the mid-Holocene warm and dry period.

Life's Roles

Despite a general tendency in many places toward a more settled existence, people in the Middle and Late Archaic still pursued mobile lives. Christopher Ruff, who has examined skeletons from Tennessee River shell heaps, has identified differences in femoral bending rigidity, or leg strength, between males and females.[26] This work suggests that mobility was greater for males than for females, presumably because men routinely spent much of their time in arduous hunting trips over rough terrain.

Funerary artifacts indicate that what people did in life and how they treated one another were mostly determined by their age, sex, and ability.[27] At Read, infant burials had the fewest artifacts, and atlatl weights and hooks were mostly found with adult males. People older than forty-five were buried with fewer objects than younger adults. Individuals who would have been considered old at the contemporaneous Black Earth site likewise had a narrower range of artifacts. During Middle Archaic times at Koster, a few individuals with debilitating conditions were buried amid habitation debris, not elsewhere with other group members. Taken together, these burials show that people who possessed the most productive and reproductive potential were more highly regarded by their fellow group members than those who were old or infirm. In short, a person's worth was measured by his or her contributions to group survival. The situation was similar to what was observed by the early nineteenth-century Lewis and Clark expedition. In Meriwether Lewis's words:

> Those nations treat their old people and women with most difference [deference] and rispect [respect] where they subsist principally on such articles that these can participate with the men in obtaining them; and that, that part of the community are treated with least attention, when the act of procuring subsistence devolves intirely [entirely] on the men in the vigor of life.[28]

Occasionally, artifacts found alongside skeletons provide clues about the lives of specific individuals, either the people who had died or those who put the items in the graves. In a burial at Black Earth they included small bones, stones and tools jumbled together.[29] Presumably these otherwise unrelated items—they have no obvious functional relationship to one another—possessed some ritual significance. If so, this cluster of objects is an early example of the medicine bundles that continued to be used into the historic period.

Growing Native Plants

Studies of plant remains over the past several decades have greatly altered ideas about Middle to Late Archaic life. In fact, Bruce Smith has argued that eastern North America—specifically the southern Midwest and Midsouth—was one of several places in the world where plants were independently domesticated.[30]

The long road to agricultural economies began with campsite clearings.[31] When repeatedly occupying the same places, people felled trees to break the forest canopy, thereby creating sun-drenched openings, and they enriched the soil with everyday waste. These settings were conducive to the growth of pioneering weedy plants, some of which proved to be valuable as food, especially their seeds. The next steps toward agriculture involved little more than tolerating useful plants that thrived in these clearings, or even encouraging their growth through occasional weeding and watering. Today, we are familiar with some of the descendants of Late Archaic cultivated plants (cultigens), notably sunflowers, acorn and scallop squashes, crooknecks, and fordhooks. Other plants that were once important—goosefoot, marsh elder, maygrass, erect knotweed, and little barley—are not as widely known and, if recognized at all today, are regarded as weeds.

Cultivated plants first appeared across a broad area stretching from central Illinois southward to northern Alabama, and from Missouri and Arkansas eastward to the western Appalachians.[32] Cucurbits also extended into the Northeast. While people dispersed the plants beyond their natural ranges, the mix of species that they grew was not always the same. By the beginning of the second millennium BCE, at least four plants had become domesticated, with the earliest signs of changes from their wild ancestors occurring as much as a millennium earlier. The morphological markers indicating a domesticated status are testa (seed coat) thickness for goosefoot; achene (dry fruit containing a seed) size for marsh elder and sunflower; and rind thickness for cucurbits. Changes in the seeds are thought to encourage quicker germination and seedling growth, characteristics that gave the plants a selective advantage in the dense stands that grew in the organic-enriched soil that built up where people settled for long periods of time.

Such hardy plants, which quickly invaded old campsites, were a reason to return repeatedly to spots where other essential foods were plentiful. The people who grew these plants were undoubtedly concerned with minimizing the risk of food shortages. Seeds could have been stored for use during the late winter months, a lean time of the year when a little extra to eat could mean the difference between life and death. The seeds must have been especially valued when shortfalls occurred in the animals and plants that people usually targeted as food.

Over several millennia, these cultigens became increasingly important across much of the Eastern Woodlands, a lengthy move toward agriculture spurred on by pressing local needs at each step of the way. Actively caring for gardens took more work than simply collecting wild plants, but the availability of a convenient, reliable, and nutritious source of food offset any disadvantages from tending these hardy weedy species.

Agricultural economies were not a foreseeable end toward which generations of prescient hunters-and-gatherers unerringly headed. People could not have anticipated, nor would they have cared about, any benefits that crops might provide for some distant generation. Instead, imperfect knowledge was used to make choices about how to satisfy immediate needs. Humans are remarkably adept at dealing with short-term problems, such as working out how to get enough to eat. They are, however, mainly blind to the long-term consequences, either good or bad, of their actions.

It is noteworthy that the earliest domesticated plants appeared at the same time as overall population growth picked up after thousands of years of stagnation (see box pp. 32–33). Considering the fuzziness of dating the earliest domesticated plants and change over time in the numbers of sites, the convergence in timing is remarkable. Overall population growth across huge areas took place within the context of long and varied histories of increases and decreases in the sizes of individual groups. During the bad times that inevitably occurred, weedy plants, quite possibly stored seeds, could have made all the difference to people whose lives hung in the balance. Although an up-and-down pattern of change over time in local population size remained the same, the declines for people who cultivated plants might not have been quite as severe, on average, as they were for their predecessors. That would favor gradual overall growth; however, from any individual's limited temporal and geographical perspective, that tendency was not noticeable.

Alliances and Antagonisms

By about 4000 BCE, in the Middle Archaic, the exchange of materials from distant places, among them copper, marine shell, steatite, banded slate, and colorful cherts, had taken off.[33] If the variety and number of non-local artifacts bear any relation to the level of communication among different groups of people, they must have had more contact with one another than before.

Artifacts fashioned from non-local materials were in circulation for long periods of time as they were passed from one person to another before ending up far from where they originated. Beads made from marine whelk shells found in graves in the Kentucky middens provide a clue about how valued objects moved from one residential group to the next.[34] Most people buried with the beads only had a few of them, but some had thousands. The overall pattern is consistent with a situation where much of the intergroup contact took place through a few well-connected people. That is, most of the non-local items passed through their hands. They, or their immediate family members, were buried with correspondingly more of the marine-shell beads than other people. There is no other evidence indicating that these individuals enjoyed anything more than context-specific roles in their communities that provided them with greater access to people in neighboring groups, along with whatever unusual objects they might possess. Nevertheless, these burials are early examples of social differentiation that would become more common in the millennia to follow.

Judging from what took place in more recent small-scale societies elsewhere in the world, the social significance of the non-local objects outweighed any value stemming from their rarity, beauty, or utility. People living far from the sources of such raw materials as copper and marine shell would have had no idea about their true origin. Even the most widely traveled people could have had only limited, and probably fanciful, knowledge about what lay beyond their own experience or that of their elders and acquaintances in neighboring groups. In that regard, they were much like New Guinea highlanders who, when first contacted in the early 1930s, did not know that their highly valued shells came from the sea or, indeed, that the sea even existed.

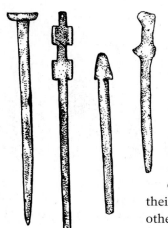

Figure 29 Carved bone pins, such as these pins from Black Earth, Illinois, have been found at a number of Middle Archaic sites. The longest pin is 6.5 in. (16.5 cm).

Neighboring Middle to Late Archaic groups had regular contact with one another, at least enough to share items that must have had some readily recognized meaning. Distinctive carved bone pins dating from 4000 to 3000 BCE, for example, occur at sites across the southern Midwest [**Figure 29**].[35] From their positioning in burials, some were probably hairpins while others were fastened to garments. They would have been easily noticed, marking the wearer's social identity. Not far to the south, along the Green River in western Kentucky, bone pins were also common—they were, after all, of practical value. But the Kentucky pins were typically plain, unlike those in the southern Midwest.

Such regional patterning is also indicated by a particular kind of large stone point, often found in caches, from northeastern Mississippi and adjacent states.[36] The same could be said about copper objects, including projectile points, in the Great Lakes area, especially Wisconsin. This copper came from multiple locations, mainly the Keweenaw Peninsula and Isle Royale in Lake Superior, which are marked today by pits where digging took place. Some of these items have been found in burial contexts, consistent with the social and ritual value placed on them.

The bone pins and other conspicuous objects presumably marked mutually recognized identities or relationships, perhaps real or fictive kin affiliation, individually negotiated trade partnerships, or shared ritual knowledge. Social networks that linked the inhabitants of far-flung areas would have facilitated movement, when necessary, into the territories of other groups. In short, regional constellations of groups were in place, although today they are seen only imperfectly through the distributions of a few distinctive artifacts.

Greater numbers of items moving among neighboring groups, along with whatever was established and reinforced by those interactions, coincided with the shift to a more settled way of life.[37] Social mechanisms facilitating cooperation must have benefited these hunter-gatherers in times of need. Anything that lessened the dire consequences of food shortages enhanced the chances of long-term survival. After all, everybody experienced occasional lean years, especially in the midcontinent during the mid-Holocene warm and dry period, making firm and readily recognized ties among groups indispensable.

Sometimes, however, contacts between Middle to Late Archaic groups resulted in bloodshed.[38] Stone and antler-tip projectile points have been found lodged in bones [**Figure 30**], and some of these unfortunate people were scalped or decapitated. While people fought one another in earlier times—one Early Archaic (8000 to 6000 BCE) skeleton from Kentucky has a projectile point embedded in a bone—little is known about these conflicts because human remains predating the Middle Archaic are scarce. It is also difficult to say how widespread or common fighting was during the Middle

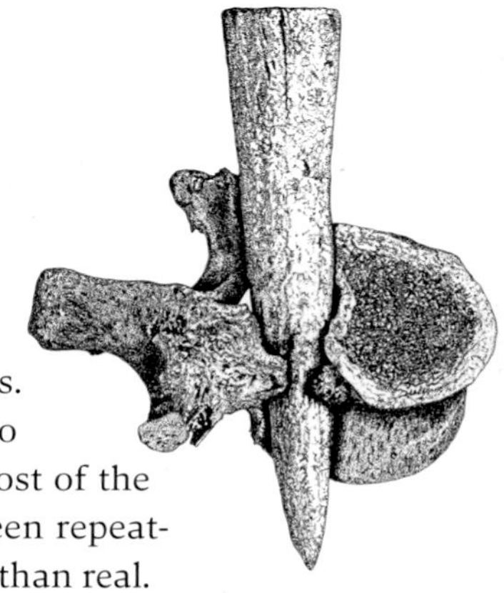

Figure 30 An antler point is embedded in this human lumbar vertebra from Indian Knoll, Kentucky. It is probably from a dart that was hurled forcefully by an atlatl.

and Late Archaic periods. Many of the known victims of violence were buried in the midcontinental middens. But these individuals are a biased sample of all people who existed at that time because the debris heaps also yield most of the best-preserved skeletons. The connection, therefore, between repeatedly occupied middens and conflict may be more apparent than real.

All that can be said with certainty is that people who frequented the big debris heaps were occasionally picked off by their enemies. Tensions were likely to erupt into outright violence when people were unwilling or unable to relinquish claims to especially favorable places. That is, fighting might break out when differences could not be resolved by simply walking away. Conflicts probably broadened and intensified when neighboring groups also fell on hard times, making it difficult for people to move or expand their territories when everyone else was also desperately searching for food.

It is not at all surprising that worsening intergroup relations coincided with a greater exchange of items from distant places. Uncertainty over what might happen when separate bands met encouraged customs that allayed suspicion and fear. Gift-giving is a good, although not always successful, means of smoothing social interactions.

Early Mounds

Middle and Late Archaic people rarely built mounds, but when they did so their efforts were often impressive. Even the smaller mounds are important for being among the earliest examples of formally organized and permanently marked burial places maintained by people living an increasingly sedentary existence.

Mounds and Occupations

The most striking mounds were built in the lower Mississippi River valley.[39] One of the earliest mound complexes is Watson Brake in Louisiana [**Figure 31**]. Joe Saunders

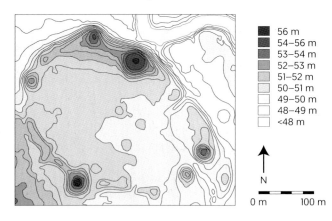

56 m
54–56 m
53–54 m
52–53 m
51–52 m
50–51 m
49–50 m
48–49 m
<48 m

N

0 m   100 m

Figure 31 Mounds were arranged in a ring at Watson Brake in Louisiana. The site, similarly to many others at this period of time, had easy access to wetlands where food was readily available.

and his colleagues have done much to clarify when it was built. Eleven mounds are connected by a low ridge about 3.5 feet (1 meter) high, and together they form an oval about 919 feet (280 meters) in diameter. The mounds are from 3.5 feet to 15 feet high (1 to 4.5 meters), except for one that reaches 24.5 feet (7.5 meters). They were built on a low terrace near the Ouachita River in northeastern Louisiana. The material used to build the mounds, which varied from one part of the site to another, was dug from areas close by, including the nearby terrace edge. That minimized the most labor-intensive part of mound-building: carrying earth by hand.

Watson Brake has been known about for a long time—the number of mounds and their large size meant the site could not be missed. Its true significance, however, was only recognized when calibrated radiocarbon dates showed that mound construction began as early as 3500 BCE, and took place for about half a millennium afterward, although it does not seem to have been a continuous process. The early date for the initiation of mound-building, which surprised everyone when first announced, is a fine example of a single discovery that has had a great effect on our perceptions of prehistory. Archaeological work usually adds only incrementally to existing knowledge, but the dating of Watson Brake provided a great leap forward in our understanding of the past.

Today, it is recognized that a number of mound sites in the Southeast were roughly contemporaneous with Watson Brake.[40] Although evidence for early mound construction is now well established, we cannot yet say why people chose to pile up so much dirt. Excavations at two sites with multiple mounds, Watson Brake and Frenchman's Bend [**Figure 32**], also in Louisiana, shed little light on the reason mounds were constructed or the roles of these sites in the region. But use of the immediate site surroundings by people living in the area is indicated by the amount of food obtained from nearby wetlands. Little was found in the way of non-local stone used to fashion tools and other objects. The excavated material, therefore, is consistent with an orientation toward local areas and only limited contact with people from afar.

A larger and better-known site in northeastern Louisiana is Poverty Point, which continued a mound-building tradition that started with Watson Brake and its contemporaries. Poverty Point, for the most part, dates to the end of the Late Archaic period.[41] Mound construction began here as early as the mid-second millennium BCE and lasted for more than a half-millennium thereafter. There are six curved ridges of soil accompanied by several mounds at Poverty Point (see box pp. 52–53). Postmolds, hearths, and other features have been identified in these soil ridges. The tallest of the mounds at the site, at about 72 feet (22 meters), is remarkable for any prehistoric mound. The soil used in building it indicates it was thrown up in short order—in months, not years. Some of the soil was specially selected for its appearance, not because it was conveniently located nearby. Nothing seems to have been put on top of the mound, the highest part of which is a fairly narrow ridge. Perhaps its significance centered on its visual impact. Other mounds, however, were built in separate stages, with the resulting surfaces used for unknown purposes before being covered with yet more earth.

Numerous artifacts have been found at Poverty Point, including small stone tools, or microliths, used for cutting, drilling, and scraping. There are also many

Figure 32 One of the Frenchman's Bend, Louisiana, mounds, which are now surrounded by houses and a golf course.

beads and small animal-like figures fashioned from various materials [**Figure 33**]. Much of this material, including galena (a lead mineral) and copper, originated in distant places, often hundreds of miles from the site.

Poverty Point was not the only site with mounds in the lower Mississippi River valley and adjacent Gulf Coast from approximately 1700 to 600 BCE, although it was the largest.[42] As one might expect, Poverty Point's big mounds and unusual artifacts have prompted considerable speculation about the nature of this society. Whatever took place was apparently rooted in a cultural tradition stretching back to the time of Watson Brake. Perhaps the people who lived around these sites, maybe even those who inhabited distant places, periodically congregated at the mounds. When doing so, they probably took part in commonplace, but nevertheless important, social interactions, such as arranging marriages, reinforcing kin ties, establishing trade partnerships, and forging intergroup alliances. Such gatherings of people were made possible by the proximity of rich, reliable, and easily harvested resources, especially those from nearby extensive wetlands. The mere presence of a mound—a prominent landmark built through sustained collective effort—may have

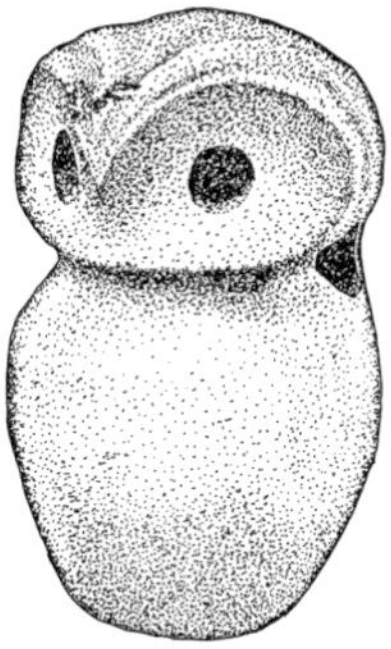

Figure 33 Many small fancy objects, such as this jasper owl bead, have been found at Poverty Point, Louisiana. Height 1.1 in. (2.8 cm).

Poverty Point

Poverty Point is located about 15.5 miles (25 kilometers) west of the present Mississippi River channel in northeastern Louisiana.[43] It consists of curved earthen ridges and several mounds, and sits on the edge of Maçon Ridge, overlooking swampy land to the east [**Figure 34**]. Of the five mounds near the ridges, one has been likened to a bird, another is conical, and the rest are platforms [**Figure 35**]. An additional bird-shaped mound is located north of the main group. The bird mounds—one must have a vivid imagination to see them as such—are elongated and have ramps jutting from one of the long sides. They are big: one is 72 feet (22 meters) high and the other 51 feet (15.5 meters). The conical mound is also a respectable 24.5 feet (7.5 meters). South of the main group is a seventh mound that seems to have been built before the rest.

The six nested, curved ridges of debris-laden soil are each about a meter high. The outside diameter, measured off the outermost ridge, is about three-quarters of a mile (1.2 kilometers), and the inside diameter, defined by the innermost ridge, is about half that distance. Just beyond the ends of the curved ridges, the land drops steeply to Bayou Maçon. The largest mound is situated midway along the outer ridge, and its elongated ramp points toward it. Why the ridges were built remains a mystery, although hearths, postmolds, and other features have been discovered in them.

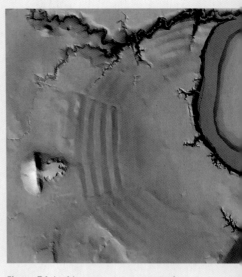

Figure 34 In this computer-generated view of Poverty Point, Louisiana, the largest mound at left center is shown next to low, curved ridges that end at a steep bank overlooking a marshy area. The ramp that extends toward the ridges is lower than the rest of the mound. A smaller mound is visible in the upper left-hand corner.

Figure 35 The biggest mound at Poverty Point is located adjacent to low earthen ridges, which can be seen at top center.

Exactly what went on at Poverty Point is a matter of debate. People lived there, but how many there were, how long they stayed, and what they did at the site are questions that require more work to answer. It is probable that people from the surrounding area periodically congregated at Poverty Point for the kinds of social interactions common to all groups of people, such as finding marriage partners and renewing bonds of kinship and friendship. As for hauling dirt to build mounds and ridges, all that can be said for sure is that it was considered necessary to create a space within which socially and ritually significant events were conducted.

been enough to draw people back to a traditional meeting place that was imbued with social and supernatural significance. A sense of community was reinforced by the combined work of generations of people that resulted in enough earth being moved to make a coherent, readily apparent, and symbolically meaningful site plan.

Although big mounds are impressive, they alone do not indicate the existence of organizationally complex societies and large populations. Mound construction requires only modest investments of effort if it is stretched out over a sufficiently long period. The occupations of Watson Brake and Poverty Point spanned several centuries, if not longer, and it is reasonable to suppose that much of the mound-building took place intermittently over many generations.

The biggest of the Poverty Point mounds, however, is a notable exception. Its seemingly rapid construction necessitated a considerable investment of labor over a short period of time.[44]

We do not know why numerous people journeyed to Poverty Point, and perhaps other sites. Large, culturally diverse, and impermanent groups, however, are known from the historic period, most memorably the one that overwhelmed George Armstrong Custer's command at the Little Bighorn in 1876. It is not inconceivable that many people occasionally gathered at Poverty Point several thousand years earlier. Once there, they were motivated to move vast amounts of earth, and the monuments they produced left a lasting impression on generations to come, even to the present day. Participating in mound-building, even visiting the location of such great effort, presumably fostered a sense of shared identity and experience. The earthen constructions, a visible connection to a deep past, marked a place of sacred and secular significance. Through the collective effort of building mounds, the site became a natural location for many people to congregate year after year.

Much has been made of the ornaments and other objects found at Poverty Point, but their mere presence means little. Craft specialists, a hallmark of complex societies, are not always needed to produce attractive or well-made objects with commonly available tools. Members of small-scale societies around the world are known to make aesthetically pleasing objects that require great perseverance, time, and skill. More interesting is what the beads and tiny figures, as well as many varieties of chert, might indicate about how they got to the site in the first place.

Figure 36 Mounds at Horr's Island, Florida, were constructed of sand and shell.

It is undoubtedly true that many more unusual materials and objects ended up at Poverty Point than left it.[45] The preponderance of non-local items was sufficient to be recognizable in the materials that were intentionally left behind, discarded, or lost here. This imbalance suggests something other than simple reciprocal exchanges among people, which were typical of the Late Archaic period elsewhere. Perhaps the periodic gatherings of people included individuals who carried easily portable items that were critical when performing their social and ritual duties.

The size and structure of the society centered on Poverty Point is a matter of debate. Whatever was going on there and at associated sites could be labeled complex in comparison to the majority of Eastern Woodlands hunter-gatherer societies at that time.[46] After all, impressive amounts of earth were moved and many non-local items were brought to the site. Yet there is no compelling evidence pointing toward the existence of permanent leadership positions or a hierarchical organization where one or more social groups dominated others. The complexity in social relationships and interactive behavior at Poverty Point seemingly did not involve the establishment of a society along the lines of the chiefdoms that emerged about two millennia later. Certainly, some individuals at Poverty Point must have enjoyed more influence than others. Leaders, even if the positions were only temporary, would have been needed in large and diverse groups of people. But their ability to inspire and persuade others might have been sharply limited to a narrow range of social or ritual settings, similar to what occurred in many historic-period tribes. There is no reason, except for big piles of earth, to think otherwise.

Other southeastern mounds dating to this period are mostly located in Louisiana and Florida.[47] Horr's Island on Florida's southwestern coast is one such site [**Figure 36**]. It consists of several mounds associated with a deep midden, part of which is an asymmetric shell ring. One mound was constructed in a series of separate building episodes that eventually produced a 19.5-foot (6-meter) pile of sand and shell. First, a low sand mound covered by shell was built on a dune. Later, more sand

and shell were added, and finally a thick shell cap. Three other such mounds at Horr's Island ranged from 5 to 13 feet (1.5 to 4 meters) high. The piles of shell and sand were deliberately built; they were not mere heaps of waste material. While it is not known how they were used, they presumably had some ritual or social significance for the people whose nearby settlement produced an extensive shell midden.

Burial Mounds

Midwestern mounds are small in comparison to the largest ones that dot the lower Mississippi River valley and Gulf Coast. People of the Middle to Late Archaic period in west-central Illinois and adjoining Missouri occasionally buried their dead in natural knolls or low mounds, typically only a few feet high, on tall bluffs overlooking adjacent floodplains.[48] The mound and natural knoll distinction is of little consequence because the two appear so much alike. Additions of soil only accentuated existing rises on generally narrow ridge crests.

Using information from Late Archaic cemeteries, including mounds, Jane Buikstra and Douglas Charles have argued that some groups in west-central Illinois and neighboring Missouri were more mobile than others.[49] Most of the human remains found in cemeteries along the Illinois and Mississippi rivers were from burials of intact bodies. A relatively settled existence in resource-rich parts of a river valley [**Figure 37**] meant that it was a simple matter to inter people in a nearby cemetery. Conspicuous cemeteries could have marked claims to the best places to live. Formal burial grounds are used by many people around the world to signal control over valued, but limited, resources, such as land.

Figure 37 A transition to a more sedentary way of life involved settlement in places where food was especially abundant and reliable. In the midcontinent, people favored places alongside rivers, lakes, and swamps.

The situation was different in contemporaneous cemeteries located along small streams that creased the surrounding uplands. There, piles of disarticulated bones were commonly buried. The people who lived between the major rivers were probably more mobile than those in the main valleys. That was because, in the uplands, the most productive patches of land were smaller and more widely distributed than they were in the big river floodplains. Bundles of defleshed bones were far easier to carry over long distances to burial grounds than heavy decomposing bodies.

The Late Archaic burials indicate that even groups in close proximity to one another might have practiced somewhat different ways of life. That is not surprising, considering how different communities depended entirely on the abundance, distribution, and reliability of seasonally available resources. All environmental settings were not the same, and neither were the lives of the people who relied on them.

A Time of Change

Whatever the specific meanings attached to mounds, large or small, they must have stemmed from a desire to claim rights over particular places and, for sites such as Poverty Point, to foster cooperation among neighboring groups. Such changes were related to the rising numbers of people who occupied the Eastern Woodlands. More people, on average, increased the possibility that a group might impinge on the foraging territory of its neighbor. Regular communication that involved exchanges of items of symbolic or personal significance presumably eased tensions before they spiraled out of control. Efforts at maintaining peaceful relations, however, were not always successful, as shown by the remains of people who were killed and mutilated by their enemies.

Over the long run, the transformation from a hunting-and-gathering way of life to one based partly on cultivated plants—that is, a more intensive use of smaller areas by increasingly sedentary people—was, once begun, irreversible. Population growth, which accelerated during Late Archaic times when domesticated plants first appeared, ensured that for their distant descendants there could be no return to a purely hunting-and-gathering existence.

Chapter 4

Builders of Burial Mounds and Earthworks: Early to Middle Woodland

In the Eastern Woodlands, several transformations in how people lived took place in the first millenium BCE. A rich ceremonial life, which had undoubtedly been present all along, took a new and dramatic turn with the construction of elaborate burial mounds. Key community members were often singled out for burial in special tombs with highly valued artifacts. In some places, earthworks enclosing many acres of ground were also built. In the midcontinent, native cultigens, several of which had been domesticated earlier, were consumed in much larger quantities than ever before. Pottery was adopted where it was previously absent, and became more common in the Southeast where it dated back to the Late Archaic period. The widespread use of pottery is, in fact, a convenient marker for the beginning of the Early Woodland period. More importantly, it signals the emergence of new ways of preparing food, much of which was grown in gardens. The overall population continued to increase, and contacts among neighboring groups broadened and deepened [**Figure 38**, see p. 58].

Early Woodland societies had appeared by the opening centuries of the first millennium BCE, and they lasted for the next 500 or more years. In the Midwest and Southeast, the following half-millennium or so, ending around 400 CE or a bit later, is referred to as Middle Woodland. In the Northeast and along the Eastern Seaboard, Middle Woodland is said to continue much longer, to as late as 1000 CE. Regional differences in when cultural intervals are said to begin and end are related to the quality and quantity of radiocarbon dates, as well as the somewhat arbitrary business of dividing up continuous technological and social change. But there was also true variation in local cultural sequences, with some developments being more apparent, starting earlier, or lasting longer in certain places than in others.

Two terms—"Adena" and "Hopewell"—are often applied to Early and Middle Woodland artifacts and sites [**Figure 39**, see p. 59]. Adena comes from the name of a mound in Ohio excavated over a century ago. For the most part, it refers to Early Woodland sites in the middle Ohio River valley, including southern Ohio, northern Kentucky, southeastern Indiana, and western West Virginia. But the actual ages of many of these sites are not known because they were excavated before radiocarbon dating was developed. For example, Adena mounds in Kentucky and parts of Ohio

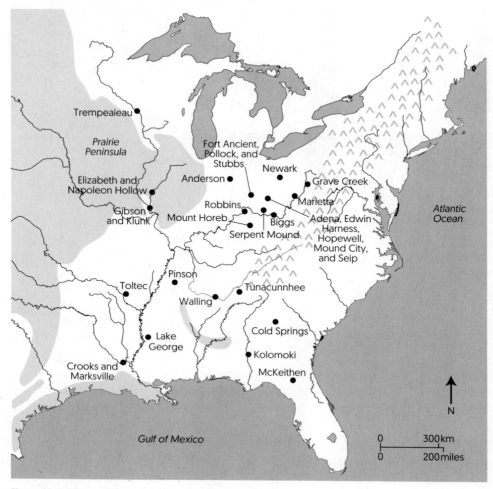

Figure 38 Selected sites mentioned in Chapters 4 and 5.

are thought to have been used as late as the initial centuries of the first millennium CE, squarely within Middle (not Early) Woodland times. Middle Woodland sites, especially those from Ohio, are sometimes labeled "Hopewell." The name comes from an earthwork and mound complex where numerous extraordinary artifacts were found, many of which were dug up for the World's Columbian Exposition in Chicago in 1893.

Burial Mounds

One of the notable aspects of Early to Middle Woodland societies is their tendency to construct mounds [**Plate 2**]. Not everyone built them, but it was nonetheless a common practice, especially in the Midwest and Southeast. While studies of mounds have focused on funerary practices, they were more than just locations for burial.

Figure 39 The name Adena comes from a large mound in Ohio, excavated in 1901.

In the Early Woodland period, mounds varied greatly in size and in how they were built.[1] Many were unimposing with simple construction histories. They include those associated with so-called "Red Ocher" burials in the upper Midwest. Far to the south, along the Gulf and Florida's Atlantic coasts, can be found a sparse scattering of mounds that tended to be no taller than a person's height.

Some of the largest and most impressive mounds were built in the middle Ohio River valley. Referred to as Adena, and dating to both the Early and Middle Woodland periods, they played a prominent role in the now-discredited moundbuilder myth. They include the 62-feet (19-meter) high Grave Creek mound in West Virginia [**Figure 40**]. It was considered enough of a curiosity 200 years ago that the men of Lewis and Clark's Corps of Discovery Expedition stopped to see it on their long trek westward to the Pacific.

Figure 40 The Grave Creek mound along the Ohio River in West Virginia, as shown in a century-old postcard.

Outside of the middle Ohio River valley, mounds were generally uncommon through much of the first millenium BCE. But by the Middle Woodland period, beginning about 2,200 years ago, many earthen mounds were being built across much of the Midwest and Southeast. Some of them were quite large, but the great majority were circular-to-oval piles of earth that were rarely more than a few yards high. Among the most notable of the big mounds were elongated piles of earth covering mortuary structures associated with geometric earthworks located mainly in southern Ohio. These Middle Woodland mounds might appear similar from the outside, yet they differ greatly in how they were built, the ways graves were constructed, and the number of people buried in them.

Adena in the Middle Ohio River Valley

Many Adena mounds were built over places where large wooden structures had once stood.[2] Some of these areas were used for a long time before mound-building commenced, as shown by postmolds for many buildings beneath the C&O, Riley, and Wright mounds in Kentucky [**Figure 41**]. Elsewhere, mounds covered only single structures, such as at Crigler, Morgan Stone, and Robbins, also in Kentucky. Here, initial mound construction conformed closely to the locations of the earlier building. Together, the wooden buildings and earthen mounds indicate continuity in the use of ceremonial space, even if what took place in these areas varied over time.

The buildings and enclosures where mounds were later built were mostly circular, although some were rectangular. Frequently, the postmolds defined areas so big that the structures could not have been roofed over. The buildings that had roofs were often constructed in a style unique to Adena sites: their circular walls consisted of pairs of outwardly slanting posts [**Figure 42**]. Their size and contents indicate they were not used for domestic purposes, but often played a part in mortuary ceremonies before

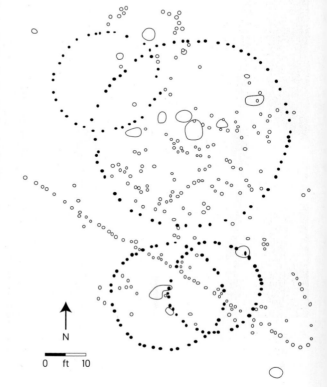

Figure 41 Some Adena mounds covered places where wooden structures once stood, such as at the C&O site, Kentucky [shown here]. The postmolds for four circular structures are shown in black. The replacement of one structure after another, eventually ending with a mound that covered the place where the buildings once stood, underscores continuity in the use of sacred space.

N

0   ft   10

being destroyed and covered by earth. Ashes and charred wood at the Morgan Stone mound show that its building, and the body within it, were burned before being buried. Something different happened at the largest of the Robbins mounds. Here, a small pile of dirt was deposited over a cremation within a building. Only later was the structure taken down and covered by more earth.

Adena mounds also contained graves, often many of them. At Robbins, the sequence of burials was occasionally interrupted by caps of soil that covered much or all of the mound.[3] The soil layers created new and somewhat smoother surfaces, so the mound's enlargement involved more than just the addition of new graves to an ever-expanding pile of earth. This periodic renewal of mound surfaces was presumably connected to ceremonies that reconsecrated the ground. Regardless of whether that took place at a fixed interval or when something unusual happened in the local social group, people repeatedly returned to bury their dead after earlier graves had been sealed by layers of earth. The renewal of sacred places so evident at Robbins would continue to be a common practice that extended to the end of prehistory and beyond.[4]

The most elaborate Adena graves consisted of large logs stacked against low earthen walls, along with other logs forming roofs and often floors.[5] Impressions in the soil reveal that bark was frequently left on the tree trunks. Cross-sections through these graves show that dirt eventually settled into them from above, presumably after the roof supports had decayed.

Figure 42 Partially excavated soil stains, where paired posts and four internal supports once stood, are visible in this excavation of the Crigler mound in Kentucky. By this point in the work, which was undertaken during the Great Depression, only part of the mound remained standing.

Stacked Cemeteries at Robbins

The two Robbins mounds in northern Kentucky were excavated during the Great Depression.[6] The largest—about 130 feet (40 meters) in diameter and 20½ feet (6 meters) high—is an excellent example of how an Adena mound eventually attained its final size. The WPA excavators were so skillful at drawing mound cross-sections that many decades later it is possible to reconstruct the mound's appearance at different points in its long history [**Figure 43**].

The first step in building this mound involved dumping a little earth over a cremation within a circular wooden structure. A heap of soil was then deposited to cover the spot where the structure, by then no longer in existence, had once stood. More soil was later added to create new graves and to cap earlier ones, enlarging the mound.

Individual graves, typically log tombs, were added to the margins and top of the mound, expanding its girth and increasing its height. Many graves, particularly rectangular log-lined tombs, were bordered by earth on all four sides. When tombs were positioned on the sides of the mound, one or more edges of the graves required the addition of only a little more soil. Much of the effort in making the tombs was spent on chopping down big trees for the logs that lined them.

The addition of graves stopped several times during the mound's construction, at which point the cemetery was partially or completely covered by a layer of earth. New graves were then added as before, until they too were capped by more soil. Eventually old graves settled and log roofs collapsed, creating low spots in the mound's surface. These depressions were used for new tombs or were filled when more soil was laid down for additional graves.

The overall result was a mound that was sometimes more peaked than it was at other times. When construction was complete, the highest point was no longer perfectly centered over the original wooden structure. Although there was continuity over time in the use of this burial area, there was no plan from the beginning for the mound's ultimate structure and appearance.

Figure 43 In 1939 and 1940, a WPA crew dug the large Robbins mound in Kentucky.

Figure 44 Many pipes, some more ornate than others, have been found with Adena burials. This stone pipe, partly restored, is from the Crigler mound in Kentucky. Length 6.6 in. (16.7 cm).

Each log-lined tomb held the remains of no more than a few individuals, mostly skeletons lying on their backs. Highly valued objects were often worn by these people or were placed alongside them [**Figure 44**]. Among the notable artifacts, mostly from graves, are copper bracelets and breastplates, marine-shell beads, pieces of cut mica, and small carved stone tablets.[7] Broken pottery has also been found, perhaps from some kind of graveside ritual.[8]

Many Adena mounds were enormous, but the labor needed from any single family when constructing them need not have been great.[9] Mound-building tended to involve numerous additions of small amounts of soil, often associated with the incorporation of new graves. That work was well within the capacity of even small communities, who would deposit new layers intermittently on the ever-growing piles of earth. As shown by Robbins, the shapes of some mounds changed with the passing years. Therefore, their configuration was primarily a matter of expedient choices about where soil should be piled up on an irregular surface. It was not a product of an overarching design established at the outset and faithfully maintained for a long time thereafter.

Middle Woodland in the Middle Ohio River Valley

Middle Woodland mounds, mainly those located in southern Ohio, sometimes covered the remains of large structures that had walls consisting of rows of upright poles and, occasionally, additional posts that supported roofs.[10] These buildings frequently had only a single room, although elsewhere several rooms were connected by short, narrow passageways. Inside were cremations, piles of disarticulated bones, and intact skeletons, all indications of the buildings' lengthy use. It is difficult to tell how many people ended up in the structures, because of poor bone preservation and bad early excavation techniques. Despite such problems, structures in Ohio's Seip Mound 1 [**Figure 45**],

Figure 45 A large mound at Seip in Ohio is open to the public.

the Edwin Harness mound [**Figure 46**], and Mound 25 at Hopewell contained the remains of at least 132, 178, and 102 people respectively. The true numbers of individuals are surely underestimated, although it is difficult to say by how much.

Artifacts were also placed in these buildings, although not always along with human remains. Some objects were intact, whereas others were destroyed when they were deposited in the buildings or when bodies were burned. Great hoards of artifacts have occasionally been found, including items made from copper, mica, and obsidian. Some of the objects were carefully wrapped before being placed in the structures. Copper artifacts, especially breastplates [**Figure 47**] and axes, occasionally have impressions of textiles or, more rarely, scraps of woven materials bound to them.[11] Both vegetable fibers and rabbit fur were used to make the fabric found at Seip, some of which was painted.

A meticulously studied rectangular building in Mound 13 at Mound City in central Ohio is a good example of one of these structures.[12] Part of the mound, which measured about 70 × 90 feet (21 × 27 meters) and was more than 3 feet (1 meter) high, was excavated in the 1920s after it and others nearby had been damaged by the army's construction of Camp Sherman in World War I [**Figure 48**]. The mound was partly covered by a barracks, which made digging it that much more difficult. Further excavations took place about forty years later when the National Park Service developed the site for the public. James Brown has combined information from both excavations, permitting the identification of two sequential structures. The later one, a rectangular building defined by soil stains where vertical wall posts

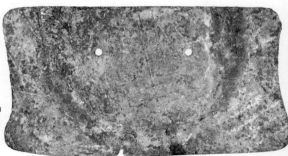

Figure 47 Remnants of paint and two suspension holes are visible on this copper breastplate from Seip, Ohio. Length 11.1 in. (28.2 cm).

Figure 48 Mounds within the army's Camp Sherman in Ohio—now known as Mound City—were excavated in the 1920s. Laborers dug alongside, and even under, barracks, making the work harder than it would have been otherwise.

once stood, measured about 44 × 56.4 feet (13.4 × 17.2 meters). Scattered across the middle of the building were bits of mica, pieces of artifacts, and burned bones that had been trampled into the floor before it was sealed by a thin layer of sand. The ground next to a specially prepared crematory basin, which was slightly more than 4.3 feet wide and 6 feet long (1.3 × 1.8 meters), was scorched by hot fires. Also discovered were four low, earthen platforms with the burned bones of several people and fragments of artifacts; thirteen piles of burned bones, some with ornaments; and a shallow burial with broken artifacts. Most remarkable of all was the Great Mica Grave, a shallow depression with a raised rim measuring 6.5 × 7 feet (2 × 2.1 meters). The soil of the rim was mixed with many items, including beads, perforated animal teeth, pieces of galena, and broken pipes. The grave was lined with sheets of mica, and it contained the cremated bones of four people, a copper headdress, and a circle cut from mica. Earth, sand, and still more mica were then added to cover the grave.

Despite the impressive contents of many of Ohio's Middle Woodland mounds, not all of them covered structures, numerous bodies, and valuable objects. One such mound, Armitage, was about 6.6 feet (2 meters) high with a diameter of 80.7 feet (24.6 meters).[13] Within it, excavators found human bones, hearths, postmolds, and impressions of logs. One skeleton was surrounded by bark, whereas the other burials consisted of fourteen piles of cremated bones. The posts predated the mound, and they were taken down before the human remains were buried. People returned to Armitage several times before the mound reached its final dimensions. When they did so, the evidence suggests that they lit small fires and added more earth.

Illinois in the Middle Woodland Period

Middle Woodland mounds along the central and lower Illinois River and adjacent Mississippi River are particularly well known. They are commonly lined up along

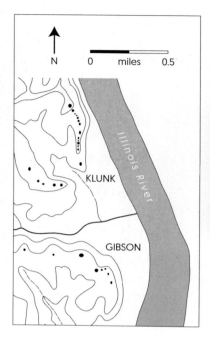

Figures 49 and 50 (Left) The Gibson and Klunk mounds are just two of many Middle Woodland mounds (black dots) on steep bluffs that provide panoramic views of the wide Illinois River floodplain. These two overlook Kampsville, a base of archaeological investigations since the 1950s. The contour lines are at 100-foot (30-meter) intervals. (Above) Views from Middle Woodland mounds bordering the Illinois River valley can be quite remarkable, as here, in 1972, at L'Orient where the river can be seen immediately below the site.

narrow ridges on steep bluffs overlooking valleys, although others are located on floodplains, including some of the largest ones [**Figure 49**].[14] The prominent positions of bluff-edge mounds made them easily visible from the nearby bottomland, where people spent much of their time [**Figure 50**].

The contents of these western Illinois mounds differ, although many of them had central log-lined tombs surrounded by simple graves.[15] Before mound-building commenced, organic-rich surface soil was sometimes removed. Mound-fill, which can be piled deeply, might consist of numerous basket loads of earth or blocks of sod, with the grassy side of the latter generally facing downward.[16] Some believe that layers of clay-rich soil were added to finish the mounds. These supposed caps, however, are usually no more than soil horizons that have developed naturally over the many centuries since the mounds were finished.

Rectangular central crypts typically held the remains of only a few people. Occasionally, the tombs were replaced, with one built over an earlier tomb, resulting in mixed deposits of soil from separate construction episodes that are difficult to tease apart. The log-lined tombs were surrounded by low ridges of earth that were at times covered with thin layers of brightly colored clay. Under favorable conditions, which rarely occur, the impressions of decayed grass or mats can still be seen on these surfaces, as well as bone pins that once held the coverings in place. Intact skeletons and disarticulated bones that were pushed to one side to make way for new bodies have been found in the tombs. Individual bones, as well as small parts of skeletons that were presumably once held together by desiccated soft tissue, were also sometimes moved to the earthen ridges bordering the burial pits. Some tombs held only scattered human remains, indicating that most of the bones were picked up after the flesh had rotted off them. It appears that the practice of placing bodies in graves, and subsequent frequent rearrangement or removal of bones, was as important for reaffirming group identity through a sense of shared burial treatment as it was a means of commemorating a particular person's life and disposing of his or her corpse.

Fine objects were often placed alongside bodies in the log-lined central tombs.[17] Among them were: stone pipes; chipped stone blades and tools; freshwater pearl beads; perforated bear canines; cut and polished pieces of bone from carnivore and human jaws; sheets of mica; marine-shell cups and beads; and copper earspools, panpipes, and celts (ax heads). Well-made pots with decorated and polished surfaces were also put in the tombs.

Simple graves were located around the central tombs. These pits were only just large enough to hold a single body, which was generally laid out on its back. Although these people were often buried with artifacts, the objects were rather unimpressive when compared to what was put in the central tombs.

Elsewhere in the Middle Woodland Period

Mounds elsewhere in the Eastern Woodlands might share some, but not all, of the features discussed above, as shown by those along the Mississippi River near Trempealeau in southwestern Wisconsin.[18] Several rectangular tombs from 6.5 to 11.2 feet (2 to 3.4 meters) long and from 0.9 to 2.3 feet (0.3 to 0.7 meters) deep were found when digging these mounds. The tombs were surrounded by low ridges composed of soil removed from the pits. Strips of bark from several kinds of trees lined the tombs and extended out to cover the adjacent ridges. The bark in one was still several inches thick when excavated, despite the decay and compaction that had taken place over many centuries. The tombs held fully laid out skeletons and bundles of disarticulated bones from two to as many as several dozen people. In one of them, small piles of bones, including both skulls and long bones, were placed on a narrow ledge between a central pit, which held additional skeletons, and the surrounding ridge of soil. Presumably bones had been pulled out of the main pit to make room for later burials and placed on the ledge. Many fine objects, including those made from copper, accompanied the burials. But despite the presence of these crypts, the numerous peripheral graves so typical of mounds in Illinois were not found at Trempealeau.

Several rectangular tombs interspersed with burials of individual skeletons were excavated in a Helena Crossing mound on the heavily eroded edge of Crowley's Ridge, which overlooks flat Mississippi River bottomland in east-central Arkansas.[19] The tombs were built with large logs, and they resembled those in the Illinois Middle Woodland and Ohio Valley Adena mounds. A dispersal of both elaborate and simple mortuary features throughout the mound is reminiscent of some Adena mounds. Similar to Middle Woodland mortuary contexts elsewhere, fancy artifacts were found at Helena Crossing, including those fashioned from copper, marine shell, and mica.

Other ways to bury the dead have been discovered in Middle Woodland mounds. At Trempealeau, for example, dirt was sometimes simply piled on human remains that had been placed on the ground.[20] Fully extended skeletons and groups of disarticulated bones were laid down on specially prepared surfaces where as much as 1 foot (0.3 meters) of the original topsoil had been removed.

Mounds in many places held burials distributed in no apparent order. They include the Copena mounds, which were often about 6 feet (1.8 meters) high, in the middle Tennessee River valley of northern Alabama [**Figure 51**].[21] Intact skeletons,

Figure 51 Many Copena mounds were small, such as this one at the Walling site in Alabama, which was photographed in 1941.

Figure 52 Tunacunnhee's Mound C, excavated in 1973, was covered with stone slabs.

some in puddled clay graves or wooden canoe-like troughs, as well as cremations and bundles of bones, have been found in them. Much like what happened elsewhere, various objects were buried with these people. In fact, Copena was named after the *cop*per and gal*ena* found in these mounds.

Four low mounds at Tunacunnhee, at the base of Lookout Mountain in northwestern Georgia, illustrate the variation in mortuary proceedings that might occur at a single site [**Figure 52**].[22] Three earthen mounds were covered with stone slabs and a fourth was composed almost entirely of rock. Some of the bodies they contained were laid out in extended or flexed positions, while others were cremated or defleshed before burial. The artifacts were particularly diverse considering the small number of burials in each mound. Among other objects, they included not only rather plain stone tools, but also bear canine ornaments, copper breastplates, and, rarer still, shark teeth and panpipes covered with copper and silver.

Beyond Burial Mounds

Two Tunacunnhee graves deserve special mention because of their positioning beyond the outer limits of the mounds. A similarly located pit containing scattered human remains was found at Elizabeth in west-central Illinois.[23] These two sites make it clear that mortuary-related activities were not restricted to mounds, but signs of them are rarely uncovered because few archaeologists bother to look for them.

At Elizabeth, a deposit of debris including obsidian flakes was located on a steep hillside no more than 164 feet (50 meters) away from the mounds.[24] It is a remarkable find because obsidian is rarely found in Illinois. The flakes must have been buried during ceremonies that took place in the area around the mounds. Excavations were also undertaken near Elizabeth at a campsite, Napoleon Hollow, located below the mounds. Michael Wiant and Chip McGimsey found that the Napoleon Hollow materials differed from normal habitation debris. Many more Hopewell pots, blades, and unusual kinds of stone, including obsidian, came from the site than expected, and there seemed to be too few ordinary hunting and agricultural tools. Good cuts of meat were brought to the camp, judging from a disproportionately large number of bones from the fleshy parts of deer. The Napoleon Hollow findings are consistent with those of an excavation of a habitation area near the Tunacunnhee mounds, which yielded pieces of copper and mica. It appears, therefore, that people periodically assembled at special camps for ceremonies that included, but were not restricted to, the burial of the dead in nearby mounds.

Ceremonial Platforms

While most Middle Woodland mounds were domes of earth of varying height, flat-topped rectangular and circular mounds were also built in the Midwest and Southeast.[25] Archaeologists were once reluctant to believe that earthen platforms were built at this time, but studies of old field notes and collections, along with new excavations, have shown that they were widely, if thinly, distributed during the Middle Woodland period.

One platform used for burials was identified at the Crooks site along a Louisiana bayou.[26] Within Mound A, which measured 83 to 86 feet (25.3 to 26.2 meters) at its base and 17.3 ft (5.3 m) high, there was a low platform later covered by two major episodes of mound construction. The initial platform had a 45 × 70 feet (13.7 × 21.3 meters) flat top that was 2 feet (0.6 meters) high, on which several pits, charred material and ash, and three hearths were found. More than a thousand burials, containing both intact skeletons and disarticulated bones, were in the mound. Almost 400 of them were in the upper part of the platform or placed on its surface. The rest were in soil that was added later to cover the platform. Bodies often had been buried in shallow graves, at least some of which were lined with mats. Most of the bones were from adults, but poor preservation presumably reduced the number of juveniles that could be identified. Only a few individuals had artifacts with them, including pottery, chipped stone tools, and copper earspools and beads.

Mound A at McKeithen in northern Florida is another such platform.[27] The site is associated with the early part of a Gulf Coast cultural tradition known as Weeden Island, and it was contemporaneous with some of the latest mound construction covered in this chapter. Graves were dug into the Mound A rectangular platform, and empty pits show that bones were removed once bodies had decomposed. Soft tissue would have quickly decayed in shallow graves in this hot, humid climate. Hearths and posts were also present, as were two small piles of animal bones. The bones, mostly from deer, were presumably all that remained of feasts that took place on or near the mound.

Some platforms were used for something other than the burial of the dead. Examples include the Capitolium mound at Marietta in southeastern Ohio, a mound designated Ma°50 at Walling in northern Alabama, the Ozier mound at Pinson in western Tennessee, and Mound A at Cold Springs in north-central Georgia [**Figure 53**].[28] The Capitolium was partly excavated during a renovation of a public library that today sits on the mound. During the dig, it was discovered that the original topsoil had been removed before thin horizontal layers of sand and gravel were laid down. These deposits were in turn covered by more earth that enlarged the mound upward and outward. Fires were lit on various construction stages as shown by patches of burned soil. At Walling, a few layers of fill had been placed over an earlier debris-laden midden. Pits, hearths, and postmolds were found when the mound was dug, but there were no obvious patterns to the posts that might indicate the presence of substantial structures. At one point, small amounts of colorful clay were laid down, seemingly intentionally. At the Ozier mound, at least six building stages, each covered by a shallow layer of sand, were identified in soil cores. Hearths were found in excavations of the uppermost sand layer. The Cold Springs mound was built in at least five stages. The maximum horizontal dimensions of the mound were essentially established by the first construction episode, so each new deposit raised it upward, not outward. Numerous features, mostly scattered postmolds, were found on these surfaces.

It is unlikely that whatever took place on each of these platforms was exactly the same because the mounds were used by different and widely separated groups of people. But the events all involved carefully prepared and periodically renewed

Figure 53 The Ozier mound at Pinson in Tennessee is a large Middle Woodland mound.

surfaces, occasionally of layers of different colors. The ceremonies held on each mound, regardless of their specific form or purpose, included the lighting of fires and the erection of posts.

Geometric and Irregular Earthworks

In addition to mounds, there are other types of Adena and Middle Woodland earthworks, particularly in central Ohio southward into central Kentucky. There are also some farther afield, such as 20IA37 in central Michigan, Golden Eagle in west-central Illinois, Mann in southwestern Indiana, 15FU37 in western Kentucky, Pinson in western Tennessee, Little Spanish Fort in west-central Mississippi, and Marksville in east-central Louisiana.[29] Time has not treated them well, but a number have survived, sometimes through sheer good fortune. For example, part of the Newark earthworks in central Ohio has been preserved by being part of the Moundbuilders Country Club golf course [**Figure 54**, see p. 72].

One way to provide a taste of the rich diversity in earthwork shapes and sizes is to discuss them in terms of three categories: small enclosures, usually circles or rectangles with rounded corners; large circles, squares, and other shapes; and hilltop enclosures conforming to local topography. But before going any further, one must realize that any such classification masks a great deal of variation in size, layout, and construction detail.

Small Enclosures

Small enclosures consisted of low embankments, often with internal shallow ditches and gaps for easy entry.[30] The sizes of 226 of the enclosures in Ohio, Kentucky, West Virginia, and Indiana range from 0.03 to 3.34 acres (0.01 to 1.35 hectares). These enclosures were frequently built close to one another, and at least some of them

Figure 54 An enormous earthwork complex at Newark, Ohio, includes this octagon and circle. Mounds can be seen just inside gaps in the octagon's walls. Access to the interior of areas encompassed by earthen embankments was often impeded by mounds or other architectural features of symbolic significance.

surrounded wooden structures or mounds, including the Mount Horeb circle and the Marietta Conus.

The Mount Horeb earthwork [**Figure 55** and **Plate 3**], which sits on the crest of a hill in the rolling horse-farm country of central Kentucky, consists of a circular shallow ditch surrounded by a low embankment.[31]

The excavators of this Adena site uncovered a row of postmolds along the ditch's inner edge. The posts would have screened the earthwork's interior from view, as the embankment was not sufficiently high to do so. The earthen embankment, ditch, and wooden wall, in that order from outside to inside, make no sense from a

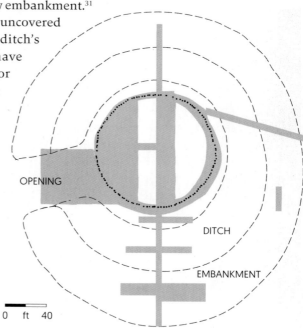

OPENING

DITCH

EMBANKMENT

0   ft   40

Figure 55 A circle of postmolds, marked by black dots, was found just inside an earthen ditch and embankment at Mount Horeb, Kentucky, when it was partly excavated (shaded area) during the Great Depression.

defensive point of view. Instead, the earthwork must have had some ceremonial importance. The excavators did not find the refuse normally present on village sites, so there was no occupation of any consequence near the circle. This is consistent with Mount Horeb once being a ritually significant structure used on only special occasions.

Mount Horeb was probably not the only circular embankment with a wooden wall. Frank Cowan and his colleagues, for example, found a similar large ring of postmolds when conducting excavations at the Stubbs earthwork in southwestern Ohio.[32] The postmolds are thought to be located where a low circular earthwork, which is no longer visible, was recorded in the early nineteenth century. The posts appear to have been taken down before they rotted, and the empty holes were filled with earth that often contrasted strongly with the surrounding natural soil. The work at Stubbs is noteworthy because it shows that it is still possible to add to information about earthworks that disappeared long ago.

A particularly fine example of a circular embankment and ditch can be seen today in Marietta's Mound Cemetery.[33] Here, a low ridge and correspondingly shallow ditch surround a high conical mound known as the Conus [**Plate 4**]. Just as at Mount Horeb and many other circles, the earthen ring is positioned immediately outside the ditch.

Marietta's Conus fills much of the space within the embankment and ditch, but that is not true of all of the mounds within small circular earthworks. Several examples include Spruce Run and Wright in central Ohio, the Anderson Great Mound in east-central Indiana [**Figure 56**], and the Biggs mound in northeastern Kentucky

Figure 56 A circular earthwork at Anderson, Indiana, which can still be visited today, is shown in this early twentieth-century postcard.

Figure 57 The small Biggs mound in Kentucky was surrounded by a ditch and embankment. Photographed in the early twentieth century.

[**Figure 57**].[34] Fires and cremations were an important part of rituals that took place at these sites. Sequentially built clay platforms, each blanketed by ash, were found in the Anderson Great Mound. Ash, charcoal, and burned bones were spread across the ground covered by the Biggs mound. A few features, including postmolds, were also noted in excavations at Anderson and Biggs. Little is known about Spruce Run because it was dug well over a century ago, yet it too covered a layer of ash. The Wright mound contained two cremations and three other burials. Once again, there were similarities in what took place at widely distributed sites.

Large Earthworks

Much larger geometric earthen enclosures were also built.[35] They include the roughly oval Adena earthwork known as Peter Village, which is within sight of Mount Horeb. Its low embankment and exterior ditch enclosed about 23 acres (9 hectares).

Most of the large earthworks, however, were constructed in central and southern Ohio during Middle Woodland times.[36] These geometric embankments, often with adjacent ditches, usually formed circles, squares, octagons, and parallel lines. The great majority of them, at least those mapped by Ephraim Squier and Edwin Davis in the mid-nineteenth century before many were leveled, enclosed areas of several acres up to about 50 acres (20 hectares), although a few were much bigger. While the geometric earthworks are certainly impressive, recent mapping and remote sensing work confirms what has long been suspected: their overall shapes were not as regular as might be imagined from Squier and Davis's hasty mapping of them almost two centuries ago.

Hilltop Enclosures

The shapes of the geometric earthworks contrast strongly with those of enclosures that encircle hilltops.[37] Many of the hilltop enclosures have also been found in Ohio, although some occur elsewhere. Walls of earth and stone were built along the edges of hilltops or slightly downslope from them. Sometimes they ringed entire hilltops, such as at the huge Fort Ancient earthwork in southwestern Ohio that enclosed about 125 acres (51 hectares). Embankments at other sites, including at Pollock in the same part of the state, merely cut across places that provided relatively easy access to the tops of hills.

At least some of the Middle Woodland sites had wooden walls that enhanced the visual effect of earthen embankments by making them higher.[38] Such walls have been traced in Robert Riordan's excavation of the Pollock earthwork. One of these walls consisted of a wooden framework once thickly plastered with mud (daub). It burned, producing a lot of distinctive reddish fired soil, and then toppled over. The wall remnants were later covered with soil, thus preserving them. Elsewhere, a wooden fence lacking a daub covering was built on a low earthen ridge. It was also later covered by earth.

Features that survived long enough to be recorded often blocked openings in the embankments, such as mounds just inside breaks in the walls of a number of the large squares and octagons.[39] The hilltop embankment at Fort Ancient is an especially good example of where gaps in an earthwork are partially obstructed. Mounds, stone circles, ponds, and specially prepared walkways were placed in or near these openings. One gets the impression that gaps in the Fort Ancient earthwork were more important than the earthen embankments. The walls forced people to pass through openings filled with symbolically significant obstacles and paths.

Building Embankments

Nobody knows how long it took to build an earthwork. This work did not necessarily require a particularly large number of people if stretched out over multiple generations.[40] Two or more embankment construction stages have indeed been identified at several sites. But not all of these excavations have revealed discrete construction episodes. An absence of such soil distinctions, however, does not necessarily discount the possibility that the enclosures were built over many years. They could have been made by progressively extending incomplete embankments rather than by adding new soil to increase the height of existing, and already fully formed, enclosures. Only the latter construction method would show up as separate building episodes in excavation trenches that cut across the earthen ridges. Creating an enclosure by lengthening incomplete ridges of soil meant that its ultimate shape and size had to be anticipated in advance and marked out in some fashion. But despite claims to the contrary, it would have been no great feat to lay out a geometric earthwork, as the ever-practical archaeologist Gerard Fowke noted a century ago.

At some sites, efforts were clearly made to keep work to a manageable level.[41] Soil came from nearby borrow pits and ditches alongside the embankments, or it was simply scraped up from the ground close to the earthen ridges. Anyone who

Figure 58 Part of the Newark earthwork in Ohio was preserved in a park, shown in this early twentieth-century postcard.

has moved dirt or large rocks knows from first-hand experience that carrying them over anything more than a short distance far exceeds the effort spent digging soil or grubbing stones out of the ground. So whatever the symbolic significance, if any, of paired embankments and ditches [**Figure 58**], there was a practical reason why they were next to one another. For example, the 16.5-foot (5-meter) high embankment of the 1,201-foot (366-meter) wide Great Circle at Newark was located adjacent to a deep ditch. A ditch positioned right next to an embankment, in this instance inside of it, had the added advantage of accentuating the appearance of the latter's height. The easiest soil to dig was also used to make up the bulk of the earthworks. Hard clay at Marksville was avoided in favor of overlying looser soil, lessening the problems faced by people who had only simple digging tools at their disposal. Debris-laden surface dirt was similarly used in at least some of the embankments in Ohio.

Piling up earth, however, is not the entire story. The original surface soil was commonly removed before earth was laid down to form the embankment walls.[42] At some sites, the surface layer was stripped from much larger areas that extended across much, and perhaps all, of the enclosures. The walls themselves were mainly made of subsoil, so it is unclear what happened to the dark, organic-rich soil that had been scraped away.

Serpent Mound

The Serpent Mound in southern Ohio [**Plate 5**] does not fit comfortably into any of the three categories noted above. This long, low embankment snakes its way down a narrow ridge.[43] The tail forms a tight spiral, and the other end widens where it abuts an oval embankment, commonly interpreted as the head, although some have likened it to a snake swallowing an egg. Recently the dating of the Serpent has been questioned. Long thought to be an Adena site, radiocarbon dates from small excavations raise the possibility that the earthwork might be no more than a thousand years old. Middle Ohio River valley people at that time are not known for building large earthworks—only a few mounds—although they had a high regard for snakes, as indicated by small pieces of copper fashioned into sinuous serpents. Perhaps both sets of dates are correct if the Serpent Mound was repaired or modified over many centuries. Lengthy and complex histories of monument use by culturally distinct societies are known from other parts of the world, and that could have happened here as well.

Earthwork Use

All of these earthen enclosures surely served ritual purposes instead of defensive needs. The embankments were often penetrated by more openings than would be prudent if the intent was to keep enemies at bay. The Fort Ancient hilltop wall had around seventy of them.[44] Furthermore, the perimeters of many earthworks were much too long to be defended by the people who lived nearby. Saying that earthworks held some ritual significance, however, is not very revealing. Clearly many of the Ohio Middle Woodland earthworks enclosed spaces used for burial purposes, but that alone did not require such large enclosures. So it is not surprising that excavations within and near the earthworks, although limited, have turned up evidence of other activities, most notably large wooden rectangular and circular structures in and around the earthworks, including those at Seip, Stubbs, and Hopeton.[45]

One such wooden construction, the Moorehead Circle, was recently identified within the Fort Ancient hilltop earthwork.[46] Excavators uncovered parts of what were three concentric rings of upright posts, within which were a pit, structure, and more posts. Often the posts were removed and replaced before they had decayed and fallen down on their own, indicating care was taken to maintain the appearance of this sacred space. The Moorehead Circle shows there are many more surprises to be found in sites that have been subject to archaeological investigations for as much as a century or more.

Work by Jarrod Burks, among others, using remote sensing methods has provided new perspectives on large parts of earthworks that were first recorded as long ago as the early nineteenth century.[47] At the Steel Group in southern Ohio, for example, the remnants of more small earthen enclosures were identified than were visible, or at least mapped, when the site was originally described. The work there, in conjunction with excavations at Stubbs and Fort Ancient, show that the ceremonial grounds were packed with far more ritually and socially significant architecture than meet the eye today. All of the wooden structures and small earthen enclosures would not have been contemporaneous, but these sites still must have been quite busy places when people periodically congregated there.

Precious Objects from Distant Places

Adena and Middle Woodland societies are noteworthy for their exchange of non-local raw materials and artifacts of great symbolic significance. The people buried in

Figure 59 Numerous obsidian bifaces (stone implements flaked on two sides to make a cutting edge) were uncovered in Mound 25 at Hopewell, Ohio. The bigger one shown here is 9.6 in. (24.4 cm) long. Bifaces that size had ritual, not practical, value.

the Adena mounds possessed numerous items fashioned from copper, such as bracelets, as well as mica cut into various shapes. The intensity and geographical scope of interaction among different groups increased during Middle Woodland times, as indicated by the overall quantity of items, how far they were carried, and the number of widely dispersed societies that participated in these exchanges. Among these materials, which were often passed along as finished objects, were copper from Lake Superior; silver from Lake Superior and, especially, Ontario; galena from Missouri and Illinois; mica from the southern Appalachians; chert from various places, including Ohio, Indiana, and Illinois; pipestone from Ohio and Illinois; alligator teeth from the lower Mississippi River valley eastward to Florida; marine shells from the Atlantic and Gulf coasts; Knife River chalcedony from North Dakota; and obsidian from Yellowstone in Wyoming.[48] The distance over which the obsidian was transported is remarkable—Yellowstone and the main concentration of Ohio earthworks are separated by about 1,430 miles (2,300 kilometers). It is not known whether this obsidian was carried overland or in canoes along rivers. If by water, the longest stretch being the Missouri, the journey along meandering rivers was more than twice the straight-line distance.

Many more objects made from non-local materials ended up in Ohio than elsewhere [**Plate 6** and **Plate 7**].[49] The uneven distribution of obsidian artifacts and debris east of the Mississippi is particularly remarkable, especially since the overwhelming majority came from Ohio, notably from two Hopewell site mounds [**Figure 59**]. Excavations at Hopewell also uncovered large caches of copper and mica objects [**Figure 60**]. Mound 2 held a cache of more than 8,000 large oval chert bifaces [**Figure 61**]. Small groups of the bifaces were covered with earth as if they had been laid down as separate bundles. Impressive hoards have also been found at other sites, including Fort Ancient and Edwin Harness, among others. At Fort Ancient, more than fifty copper artifacts, mostly breastplates and earspools, were accompanied by about twice as many from cut mica. One hundred or more pieces of cut mica were found in a grave at Edwin Harness.

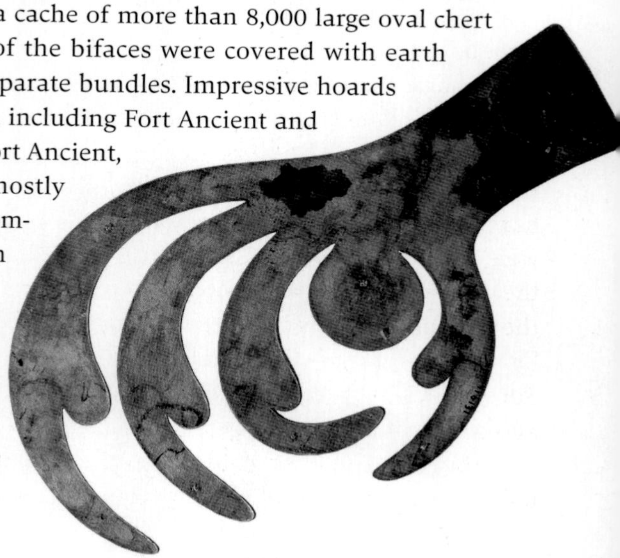

Figure 60 A mica cutout depicting a bird's claw came from the Hopewell site in Ohio. Height 11 in. (27.9 cm).

Figure 61 Excavations in Hopewell's Mound 2 yielded many chert bifaces, including those piled outside a tent in this early 1890s field camp.

Several other places in the Eastern Woodlands also have unusually high numbers of non-local artifacts.[50] Many fine objects, such as copperwork and marine shells, were buried in the Illinois mounds. At the Baehr site, one of two deposits of chert bifaces contained over 6,000 items. Small piles of bifaces had been placed on the ground and then covered with a little dirt, just like what took place in Hopewell's Mound 2. Turning to the Southeast, more copper artifacts have been found in the Copena sites than anywhere else in the South. Individual sites, such as Tunacunnhee, have also produced unusually large numbers of remarkable finds.

Although numerous non-local objects, both raw materials and finished artifacts, have been found in southern Ohio and in such places as west-central Illinois, they would hardly have been noticed on a day-to-day basis. Most of them have been found in contexts related to special ritual activities, often those connected to a commemoration of the dead. They are not much in evidence in common residential sites. Efforts were probably made to prevent objects imbued with ritual significance from being harmed through casual contact. Others, valued principally because of their rarity, were probably collected by kin groups for later use in impressive displays that boosted their standing within local communities. The discrete piles of bifaces that made up the enormous hoards at Hopewell and Baehr are consistent with contributions made by separate groups of people. Burying valued items, often destroying them when doing so, effectively removed them from circulation. They therefore remained strange and wonderous, enhancing their social and ritual significance.

Many items that originated elsewhere must have been passed from one individual to the next, presumably as part of ceremonies that involved displays of wealth

Remarkable Discoveries at Hopewell

Hopewell in central Ohio, originally known as Clark's Works, is noteworthy because some of the most impressive artifacts from the Eastern Woodlands have been found there.[51] Many of them were uncovered when digging for items for the World's Columbian Exposition in 1893; others were discovered during excavations in the early 1920s.

The site consisted of a square embankment adjacent to the much larger Great Enclosure. The Great Enclosure was a roughly rectangular ridge and exterior ditch that encompassed more than 100 acres (40 hectares). In the mid-nineteenth century CE, the embankment was still about 4 to 6 feet (1.2 to 1.8 meters) high. Within the Great Enclosure were two additional embankments, one surrounding the largest mound at the site, Mound 25. It measured as much as 189 × 550 feet (57.6 × 167.6 meters) and was about 21 feet (6.4 meters) tall. It is not known how many mounds were originally at Hopewell, but there were probably around forty, most of which were small.

The mound excavations yielded impressive artifacts, often buried together in single deposits [**Figure 62**]. Mound 25 contained a great number of them, including more than one hundred obsidian bifaces and a large cache of copper items, such as axes and breastplates. The obsidian points were intended for display. Many of them were so big they had no practical value, and they were often rather oddly shaped. In excess of 500 copper earspools were found elsewhere in the mound, including a considerable number stuck together in a mass. The other mounds also produced many noteworthy objects. Mound 11, for example, had about 300 pounds (136 kilograms) of obsidian, and several thousand sheets of mica were buried in Mound 17.

Figure 62 A large cache of copper artifacts (bottom center) was found in Mound 25 at Hopewell, Ohio, when it was excavated more than a century ago.

or generosity. There is reason to believe, however, that a down-the-line movement of these objects was not the entire story.[52] Indeed, it is difficult to see how such exchanges could account for huge accumulations of non-local artifacts, such as the piles of obsidian, copper, and mica at some of the Ohio sites. The obsidian is especially interesting because enough of it reached the Hopewell site to form two immense deposits, far more than has been found elsewhere in the Eastern Woodlands. As James B. Griffin pointed out decades ago, a few people might have traveled long distances to get the obsidian, among other raw materials.

The disproportionate number of elaborate items, many fashioned from non-local materials, in southern Ohio must have been related to its reputation as a ritually potent landscape. People presumably journeyed to the many large earthworks, carrying ritually significant objects when doing so.[53] Perhaps they went to Ohio to acquire the knowledge that the builders of the greatest mounds and earthworks were thought to possess. Upon arriving in such places as present-day Chillicothe, the location of many earthworks, including Hopewell and Mound City, visitors from afar would have been awestruck by the sheer number and scale of sacred constructions. This other-worldly experience could have been augmented by participation in the creation or modification of earthworks, mounds, and wooden structures. Perhaps people from southern Ohio also set out on arduous treks to the distant sources of unusual and symbolically meaningful objects, including raw materials that could later be transformed into items laden with ritual and social importance. Such trips need not have occurred often, and some might never have been repeated. Upon their return home, the items people carried were sure evidence of their success.

Whatever took place, travel to mysterious places would have boosted the reputations of those who undertook such long journeys, the details of which were undoubtedly embroidered during frequent retelling. For people who normally never traveled far, trips resulting in the acquisition of knowledge and unusual objects must soon have become the stuff of legend in communities across much of the midcontinent and beyond.

While it is not known what prompted people to head off to distant lands or permitted their safe travel with heavy loads of valuables, it is clear that the Middle Woodland period was a time of unusual harmony.[54] The numerous skeletons unearthed at many sites show few signs of the injuries that occur when people fight one another. A reduction in conflicts among groups is consistent with permeable social boundaries that allowed at least some people to travel unscathed across long distances with unusual and ritually meaningful objects.

Where They Lived

Much remains to be learned about the mounds and what they contain, but more is known about them than about ordinary residential sites. Sparse habitation debris and pottery that tends to break apart quickly in plowed fields makes settlements hard to find.

Soil stains from posts that supported buildings, screens, and drying racks have been found in excavations.[55] Houses varied in size and shape, although most of them were rather flimsy and could have been thrown up without much effort. Hearths and shallow pits have also been identified. Most of the pits must have been used for storage purposes, although some were packed with fire-cracked rock consistent with their use as earth ovens.

Sites tend to be small, with debris rarely covering more than several acres, and often much less.[56] Where structure remnants have been uncovered, there are usually only a few buildings arranged in no apparent order. It appears that many people, perhaps the great majority of them, lived in communities where houses were strung out widely along the banks of lakes and creeks, or other especially favorable spots. Clusters of structures indicate that there were also compact villages. But, for the most part, these settlements did not consist of many households. Nor did people live in them for a long time, based on the amount of refuse left behind. Relatively few sites consist of heavy distributions of debris along with numerous features and dark organic-rich middens. These places were occupied by larger numbers of people, for longer periods of time, or both. Scattered around such permanent settlements, regardless of their layout or duration of use, were temporary camps used when hunting, fishing, or collecting wild plants.

Settlements were often clustered in the vicinity of the big Ohio earthworks, which comes as no surprise because earthworks were often situated in resource-rich stretches of river valleys.[57] Here again, households were usually widely dispersed, as indicated by bits of pottery and stone spread thinly across modern farmers' fields. The earthen complexes themselves, however, were used for ceremonial events, not for domestic purposes.

Coastal sites likewise vary in size, and many of them are composed primarily of discarded shells from innumerable meals.[58] Judith Bense has found that shell deposits along the Gulf Coast range from shapeless dumps to big rings and long ridges conforming to nearby shorelines. Pits, hearths, and postmolds have been identified in them. The sites, including many shell middens, seem to be distributed in clusters along the coast. Here, too, people were unevenly spaced across the land. Each group of sites features at least one large midden, sometimes accompanied by mounds.

Only rarely is it possible to get a glimpse of daily life beyond the tools used and food eaten, the construction and arrangement of houses, and the burial of the dead. Therein lies the importance of one of five figurines from the Middle Woodland Knight mounds in west-central Illinois.[59] A woman is depicted grasping an arm and a leg of a child who is draped across her back [**Plate 8**]. It must have been a common sight because this way of holding children was also noted as occuring more than a millennium later in coastal North Carolina [**Plate 9**]. Late sixteenth-century English colonists regarded it as a "strange manner of bearing their children, and quite contrarie to ours."[60] Even younger children during the Middle Woodland period were apparently often strapped into cradleboards, which produced a slight flattening of the back of the head.[61] That unintentional cranial deformation was widespread, and it too had a considerable time depth, extending to the historic period.

Cultivating Gardens

About 2,000 years ago, in the Middle Woodland period, there was a major shift in diets in the midcontinent.[62] From that point onward, many people relied heavily on weedy plants, grown in gardens, that were prolific producers of starchy and oily seeds. Productivity near settlements correspondingly increased, most importantly through the addition of a readily storable harvest of nutritious seeds. The heavy dependancy on a mix of native cultigens was not the first major change in diets that took place in eastern North America, nor would it be the last. It was nonetheless important because it signaled a departure from long-established ways of life that focused mostly, if not exclusively, on hunting game, fishing, and gathering wild plants.

For some decades it has been widely recognized that the move to agriculture spanned several thousand years. As we have seen, Middle to Late Archaic people had already begun to direct more of their attention toward plants and animals that were locally abundant and rapidly replenished through high reproductive rates. They included weedy plants that yielded seeds that could be eaten immediately or stored for lean times of the year.

The transition to agriculture was undoubtedly a lengthy process, but that does not necessarily mean it was as gradual as commonly thought (see box pp. 84–85). Archaeologists tend to favor interpretations featuring slow, steady, and incremental change over those involving abrupt transformations. That is because the latter have often been shown to be a result of gaps in cultural sequences, so intermediate stages are missing. Yet here is an occasion where major shifts in food production took place in sharp and widely spaced steps—meaning, in human terms, that each transition might have spanned only several lifetimes.

In the midcontinent, there is a dramatic increase in native plant seeds occurring in samples of carbonized plant remains from sites up to 2,000 years old. They sometimes virtually replace nutshells, which can be used as a measure of wild plant consumption because they preserve so well. This shift in food took place when the overall population was growing. In fact, it was the second long-lasting period of population increase, with the first occurring much earlier in Paleoindian times. Moreover, the first known domesticated erect knotweed at a midcontinental site, based on the size and coat appearance of its single-seeded fruit (achene), has been dated to around 1 CE.[63] In other places, this plant retained its wild form, despite being an important source of food. Changes in erect knotweed, as with those of other native cultigens that occurred much earlier, were connected to people altering their immediate environments, modifying the competitive pressures on seedlings as they did so.

Maize also made its appearance several centuries before it became a dietary staple, which happened in some places toward the end of the first millennium CE, and in others a few centuries later.[64] Initially, maize was rarely grown and spottily distributed, to judge from its near absence in the vast quantities of plant remains that have been studied from numerous sites in diverse environmental settings. Therefore both native cultigens and maize were around long before they rather abruptly became major components of diets over the space of only a few generations.

A Move toward Agriculture

A considerable amount of information about ancient diets has come about through the use of water screening, or flotation, to separate small bones, seeds, and nutshells from soil. It is now possible to use the botanical data to illustrate the overall trend in the intensification of food production.

In the two graphs shown here, the dots represent the charred, hence preserved, plant remains found at many sites [**Figure 63**]. Some sites were occupied at different times, so each occupation gets its own dot. The plants include nuts, mostly hickories; introduced crops, both maize and beans; and the native cultigens squash, goosefoot, marsh elder, erect knotweed, maygrass, little barley, and sunflower. All sites have more than one hundred identifiable fragments, with data gleaned from published sources. The horizontal axes show the approximate ages of the samples. The vertical axes indicate the proportions of different kinds of plants.

Most sites are from the midcontinent, which is where botanical specialists have been especially active. The sites are unsorted according to geographical location, amount sampled, season of use, or length of occupation. Therefore patterning in these data is muddier than if sites could be reliably separated according to their function.

The dots in the upper graph show, for each sample, the burned remains of plants grown in gardens (maize, beans, and native cultigens) relative to all cultigens plus nutshells. Nutshells serve as a crude measure of wild plant food. The inclusion of such plant remains as berry or grape seeds has no noticeable effect on the general pattern because nutshell dominates the wild plant material.

The lower graph is organized in much the same was as the upper one, except the dots indicate the abundance of introduced cultigens (maize and beans) relative to all cultivated plants (maize and beans, plus native cultigens). Beans are poorly represented in archaeological assemblages, so what is shown is essentially the representation of maize in samples of cultivated plants.

It appears from the data that native cultigens were first used heavily in many places about 2,000 years ago. Maize began to make a major contribution to diets as much as 1,000 years later. It is far simpler to identify the range of foods in diets than it is to estimate the amounts actually eaten. Yet despite an inability to go directly from preserved botanical materials to the composition of prehistoric meals, major shifts in the proportions of food remains—for example, plants that were cultivated instead of merely gathered—mark significant changes in how people went about getting enough to eat.

What is clear is the road to a heavy reliance on cultivated plants was long. But it proceeded in a step-like fashion. Lengthy periods of near stasis were interrupted by episodes of innovation that resulted in marked changes in diets. Those transitions took place over no more than a few centuries.

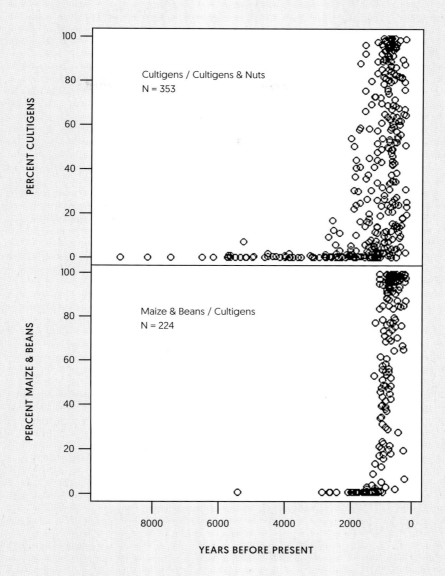

Figure 63 The road to agricultural economies was long, but it was not smooth, as shown by burned plant remains in archaeological samples from many sites (dots). The upper graph shows cultigens, both native and introduced plants, relative to all cultigens and nutshell. The lower graph shows the same for maize and beans, mostly the former, in terms of all cultigens, including native plants.

A relatively abrupt shift to a strong reliance on native cultigens during the Middle Woodland period suggests that a point was eventually reached where far-reaching technological and social innovations, perhaps including a greater need for collective labor at certain times of the year, were required if further increases in yields were to be realized. A step-wise development of agricultural economies—first to native cultigens and then to maize and beans centuries later (see Figure 63, p. 85)—makes sense if different interlocking components of human cultures are taken into account. Throughout most of prehistory, a slow overall rate of population growth meant that innumerable incremental changes in how people lived adequately satisfied additional demands for food. When one's existence hangs in the balance, people tend to opt for the familiar, as long as it works sufficiently well, rather than to experiment with something that by its very novelty is inherently risky. But particular ways of life are not infinitely adjustable. With a growth in population, there inevitably comes a time when tweaking an existing survival strategy is no longer sufficient. In this instance, a further reliance on native cultigens had to involve a major restructuring of the annual cycle of activities along with the means of organizing labor for critical tasks, such as planting, harvesting, and preparing seeds for storage. Group mobility and size, gender roles, social institutions, and so on had to change more or less in tandem. Once people committed themselves to a new way of life, the proportion of seeds in their diets skyrocketed. For hundreds of years thereafter, further incremental changes in how people lived once again resulted in sufficient increases in yields when they became necessary.

Indigenous cultigens were not as heavily used north, east, and south of the midcontinent. It was not as if these plants were totally absent—cucurbits, for example, have been found at sites dating to the mid-Holocene in the Northeast—but people did not rely nearly so much on them. In areas peripheral to the midcontinent, another thousand years would pass before people shifted from wild plants to those grown in gardens, at that point largely maize. It cannot be expected that dietary practices changed all at the same time across the length and breadth of an environmentally and culturally diverse region, and considerable variability in that process is precisely what is seen.

People everywhere continued to gather wild plants, such as nuts and berries, for food, as well as to hunt and fish [**Figure 64**]. Meat from white-tailed deer and other mammals contributed much to diets, but so too did fish from streams and wetlands.[65] The essential role of fish in many diets

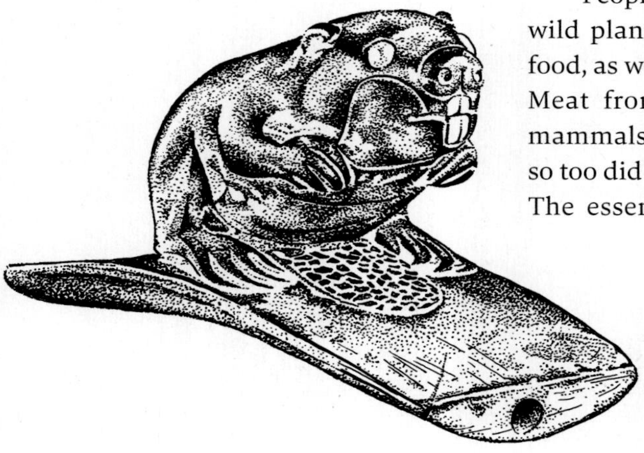

Figure 64 Animals, including those from wetlands, were sometimes depicted on Middle Woodland objects, such as on this beaver pipe from Bedford, Illinois. Length 4.6 in. [11.6 cm].

Figure 65 There are many Middle Woodland sites, including this large mound, located in a stretch of the Mississippi River floodplain in Jackson County, Illinois, that was once mainly marshy ground. The positioning of these sites underscores the importance of food from wetlands to the people of this time period.

influenced decisions about where to settle. Early to Middle Woodland sites along the Mississippi River in southwestern Illinois tended to be located near extensive backwater lakes and swamps [**Figure 65**]. Another good example is the strong wetlands orientation of food-acquisition strategies in the vicinity of Saginaw Bay in Michigan. Shellfish and fish quite naturally made up much of the diet of coastal people, as they had for quite a long time; they would continue to do so until after Europeans arrived on the continent. Shell heaps, however, can be deceiving. Fish were actually more important than shellfish as a source of food along the Gulf Coast.[66] Fish bones are just not as noticeable as shells.

Changes in diets are commonly believed to have resulted in a wider use of pottery midway through the first millennium BCE. Early Woodland vessels must have satisfied some demand that did not exist before, presumably a desire to cook seeds to make a thick porridge. While a reasonable enough explanation for the adoption of pottery in the midcontinent, people elsewhere did not eat nearly so many seeds. Perhaps these people, some of them at least, also began to place a greater emphasis on such food as acorns, which demanded greater preparation time, including prolonged cooking. Whatever happened, the earliest pots were unlikely to have been a great improvement over containers that had been around for a long time. The tilt toward pottery must have been related to some combination of cooking and storage requirements, the durability and portability of various kinds of containers, the effort to make them, the contexts of their use, and the extent of group mobility.

New food-production strategies probably played a big part in what we see as most unusual about this period of time: great ceremonies, extraordinary symbolically charged objects, and generally harmonious intergroup relations. When people switched to a heavy reliance on plants, it became possible to produce surpluses with little additional work, making this a time of relative plenty. Extra food, especially when available on a consistent basis, could be deployed to sponsor ceremonies involving mound and earthwork construction. A greater reliance on plants from gardens provided a cushion that blunted the worst effects of shortfalls in wild foods. Correspondingly fewer periods of great hunger meant that people did not have as many reasons to extend their foraging trips onto land claimed by their neighbors, who might also be experiencing hardship. A relaxation of tensions could be why some individuals, even if only a few of them, were able to travel long distances carrying precious artifacts through territories controlled by many different groups of people.

The Nature of Mound-Building Societies

Mounds provide a few clues about how Early to Middle Woodland societies were organized. Most importantly, only some community members were singled out for special mortuary treatment. These people were buried with the finest objects available, many fashioned from non-local materials, indicating certain individuals or groups had a higher status than others.

Mounds held only a small fraction of nearby populations. But access to them was not as restricted as archaeologists once thought.[67] When many of the Adena mounds were dug early in the twentieth century CE, it was believed that they contained mostly young men. But better means of estimating age and sex are available today. At Robbins, a wide range of ages and both sexes are well represented in the skeletal collection. Yet it is still true that mostly adults were buried here and at the other Adena mounds. The situation for the Ohio Hopewell mounds is similar—it was once thought that males greatly outnumbered females. A roughly equal representation, however, has been found in the adults from Seip Mound 1 and Hopewell Mound 15. At Seip, individuals of all ages were present, although there were fewer infants than expected. Finding too few infants is common in archaeological samples because mortuary customs sometimes excluded the very young from burial grounds, bone preservation is frequently poor, and excavation methods in the past often were not up to the task of finding small bones. Some combination of the above surely affects the Ohio Hopewell sample.

The central tombs in the Illinois Middle Woodland mounds provide hints about who enjoyed the highest social standing. They held juveniles and adults of both sexes.[68] At some sites, such as Gibson and Klunk in the lower Illinois River valley, mostly adults and mainly males were buried in the crypts and on the surrounding earthen ridges. It seems that women were granted access to tombs only when men were already present. But this pattern does not hold true everywhere in west-central Illinois, such as at Elizabeth. Furthermore, the men in Gibson's central tombs were somewhat taller, on average, than those in the nearby simple graves. In some communities, an imposing physical presence apparently contributed to the achievement of high status.

The people who received special treatment upon their deaths must have held positions of great respect and influence in their lineages or communities. Many of them were involved in rituals critical to the well-being of their local groups, to judge from the fragments of ceremonial costumes that have survived.[69] They included cut maxillae (the upper part of the jaw) and mandibles (the lower part), complete with teeth, from carnivores and humans. At least some of these bones must have been attached to masks or other articles of clothing. One wolf palate retaining anterior teeth, including sharp canines, was buried with someone whose upper front teeth had been knocked out long before death. The palate was probably held in the mouth as part of a mask. It was presumably a piece of a costume similar to a bear's head and skin depicted on a figurine from the Newark earthwork complex [**Figure 66**]. The same kind of head covering was shown on a pottery figurine fragment from west-central Illinois. Such ritual paraphernalia indicate a wide distribution of similar practices and beliefs. Antlers from deer headdresses have also been found, such as one from a mound at Hopewell fashioned from copper. Deer costumes might have been connected to hunting magic. It was commonly employed throughout the world by people who had no control over the whereabouts of elusive game. Perhaps deer symbolism even had a distant descendant in the antlers that signified leadership positions among the historic-period Iroquois. But if there was indeed a connection, there is no reason to believe that the precise meaning of the symbols remained the same.

Local leaders probably played a central role in maintaining contacts among neighboring, but essentially autonomous, communities. People of consequence at Tunacunnhee no doubt owed much of their success at acquiring Hopewell-style objects to their settlement's location along an important communication route.[70] A historic trail passed by the site, and its use may have extended far back into prehistory because it is a natural route through mountainous country.

Quite apart from being conspicuous displays of wealth, the objects that ended up in mounds must have been potent and widely recognized symbols that underscored connections between different groups of people and their relations with the supernatural. Many of the artifacts, such as depictions of raptorial birds and waterfowl designs on pottery, occur at sites throughout the Midwest

Figure 66 This stone figurine depicting what is probably a shaman, whose head is covered by a bear mask, was found in Newark, Ohio. Height 6.3 in. (16 cm).

and Southeast [**Plate 11** and **Figure 67**]. So by this time, if not earlier, certain beliefs had found wide currency across much of the Eastern Woodlands. Some of the objects must have been part of rituals that took place near the mounds, such as copper-covered panpipes that might have been played in ceremonies before they were buried.

As part of a rich communal ritual life, especially influential members of prominent kin groups probably orchestrated the construction of mounds. In so doing, they enhanced their standing in local communities. These were the individuals who possessed the means to mobilize the resources needed for festivals in which dirt was moved to build permanent monuments. Once the organizational changes permitting a heavier dependancy on native cultigens were in place, it would have taken little additional effort to produce food surpluses, at least in good years. This could have been done to support periodic groupings of people.

Preparations for special occasions can be impressive, as I have seen on a Micronesian island where numerous people took part in an event in a person's honor, which took place long after he had died. Vast quantities of food were laid out, far more than what could be immediately consumed, in a demonstration of the social group's strength and importance.

Perhaps rival kin groups participated in competitive displays near the mounds and earthworks to enhance their local reputations. One is reminded of the potlatches (gift-giving feasts) of the Northwest Coast, where large quantities of items, many

Figure 67 Middle Woodland pottery was sometimes heavily decorated, especially vessels used in funerals and other ritual events. This pot with a bird design is from Illinois.

having symbolic significance, were presented, distributed, and destroyed on occasions designed to enhance the prestige of the people who sponsored them.

Such events could account for the many precious items that were gathered together and then destroyed or buried in the Adena and Middle Woodland mounds. Ersatz objects were even used when real ones were in short supply. They include mica-covered clay beads mixed with pearl beads from Edwin Harness, and large bifaces of black cannel coal instead of obsidian from the GE mound in southwestern Indiana.[71] Such artifacts indicate that sleights of hand were not beyond people determined to put on the best show possible with whatever was available. Mortuary conventions were endlessly reinterpreted to meet the demands of the moment. So the particular ways bodies were handled and the artifacts placed alongside them varied greatly, even within single burial contexts, such as the structures in Ohio. The human remains and what happened to them were most probably less important than the social and ritual objectives fulfilled by the active involvement of group members in these events.

The most elaborate mortuary facilities—among others, Adena log-lined graves, Illinois Middle Woodland central tombs, and Ohio Hopewell structures—seem to have been used by some form of kin-based social group. Impressive displays related to funerals and celebrations of ancestors were perhaps important demonstrations of the living group's identity and standing within the local community. Large kin groups must have been involved because great efforts and extensive social connections were needed to collect the items consumed in the ceremonies, and much work was required to build or refurbish burial features and earthworks. Such work can be lightened by folding it into socially and ritually significant events that attract willing participants. That was no doubt done, but exactly how people were motivated to help is unknown.

Once built, the mounds served as permanent landmarks that marked long-standing connections to particular areas [**Plate 10**]. They clearly reminded all who saw them that many generations had preceded the people who currently lived nearby. The Adena mounds in central Kentucky, situated on high spots in rolling terrain [**Figure 68**, see p. 92], and the Illinois River Middle Woodland mounds, prominently located on bluff crests, are good examples of that practice. As highly visible symbols of rights to specific territories, these mounds were an integral part of the cultural landscape and how people distributed themselves across it. What they symbolized was important because survival rested squarely on undisputed access to nearby resources, especially food.

Despite the pomp and ceremony that accompanied the burial of key people, these individuals do not appear to have enjoyed special treatment during their daily lives. Judging from the burials, they possessed more precious objects, mostly ornaments, which were displayed on special occasions to mark ritually and socially significant positions. But nothing indicates that everyday life for the most influential community members was different than it was for anyone else. A lack of distinction among people during their lifetimes, in terms of residential structures, associated artifacts, and site layouts, distinguishes the Middle Woodland societies from the chiefdoms with strong hereditary leaders that arose hundreds of years later.

Figure 68 The large Wright mound as it appeared in 1937 before it was excavated. The mound was located on a high hill in the rolling Kentucky Bluegrass region.

Eventually the construction of elaborate burial mounds and the exchange of non-local objects virtually ceased. Years ago it was thought that people simply "gave up the habit of building Mounds, for some reason or other," as if it was simply a matter of choice.[72] Today it would be said that transformations in how societies were organized lie at the root of why constructing mounds and conducting associated ceremonies diminished in importance during Late Woodland times. Changes in social organization were closely related to alterations in population size, technology, subsistence practices, and intergroup relations. But precisely what happened and why it did so are hotly debated.

Chapter 5

A Time of Great Change: Late Woodland

Archaeologists once paid scant attention to the Late Woodland period, as it was considered a "slightly murky interval" dominated by rather nondescript "gray" cultures.[1] Mounds continued to be built between about 400 and 1000 CE, mainly in the Midwest and Southeast, but they were, for the most part, smaller and less elaborate than those erected just a few centuries earlier. Nor did they contain as many high-value objects as those of the Middle Woodland period. Pottery was also rather plain when compared to the finest Middle Woodland vessels [**Figure 69**].

That inattention was misguided. In the Midwest and Southeast, the areas emphasized in this chapter, populations grew during Late Woodland times while settlement locations and their configurations changed. Communication among separate groups of people broke down, with relations often deteriorating into outright warfare. Late in the first millennium CE, maize became an essential part of the diets of many people. Why that occurred and how it set the stage for a widespread development of the hierarchically organized societies in the southern Midwest and Southeast known as chiefdoms are among the most important questions facing archaeologists today.

With the Late Woodland, there are, once again, regional differences in cultural developments and how they are classified by archaeologists. In the Northeast and mid-Atlantic regions, Late Woodland is said to start somewhere around 1000 CE, following a lengthy history of societies referred to as Middle Woodland, and to continue up to the first contact with Europeans. Life at that time is covered in a subsequent chapter on late prehistory.

Figure 69 This Late Woodland ceramic vessel from the Mund site in Illinois has an exterior roughened by cords pressed into the clay when the pot was made, a surface treatment that was common at that time in the Midwest. When excavated, it was sitting upright with another pot in a pit. Height 8.9 in. [22.6 cm].

Mounds of Various Shapes and Sizes

Effigy Mounds

During the Late Woodland period, curiously shaped burial mounds, commonly called effigy mounds, were built in southern Wisconsin and adjacent parts of Illinois, Iowa, and Minnesota.[2] Their shapes have been referred to as birds, bears, panthers, turtles, and lizards, while other mounds take on more fanciful forms or are merely long ridges or domes of earth. Individual mounds tend to be poorly dated, although most of them were certainly constructed between the eighth and the eleventh or twelfth centuries CE.

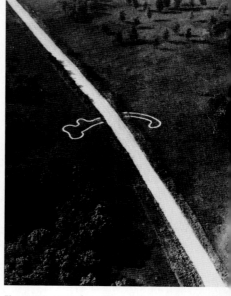

Figure 70 Many Late Woodland effigy mounds have been partly or completely destroyed, such as the Wehmhoff mound in Wisconsin, cut in half by a road, as shown in this photograph from 1927.

Effigy mounds tend to be low, but they can be as long as several tens of yards [**Figure 70**].[3] They were usually built in one flurry of effort that involved scraping up soil and carrying it over short distances. Often, the original topsoil was dug away before earth was added to form a mound. A few shallow depressions that were never filled even survived to historic times, referred to as "intaglios." The mounds contain the burials of juveniles and adults, consisting of complete skeletons, piles of disarticulated bones, and cremated bones. Frequently these were put in the head and heart areas of the animal-shaped mounds. But the few individuals who were buried in each mound were only a tiny fraction of the people who lived nearby.

Effigy mounds are not evenly distributed across the upper Midwest, nor are the most commonly occurring shapes the same in all places.[4] The mounds were often built near one another, forming clusters that might range up to a dozen or more [**Figure 71**]. Lynne Goldstein has noticed a relationship between the distributions of certain kinds

Figure 71 Many effigy mounds were located near Lake Koshkonong in Wisconsin, including this one with a long tail, a shape sometimes referred to as a panther or water spirit.

of mound shapes and environmental settings. Bird mounds occur in many places, but especially in the general vicinity of the Mississippi River, where migratory birds are common, and turtle mounds are often located near wetlands. Such associations should not be surprising because these people's lives were centered on making do with whatever was locally available.

The builders of the effigy mounds followed a hunting-and-gathering existence.[5] Pieces of pottery, stone tools, and other debris have been found near many mounds. The debris was probably left by people who congregated at these spots to hold ceremonies that involved moving earth and burying the dead. These events provided opportunities to arrange marriages and to establish cooperative relations with members of other groups. A few dozen people working for several days could have thrown up a mound while participating in festivities that accompanied such gatherings. Perhaps social groups identified by totemic markers built the mounds to establish claims to particular areas. If so, then several such groups lived in close proximity, even in single communities, because different kinds of mounds were commonly mixed together at single sites. Whatever took place, people repeatedly returned to these socially and ritually important places, as shown by the frequent clustering of mounds, although they were arranged in no apparent order [**Figure 72**].

Figure 72 Effigy mounds were often clustered together, such as those of the Lizard group in Wisconsin, shown here as dark silhouettes.

Other Late Woodland Burial Mounds

Oval to circular burial mounds were also built at this time elsewhere in the Eastern Woodlands.[6] More earth was often added as new bodies were placed in the mounds, so they gradually grew larger. In the midcontinent—from the Ozark Mountains to the Ohio Valley—mound construction commonly included great amounts of stone. Stone platforms or simple structures of stacked rocks were often, but not always, covered by earth. They can be difficult to find if not covered by a mantle of earth, especially in thick forests. One such pile of rocks—all that remained of two small limestone-slab rectangular structures at the L'Orient site—was on a narrow ridge overlooking the Illinois River floodplain. The stones were well hidden by more than a millennium of forest detritus when Michael Wiant and I stumbled across them after having examined two prominent Middle Woodland mounds located further down the ridge.

Mounds dating to this period have been excavated in west-central Illinois on high bluffs overlooking river floodplains.[7] For the most part, they were simple piles of earth for graves that each held a single skeleton. Even when used for long periods, the low mounds remained rather inconspicuous. They often appear much like natural knolls, which can also contain burials. Little consideration was given to the layout of these cemeteries. Later graves cut through earlier ones, and old bones were simply put into new graves or discarded in soil added to enlarge the mounds. The locations of burials were apparently soon forgotten, and no attention was paid to what was in previous, and presumably unmarked, graves.

Juveniles and adults, both males and females, were buried in these Illinois mounds. There is little, if any, discernible evidence for status differences among the burials, but not all people were treated alike. Disproportionately large numbers of artifacts accompanied some of them, children as well as adults. But unlike their Middle Woodland predecessors, these people were not as well endowed with rich grave goods, and they were not otherwise singled out for special treatment when they died.

Plazas and Platform Mounds

Late in the first millennium CE, distinctly different kinds of mounds were increasingly incorporated into community layouts in the southern Eastern Woodlands, especially in the lower Mississippi River valley. They were not the first mounds to be built near habitation areas, but they do represent the beginning of a site plan that consisted of a centrally located open space surrounded by mounds and domestic buildings. The plaza-and-mound arrangement became quite common during the subsequent Mississippian period, which in many places begins in the eleventh century CE. Although archaeologists tend to emphasize mounds—they command our attention when we visit sites today—the plazas were where many events that fostered a sense of group identity and community integration probably took place.

Platform mounds, such as those at sites in the lower Mississippi River valley collectively referred to as Coles Creek, were a key feature of major settlements associated with hierarchically organized societies that were developing at this time.[8] Considerable work, including mound excavation, has been done at one of these sites, Lake George, in western Mississippi. There, mound building began somewhat before 800 CE, but it greatly increased after that time. The Lake George mounds were constructed in several stages, at least some of which supported buildings. The largest, Mound C, contained burials and structures that were perhaps charnel houses. Within a few

Plate 1 [Above] Mounds, such as this one of discarded shell in St. Petersburg, Florida, are occasionally shown on old postcards. The mound, destroyed many years ago, was once an attractive centerpiece for the grounds of a hospital.

Plate 2 [Below] An impressive conical Adena mound can be seen in a park in Miamisburg, Ohio.

Plate 3 (Above) Mount Horeb is located on a hill in horse country near Lexington, Kentucky. Snow fills the ditch, which is flanked by the embankment (left) and the earthwork's flat interior (right).

Plate 4 (Above right) The Conus, as shown in an early twentieth-century postcard, is prominently located within the Mound Cemetery in Marietta, Ohio.

Plate 5 (Right) The Serpent Mound in Ohio is one of the best-known earthworks, but the date of its construction is still debated.

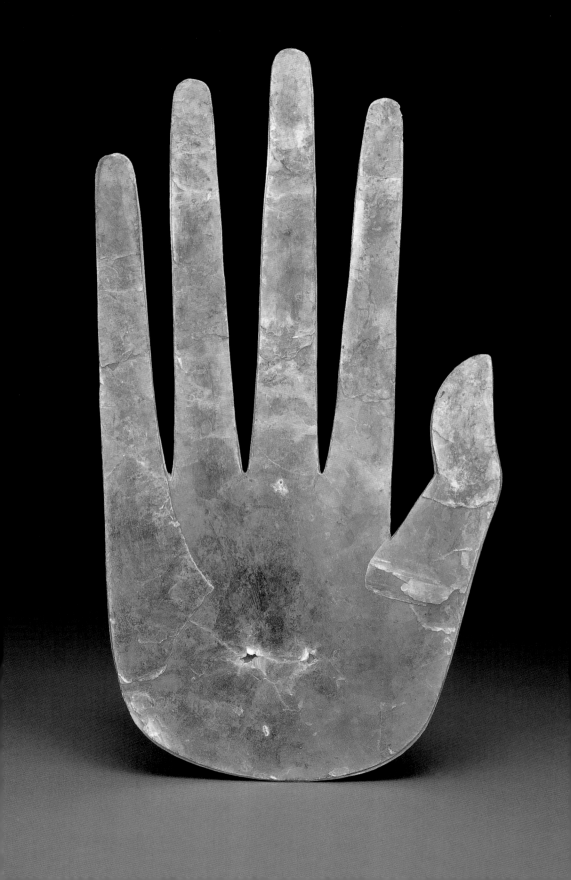

Plate 6 (Left) Mica from Mound 25 at Hopewell in Ohio was cut into a variety of shapes, including this hand with curiously elongated fingers. Length 11.4 in. (29 cm).

Plate 7 (Above) Birds of prey were depicted on some Middle Woodland objects of ritual significance, such as this copper plate from Mound City, Ohio. Length 12 in. (30.5 cm).

Plate 8 (Above) A ceramic figurine from the Knight mounds in Illinois depicts a woman carrying a child on her back. Height 3.7 in. (9.4 cm).

Plate 9 (Right) In the late sixteenth century, women in coastal North Carolina were said to carry children on their backs, in a manner closely resembling the depiction in the Knight mounds figurine (Plate 8) more than a millennium earlier.

Plate 10 [Above] The Middle Woodland Bynum mounds in Mississippi, one of which is shown here, are located along the scenic Natchez Trace Parkway. Part of the site was excavated in the mid-twentieth century.

Plate 11 [Below] This raven effigy platform pipe from the Bedford site, Illinois, was just one of the animals represented on Middle Woodland objects. Length 4 in. [10.2 cm].

Plate 12 [Above] Monks Mound at Cahokia viewed from the southeast. The first terrace, with its ramp, juts out toward the main site plaza. The edges of the third and fourth terraces, the latter only slightly higher than the former, can be seen at the top of the mound.

Plate 13 [Below] A mound at Shiloh, Tennessee, was partly composed of specially selected colorful soil, as shown in this view of the excavation in 2003. The mound, which is on the Civil War battlefield, was dug because it was in danger of being lost through erosion.

Plate 14 Monks Mound at Cahokia is by far the largest mound in the Eastern Woodlands. About one half of the earth used in building mounds at Cahokia went into Monks Mound. Today, an interstate highway, seen in the background, passes immediately north of the mound, through what was once swampy ground in an abandoned Mississippi River channel.

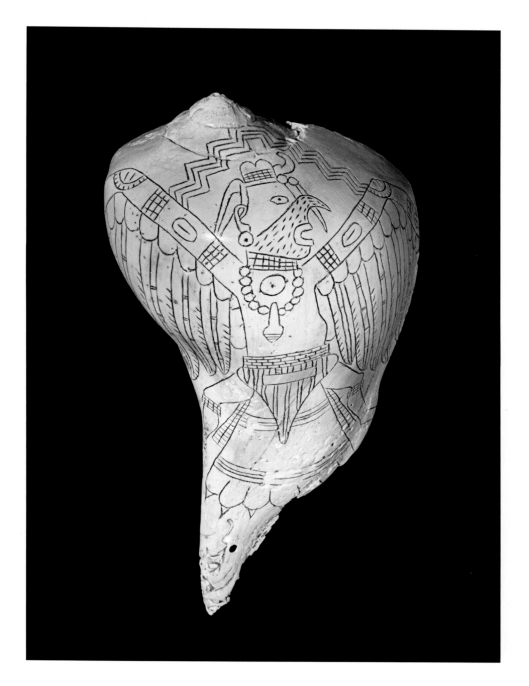

Plate 15 A large whelk shell from Spiro, Oklahoma, shows a man in bird regalia. Regardless of whether such images depict real warriors or mythical beings, they underscore a need for bold and decisive action in war. A bird's wings and tail feathers are shown, as are an earspool and a bead necklace with a shell pendant. Length 13 in. (33 cm).

Plate 16 This red cedar human figure was one of several from the Craig Mound at Spiro, Oklahoma. In the Great Mortuary, conditions favored the preservation of objects that usually decay, such as those fashioned from wood. Height 12.8 in. (32.5 cm).

Plate 17 [Above] One of the biggest mounds at Moundville is located within the plaza. Two of the mounds that surround the plaza can be seen in the background.

Plate 18 [Below] Mounds at Etowah, Georgia, were surrounded by a stout palisade and ditch. William Tecumseh Sherman visited the mounds as a young man, which gave him a feel for the lay of the land that he put to good use during the march to Atlanta in the Civil War.

Plate 19 Two stone human figures were found in a grave at the foot of a ramp for Mound C at Mississippian-period Etowah, Georgia. They were broken, seemingly when originally dropped into the pit, but it was possible to restore them. Height 24 in. (61 cm).

Plate 20 A forked-eye design resembling markings on a peregrine falcon—a bird known for swift dives on unwary prey—is shown on this copper plate from Spiro's Craig Mound. Such markings emphasized the importance of decisive, even ruthless, behavior for people of consequence. Length 9.4 in. (23.9 cm).

centuries—that is, during the subsequent Mississippian period—mounds supporting buildings that held the remains of important ancestors, along with many precious objects, would become a prominent feature of many major settlements.

Settlements with mounds also occur in the vicinity of the Gulf Coast from Alabama to Florida. Dating to the end of the Middle Woodland through to Late Woodland periods, these sites are known as Weeden Island, although there are regional differences among them. One such site is Kolomoki in southwestern Georgia.[9] It encompassed nine or more mounds, with the tallest, at 56.5 feet (17.2 meters), being much bigger than the rest. Fronting the large mound was a plaza where debris was sparse. Mound building at Kolomoki continued for several centuries, although the pace of construction varied over time, as did the settlement's overall configuration.

The most impressive mound center at this time was Toltec, in the heart of Arkansas.[10] Here, eighteen mounds surrounded two plazas, habitation areas, and a defensive embankment and ditch [**Figure 73**]. The mounds included rectangular platforms, alongside which were sometimes the discarded remains of feasts, including many white-tailed deer bones. So at least some of the earthen platforms were used for ceremonies, presumably orchestrated by leading figures in this society, that involved the consumption of great amounts of food (see box pp. 98–99).

These feasts perhaps resembled one that the late eighteenth-century naturalist William Bartram took part in when traveling through northern Florida. People of consequence, including Bartram, were served choice cuts of meat from "three great fat bears already well barbecued or broiled," along with other food, while seated in a "banqueting house" in the "public square."[11] What remained of their meal was later distributed to less notable members of the community, the "families of the town." The dignitaries then retired to a "council house," discussed weighty matters, smoked tobacco, and drank the "black drink," a stimulant made from holly that induced vomiting and was thought to have a cleansing effect. Villagers meanwhile used the square for a "frolick [that] continued all night."

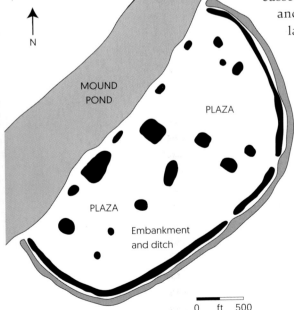

N

MOUND POND

PLAZA

PLAZA

Embankment and ditch

0   ft   500

Figure 73 At Toltec in Arkansas, mounds (black) were arranged around two plazas that were in turn surrounded by an embankment (also in black) and ditch (gray). The site is located alongside an abandoned Arkansas River channel, locally known as Mound Pond (top left). The positioning of this settlement underscores the wetland focus common to many late prehistoric mound centers.

Figure 74 Among the mounds at Toltec, Arkansas, are these two large ones. The site is open to the public.

More than one hundred years ago, Cyrus Thomas called Toltec, which dates from 700 to 1000 CE, "the most interesting group in the state" of Arkansas.[12] His warm enthusiasm about what was then known as Knapp Mounds has been fully justified by the work of Martha Rolingson and her colleagues.

Toltec is located alongside an old river channel, fittingly named Mound Pond, that was left behind by the meandering Arkansas River. A close association with a backwater lake would be seen time and again throughout the subsequent Mississippian period.

Eighteen mounds, along with habitation areas, surrounded two plazas, all of which was enclosed by an 8-foot (2.4-meter) high embankment accompanied by an externally located ditch. The ends of the curved ditch and embankment met the shores of Mound Pond. The roughly straight riverbank and curved defensive work together define a D-shaped area of 104 acres (42 hectares). The site area is naturally fairly flat, although the largest plaza is located on its highest point. Ten mounds, including the two biggest ones, surrounded this 623 × 1247-foot (190 × 380-meter) plaza. This open area has yielded little in the way of artifacts. It was deliberately kept clean, presumably in anticipation of important ceremonies.

Over time, many of Toltec's mounds have been reduced by plowing and erosion, but the two largest ones are still 37.7 feet (11.5 meters) and 49.2 feet (15 meters) high [**Figure 74**]. They towered over all the others, most of which were no taller than a person's height. Excavations in several low mounds show that they were constructed of nearby soil—these particular mounds were built in a few brief bursts of effort. In contrast, excavations into one of the two tallest mounds indicate it was built in at least five stages.

Martha Rolingson's excavations have provided a remarkable view of activities that took place on or around Toltec's mounds. She dug into a low, square platform known as Mound S, one of ten mounds that bordered one of the plazas. It was roughly 52.5 feet

(16 meters) along each side, although the back of it was slightly longer than the front. The upper portion was not intact, but it did not appear to have ever supported a building. More importantly, the excavators uncovered a deposit of many bones, mostly from white-tailed deer, at the rear of the mound; that is, on the side away from the plaza. The bones were scattered over an area of about 3,660 square feet (340 square meters). They became less frequent as one got further from the mound, indicating that the debris came from events that took place on this earthen platform. It seems these bones were exposed for only a short time before being buried, as they lacked signs of weathering and there is little evidence of damage from animals. Therefore this pile of earth was built for special use during feasts that must have attracted enough people to leave behind great amounts of refuse. Bones tossed from the mound were covered with soil once feasts were over. That was sensible, considering the overpowering stench any remaining meat would have produced in the heart of the site.

Excavators also found food debris when they worked on Mound D, another low platform that fronted the same plaza as Mound S. This mound was enlarged at least twice, and perhaps three times. The earliest platform measured 42.5 × 62.5 feet (13 × 19 meters) and the second at least 105 × 125 feet (32 × 38 meters). Debris-rich middens containing the bones of white-tailed deer were located along the sides of these two mound stages. Once again, the refuse was soon buried. A final layer of soil covered the 5-foot (1.5-meter) high second platform, although little of this deposit has survived. That layer of soil might have signaled the mound's termination as a ceremonial platform and buried even deeper the garbage that had accumulated beside the mound.

Scattered Enclosures

Mounds were not the only large construction projects undertaken at this time. In some places, low walls were put up that partially or completely encircled hill crests.

Investigations of Greenwood Village in northern Ohio show that several low embankments and shallow ditches cut across points of easy access to a high flat area otherwise bordered by steep slopes.[13] Little in the way of ordinary habitation-related features and trash was found, so this hilltop was presumably used for ceremonial, not residential, purposes.

Farther south, low rock walls (commonly called "stone forts") are thinly scattered from southern Illinois eastward into Kentucky.[14] They were often built in remote places far from major population concentrations in river valleys. The long piles of stones required no special skills to build, and rocks were carried over short distances, lessening the most labor-intensive part of the work. Often, the rocks only blocked places where access to hilltops was relatively easy, and small stone mounds were built near many of them. Debris from everyday activities can be found nearby, but it is usually scarce and widely distributed.

Because of their locations on hills, the stone walls are sometimes considered to have been defensive structures. Yet it is hard to see that large forts were necessary in sparsely populated areas. In such places, dispersal as a means of avoiding enemies would have been a far easier, but still effective, response to threats. Even if there was a need for defensive measures, nearby populations were insufficient to man the walls of the so-called forts. It is more likely that the rock walls and steep slopes delineated ritually important places much as they did earlier in time. But it is puzzling that the distributions of the Middle and Late Woodland hilltop enclosures, with the former mainly in southern Ohio, are not the same.

Villages Become Commonplace

Evidence for structures is often readily apparent at Late Woodland settlements, in marked contrast to earlier sites. Isolated houses occur, as do small groups of them, the latter presumably having belonged to closely related families. Clusters of a dozen or more structures have also been identified. Here, buildings share similar alignments or are arranged in a regular fashion, indicating coherent community layouts. One gets the impression from the amount of debris, the number of structures, and the infrequency of building remnant superpositioning that most of these villages were occupied for only a handful of years by no more than a few dozen people.

Some villages, however, were occupied for longer periods. They are marked by partial or complete ovals of dark, organic-rich soil loaded with debris where houses and other features had been arranged around open spaces. Examples of such sites include Jamestown in southern Illinois and Pyles in northeastern Kentucky.[15] The middens at Jamestown and Pyles measured 197 × 262 feet (60 × 80 meters) and 722 × 833 feet (220 × 254 meters) respectively, typical for villages during this period.

Lines of small postmolds mark the locations of the walls of structures [**Figure 75**], most of which were oval or rectangular and rather small. Individual buildings cannot have been occupied for more than a few years before they began to fall apart because the walls were made from small rot-prone posts, and few serious attempts were made to repair them. Large pits, presumably used to store food for lean times of the year, among other features, are commonly found near the buildings.

Figure 75 Excavators in 1979 at Robinson's Lake, Illinois, are shown scraping dirt off a house floor to define dark soil stains, or postmolds, where vertical wall posts once stood. At this site, as well as others in Illinois, the floors of Late Woodland houses were often dug into the ground, which provided some insulation.

Large-scale excavations give us a good idea of what the villages in the Mississippi River valley near present-day St. Louis looked like.[16] Structures dating to the end of the first millennium CE tended to surround small, open areas. Some of these spaces were completely devoid of features, whereas others contained central posts, several large pits laid out in a square, or a big building used for some unknown purpose. The overall village layout—domestic dwellings encircling public spaces where special features might be located—foreshadows elements of later Mississippian mound centers. Scattered around these villages in both floodplain and upland settings were camps, presumably used by foraging groups for only days or weeks at a time.

In most places, neighboring villages tended to be roughly the same size, and were usually occupied by only a few dozen to a hundred or so people. But that situation began to change toward the end of the first millennium CE, especially along the central and lower stretches of the Mississippi River and its principal tributaries.[17] Here, permanently occupied sites included locally important centers as well as outlying settlements, ranging from villages to isolated houses. The principal sites that included mounds were inhabited by greater numbers of people for several generations or even centuries, much longer than the surrounding small settlements. Toltec and Lake George are fine examples of such centers. The mounds at major sites were built at different times and seem not to have been used for the entire duration of settlement occupancy. But even abandoned ones fixed the basic structure of a site because they were such prominent features. The mounds, used or not, might have been linked to stories about notable events or specific ancestors, much like the monuments of many other societies elsewhere in the world. If so, then the mounds—in fact, entire settlement layouts—served as visual representations of societal histories.

Populations across much of the Eastern Woodlands continued to grow throughout the Late Woodland period. Many more sites, often with more debris, indicate bigger groups of people, longer occupations, or both. In addition to being scattered along major rivers, sites were often located far up smaller streams. An occupation of areas some distance from major rivers has been noted in several parts of the Midwest and Southeast, although it is hard to measure the degree to which the overall distribution of settlements had changed from earlier times.[18] In the midcontinent, a movement from river valleys was facilitated by a heavier reliance on native cultigens. Because it was now possible to increase the productivity and reliability of edible plants in less desirable places, people were not as tightly tethered to the richest settings. But this solution only worked for several centuries. Population growth would soon catch up with the increase in agricultural output, and something else had to be done.

A Switch to Maize

By the Late Woodland period, the starchy and oily seeds of several native cultigens had become essential parts of diets in many places.[19] The most intensive use of these cultigens was in the midcontinent, but even there the plants people relied on most heavily were not always the same. After seeds were harvested, they were probably parched in pots placed over open fires, if they were to be stored for hard times. Mistakes made while doing so probably account for the large clumps of charred seeds that were thrown away with other trash.

In west-central Illinois, and presumably elsewhere as well, a greater emphasis on these weedy plants was accompanied by a rise in workload, especially for women.[20] When looking at skeletons from this area, Patricia Bridges and colleagues found that female upper and lower limb strengths increased from Middle to Late Woodland times. That change is consistent with the strenuous work of planting and harvesting, and then the processing of food. It indicates that with a heavier reliance on native cultigens women, in particular, were involved in more drudgery than ever before.

Sometime between 800 and 1100 CE, maize began to be grown in many places, as is indicated by great amounts of charred kernels and cobs in the fill of houses and pits (see box pp. 84–85).[21] Perhaps the use of maize after centuries of neglect resulted from the introduction of a new variety better adapted to a temperate environment. Some might even argue that the sudden appearance of carbonized maize relates to a different way of preparing food that also made it more probable kernels and cobs would be burned, hence preserved. Fortunately, we have an independent means of assessing maize consumption: the stable carbon isotope signatures of human bones, a direct indication of what people ate. As it turns out, both the skeletal and botanical evidence indicate a shift in dietary composition. Within any particular region, diets changed over as little as several generations to no more than two or three centuries. From an archaeological perspective, this was a rapid transformation.

In the midcontinent, maize was grafted onto well-established plant cultivation practices. Stone hoes, most notably large ones of tabular chert from the Mill Creek quarries in southwestern Illinois, began to be widely traded in the Midwest.[22] The use of heavy hoes signals a greater need to prepare bigger areas for planting and to weed them on a regular basis. Elsewhere, maize was adopted without being preceded by a long tradition of growing native cultigens, mostly after 1000 CE and sometimes well after that date.

Long occupations of particular areas changed dense forests to vegetation mosaics ranging from shrubby growth to mature stands of trees. For example, bits of burned wood from archaeological sites in Ohio show that second-growth trees (those grown after a clearing episode) increased at the expense of those typical of old forests.[23] The benefits of this transformation in vegetation cover were many. Saplings filled a need for straight, narrow poles for houses, and edible plants and animals thrived in overgrown clearings. Regardless of what was grown in gardens, people everywhere collected nuts and berries, and hunted large and small animals. Much of this food could be obtained near settlements where active and abandoned fields were interspersed with woodlands.

Hunting practices changed across much of the Eastern Woodlands somewhere between 600 and 800 CE, which was when numerous small arrowheads first appeared.[24] Opinion is divided over whether bows and arrows were new to the Eastern Woodlands, but they certainly became common during a period that spanned only a few centuries. Light bows and arrows—as opposed to heavy spears thrown by hand or with an atlatl—would have been particularly desirable if locally depleted game forced hunters to travel over long distances in their search for prey. Such hunting practices took place in at least some places, for instance in the middle Ohio River valley where hunting camps have been found in remote rock shelters. Perhaps more importantly, bows and arrows were useful in the opportunistic hunting of small mammals and birds that frequented fields and clearings. People in the midcontinent were spending more of their time in these places, as indicated by the large quantities of cultivated plants that were consumed. A bow and quiver of arrows would have been just what was needed when people happened upon something to shoot in the active and abandoned fields interspersed with wooded areas that surrounded their settlements. The situation was similar to what occurred hundreds of years later when "Vermine Hunting" in and around maize fields was considered a "very diverting" pursuit by the inhabitants of tidewater Virginia.[25]

Figure 76 Bone fishhooks and gorges (sharp bone splinters that get stuck in a fish's gullet) are sometimes found in Late Woodland sites, such as these specimens from Illinois. Most fish, however, were caught in nets. The hook is 0.7 in. (1.8 cm) long.

The consumption of fish increased during this period of time along major midwestern and southeastern rivers.[26] This development is consistent with a more sedentary existence by greater numbers of people who placed heavier demands on what local areas could produce. People occupying wide floodplains naturally turned to fish, which were not only abundant but easily caught in shallow bodies of water [**Figure 76**]. Fish and other aquatic animals made up a correspondingly smaller part of the diets of people who lived along narrow upland streams lacking extensive backwater lakes. Major river valleys were not the only places where people spent much of their time foraging in and around wetlands. Other areas included the Saginaw drainage basin, where a large bay from Lake Huron takes a big bite out of east-central Michigan. The inhabitants of the Atlantic and Gulf coasts also continued to collect what marshes, bays, and estuaries could provide.

Life within Groups

For the most part, there is little to indicate any great differences in social standing within Late Woodland communities.[27] Grave goods tended to be utilitarian objects and small personal ornaments. Nevertheless, people were often buried in different ways in roughly contemporaneous nearby sites, and even within a single burial ground. Bodies ended up in mounds, but also in flat cemeteries, on cremation platforms, and within village sites. Often, intact bodies were buried, although many of them were either cremated or defleshed in some manner before the remains were put in the ground.

Perhaps the burial grounds are telling us that many Late Woodland societies were divided into roughly equivalent descent groups that used funerals as one means to express their distinctiveness relative to the rest of their communities. The artifacts, however, indicate that nobody enjoyed much greater access to special goods than the other people in the same burial site. Residential structures confirm this lack of social differentiation. One house within a village looks very much like the others, as long as due allowances are made for inevitable differences in household size, composition, competence, industriousness, and good fortune.

This rather egalitarian situation began to change after about 800 CE, particularly in and around the Mississippi River valley south of present-day St. Louis. Here, there developed marked differences in the size, longevity, and internal characteristics of permanent settlements. The largest sites were planned communities with one or more mounds fronting public plazas. Their appearance is one indication of the emergence of chiefdoms. A few people of high rank, presumably members of prominent lineages, were also singled out for special treatment when they died. For example, the individuals buried in small clusters of graves in Mound C at Lake George made up only some of the site's inhabitants.[28] About half of them had died as juveniles, which is typical of preindustrial societies, and their presence along with adults is consistent with the mound being reserved for members of a particular descent group. Admittance did not depend on one's achievements during a long and active life. Instead, kin-group affiliation determined who enjoyed privileges that included burial in a mound within the biggest site in the area.

Deteriorating Relations

Contacts were maintained among members of different societies, as shown by the movement of such items as copper and marine shell across long distances.[29] Nevertheless, the exchange of these objects had decreased from the level seen just a few centuries earlier, although in some places it picked up once again late in the first millennium CE. These objects would have been passed from one person to the next, probably as gifts that accompanied quite ordinary social transactions, such as arranging marriages, settling disputes, and acknowledging friendships.

The leaders of nascent chiefdoms in the south undoubtedly did whatever they could to get prized items from their counterparts in neighboring societies. These objects were used to signal high status and distributed in a manner that bolstered the positions of high-ranking people. Yet existing evidence, such as it is, indicates that even the most important residents of mound centers possessed only a few valuable objects. At Lake George, for example, the people in Mound C did not have many special goods, or at least none ended up in funerary contexts. No matter how influential these people might have been, they seemingly did not exercise direct and effective control over the long-distance movement of items fashioned from non-local materials.

Relations among many groups had deteriorated badly by the end of the first millennium CE. Victims of violence, including people shot with arrows, are evident in many skeletal collections.[30] While extremely useful when hunting, bows and arrows doubled as efficient weapons when skulking around enemy villages waiting for some hapless person to wander by.

Despite the bloodshed, fighting rarely reached a point where people could justify erecting palisades around their villages. The chance that some losses might occur must have been weighed against the greater certainty that diversions from food acquisition, among other essential chores, posed a significant threat to survival.

Yet in some places, people found it necessary to build substantial defensive works, such as at Toltec. Perhaps that was related to the kind of society that was beginning to emerge in the southern Eastern Woodlands. Chiefs at this time probably maintained only a tenuous hold over societies riven by internal factions led by potential rivals. Their historic-period counterparts were plagued by the threat of usurpers who were always on the lookout for signs of weakness. In the centuries to come, the widespread establishment of chiefdoms was accompanied by many settlements surrounded by walls, especially the largest ones. The palisades provided protection from attacks while projecting an aura of strength. They were equally effective against external enemies as internal rivals, both of which could pose a threat to the leading figures in these societies.

The Origin of Chiefdoms

Much more work must to be done before we understand the origin of chiefdoms in the southern Eastern Woodlands, but a bare outline of what took place is beginning to emerge. The following version of events relies heavily on what happened in the midcontinent, a particularly well-studied area.

The Middle Woodland shift to a greater reliance on native cultigens about two millennia ago enhanced the productivity and reliability of local resources. People began to expand into places with fewer and more scattered wild foods, which is most noticeable as a principally Late Woodland movement into settings far from major river valleys. Yet whatever gains were realized by a heavier use of indigenous crops, they were eventually offset by continued population growth.

Late in the first millennium CE, people faced a landscape that to them must have appeared full. The most favorable areas were already occupied, claimed as hunting territories, or lay between hostile groups. Venturing into no-man's-lands, let alone trying to live in them, was an increasingly hazardous business. Communities that had budded off from existing ones would have found it difficult to carve out suitable areas for themselves. More people than ever before meant there was a greater chance that hunters, inadvertently or not, impinged on their neighbors' territories. That was especially possible during bad years when hunters had to travel widely in their search for food. Viewed in that context, it is not surprising that people began to be attacked on a regular basis, as shown by skeletons with injuries from clubs and arrows.

The balance between maintaining an existing way of life and protecting oneself eventually tipped toward defensive needs. Vulnerable groups of people could no longer remain distributed along both major rivers and much smaller tributaries. They sought safety in numbers, so in many places individual villages became larger and river valleys more crowded.[31] Failure to form politically and militarily formidable groups invited disaster.

Local population densities increased quickly wherever people gravitated toward one another. Pressures on the productive capacity of local areas were correspondingly greater, causing people to seek new ways to squeeze more from the immediate vicinity of their settlements. Fortunately for them, a solution was at hand: they could shift to growing maize.

For the people of the midcontinent, maize may have been marginally more productive than a mix of indigenous seed crops, although any difference in yield was offset by higher field maintenance requirements for maize and the greater reliability of hardy native plants.[32] What probably made the difference for individual households was the efficiency and flexibility provided by maize during the critical harvest season. The yield-to-cost ratio must have weighed heavily on families whose most pressing immediate objective was their own survival. A wider range of people, from young children to the elderly and disabled, can be of real help when harvesting maize. Cobs are easily picked off stalks, and they can be dried and stored that way or shelled. In contrast, seeds from the native cultigens had to be laboriously stripped off the plants, then dried or parched before storage. The latter, in addition to taking time, involved mistakes stemming from inattention, as shown by discarded masses of charred seeds in archaeological deposits. Mature corn can also be left on the stalks until people are ready to pick it, as long as one does not mind some loss due to animals. This flexibility was critical for individual families because competing demands on the limited labor they possessed were always a problem, especially during harvest season. Late summer to early fall was the busiest time for collecting food needed to make it through a cold and barren winter.

By maximizing efficiency and flexibility at harvest time—precisely when scheduling concerns were greatest—people made a rational choice that boosted their chances of securing ample reserves for the lean months ahead. That does not mean they were any healthier than before, only that there was a shift to a new source of food that soon became an integral part of diets. The impetus to grow maize, therefore, mainly came from below through individual household decisions. It did not originate from above, despite whatever advantages the leaders of nascent chiefdoms realized from surpluses produced in good years.

Despite a gravitation toward places with the greatest productive potential, the threat of hard times could not be averted. The aggregation of people, in fact, made matters worse because increases in local population densities placed more pressures on nearby resources. When primary sources of food failed—and in the fullness of time they surely did so—it was no easy matter to switch to something else to eat. Populations by this time had risen well beyond the level where people could slip back into an exclusively hunting-and-gathering way of life in times of need. Moreover, the existence of watchful enemies made it dangerous to spread into infrequently used land where wild resources might still be abundant. Unevenness in local productivity and constraints on population dispersal gave the leaders of strong lineages in especially favorable locations an opportunity to expand their influence. The surpluses they acquired from their followers were probably used to organize special events, and doing so would have enhanced their social standing still further. Perhaps more importantly, these lineage heads were the ones who possessed the means to help others eke out a living during difficult times. Inevitably, people became indebted to situationally advantaged leaders who, over the long run, were capable of attracting and retaining the most supporters, establishing conditions favorable to the development of the first chiefdoms.

It should be emphasized that the emergence of societies structured around hereditary chiefs drawn from prominent lineages was not an inevitable outcome of the adoption of maize. After all, the transition to maize-based diets, once started, took place just as quickly in the northern Eastern Woodlands where chiefdoms never developed. These northern groups also lived in clusters of villages separated by long stretches of infrequently used and often bitterly contested land. They faced much the same kinds of pressures and adopted maize to address them, but the sociopolitical outcome was different (see Chapter 7).

Furthermore, while maize was of central importance in many places where chiefdoms developed—and it is emphasized in the archaeological literature—agriculture was not a necessary prerequisite for the emergence of institutionalized social inequality. Coles Creek people in the lower Mississippi River valley continued to rely heavily on foraging for wild plants, including acorns, for several centuries after chiefdoms had appeared.[33] On Georgia's coastal barrier islands, chiefdoms also developed without a heavy reliance on maize. Even where great amounts of maize were grown in the central Mississippi River valley near present-day St. Louis, the principal Late Woodland and later Mississippian settlements were located right next to large backwater lakes and swamps. Aquatic resources were absolutely essential if many people were to be supported over long periods of time. The central role of wetlands in chiefdom development across much of the Midwest and Southeast deserves far more attention than it has received.

Chapter 6

Chiefs Come to Power: Mississippian

By the eleventh century CE, greater political centralization, notably in the form of inherited leadership positions and ranked social groups, with both legitimized by widely shared beliefs and customs, had become increasingly common. These societies, commonly called chiefdoms, were scattered across the Southeast and southern Midwest, and they extended up the Mississippi River and its tributaries as far as southern Wisconsin [**Figure 77**]. In the sixteenth century, Spanish adventurers, notably Hernando de Soto, encountered a number of them as they cut their bloody way through the Southeast, but within a hundred years or so most of the chiefdoms had vanished. They had fallen victim to population loss, sociopolitical disorganization, and unrest following sustained contact between the peoples of the Old and New Worlds. In contrast, midwestern chiefdoms that expanded northward in the eleventh century during the Medieval Warm Period disappeared a century or more before the Spaniards plunged headlong into the Southeast. They fell apart during a time of population movement and warfare that accompanied deteriorating climatic conditions, which had taken a turn for the worse by the fourteenth century and would later culminate in the Little Ice Age.

Most of the chiefdoms of the Southeast and southern Midwest are referred to as Mississippian (the eleventh century CE to the Spanish arrival), but the two terms, chiefdom and Mississippian, are not freely interchangeable. Not all Mississippian groups—that is, those with certain kinds of distinctive pottery and houses—were chiefdoms. In some of them, a ranking of people appears to have been weak or absent, and there is little or no evidence to suggest fixed leadership positions. Moreover, not all late prehistoric chiefdoms are labeled Mississippian, even when that admittedly fuzzy category is stretched to its furthest limits.

At the outset, it should be noted that any sociopolitical category, chiefdoms included, encompasses a wide range of societies. Much work remains to determine precisely how the Eastern Woodlands chiefdoms were organized and functioned. The extent to which power was either centralized or distributed among important people seems to have varied greatly. That said, an important characteristic of chiefdoms is the existence of leadership positions that are inherited and feature a say, even a measure of control, over what takes place in a wide range of societal contexts. These positions are different from those where influence, but not control, over community affairs is

Figure 77 Selected sites mentioned in Chapters 6, 7, and 8.

earned in one way or another, and is temporary, situationally based, and limited to specific contexts. Furthermore, the character of subsistence economies, the nature and intensity of relations among groups near and far, and what lay behind the origin and eventual demise of the Eastern Woodlands chiefdoms are all topics of lively debate among archaeologists.

Markers of High Office

The prominent positions held by some individuals in Mississippian societies is indicated by the quantity and quality of burial artifacts, as well as interment in mounds. Conspicuous displays of unusual items made it clear who possessed the means to obtain great numbers of precious objects. Archaeologists quite naturally focus on artifacts that preserve well, such as those fashioned from stone, shell, and copper. But it must be remembered that other items, including what people wore, also signaled high social status and ritually significant responsibilities. Fragments of garments found in the Craig Mound at Spiro in eastern Oklahoma were made of fabric that incorporated animal hair, notably from rabbits, and brightly colored feathers.[1] The fine quality of these mantles and skirts would have been immediately distinguishable from the plain clothes, often of plant fiber, possessed by most other people.

The impressive objects found at some sites alongside the skeletons of individuals who were once leading members of their societies include elaborate headdresses and gorgets (an object, in this instance ornamental, worn at the throat) as well as eye-catching but functionally useless stone axes and maces. These were insignia of high office in the sense that they marked people who held positions of political or ritual importance, and only certain individuals were entitled to possess them. The diversity of artifacts, even within single burial contexts, is consistent with multiple paths through which people could distinguish themselves and acquire positions of influence. One cannot avoid the impression that instead of being conventional markers of specific institutions and offices, such as chief, war leader, or religious practitioner, many items were closely tied to particular individuals whose characteristics, actions, and abilities were acknowledged upon burial. The objects were perhaps so tightly associated with these people that they could not be readily passed down to someone else.

Mounds for Key People

Once again, mounds offer a wealth of information about people's lives. They were used for numerous purposes and were often essential elements of community layouts. Most of them were rather small, and, much like the mounds of other periods, are now frequently plowed down to the point where they are hardly visible. But some were massive piles of earth, and they included the largest mound ever built in the United States: Monks Mound at Cahokia in the Mississippi River bottomland of southwestern Illinois [**Plate 12**].

Mississippian mounds are often rectangular with flat tops [**Figure 78**]. Many of them once supported wooden structures that took different forms depending on when and where they were built, and how they were used [**Figure 79**]. They were prominent features of major Mississippian sites that were meant to impress onlookers. But, depending on how a mound was used, easy access to it was sometimes denied. That

Figure 78 Postmolds where wall posts once stood show that the flat surfaces of Mississippian mounds often supported buildings. This excavation in 1939 of a mound at the Rudder site in Alabama exposed the remnants of a sequence of circular and rectangular structures. Earthen platforms that had supported structures were sometimes later buried by additional layers of soil that raised the mound's height, as shown by the mound-fill to the right of the excavated postmolds.

Figure 79 A reconstructed mound and building at Town Creek in North Carolina provides an impression of what a structure sitting on an earthen platform might have looked like to the inhabitants of major settlements. Buildings were used for various purposes, for example as residences for highly ranked people and for holding the bones of prominent ancestors and precious artifacts.

is shown by rows of postmolds surrounding the bases or summits of some mounds.[2] These posts, even if they did not support solid fences, could have still marked sacred places. One such building used by the historic Taënsa of the lower Mississippi River valley was encircled by poles with skulls stuck on them. Heads rotting in the hot sun were an unambiguous warning that the sacred place should be approached only with caution on appropriate occasions.

Mound Construction

Continuity in the use of socially and ritually meaningful ground was a common feature of major Mississippian settlements, and that was as true of mounds as it was for other key parts of these sites. Special structures were sometimes replaced by earthen platforms, both of which were similarly aligned. One such example was found at Lubbub Creek in west-central Alabama. There, the orientation of the initial rectangular mound conformed to the positioning of rectangular structures and an enclosing fence that predated it.[3] Even later enlargements of the Lubbub Creek mound retained the same orientation [**Figure 80**].

N

Figure 80 Structures built on the original ground surface had the same orientation as this platform mound at Lubbub Creek, Alabama, indicating continuity in the use of space for architecture that was held in high regard by the settlement's occupants. Much of the mound (outlined) was destroyed before excavations in 1979 (shaded) exposed postmolds and wall trenches that belonged to several buildings.

0   ft   50

Dirt for mounds was often dug from large pits or scraped up from nearby areas, including village deposits and swamps. These soils show that many mounds were built in one or several bursts of effort. The people who performed this work probably did so on special occasions, such as during annual ceremonies or at critical points in their leaders' lives. Some mounds, however, required much greater investments of labor and long construction histories, as indicated by their size and separate mantles of earth.[4] It could take several generations, or even longer, before the largest mounds reached their final dimensions. Their lengthy construction often seems to have been episodic in nature, and involved massive deposits of fill laid down all at once, not an incremental process of adding a little soil at frequent intervals.

When building mounds, special soils were sometimes chosen for their visual appeal or symbolic significance.[5] Excavations in the Snodgrass mound in northeastern Alabama exposed several stages that were each separated by layers of either red or blue-gray soil. The use of such mound-fill is particularly well documented at Shiloh in western Tennessee [**Plate 13**]. Recent excavations in Mound A exposed layers of different-colored soil, notably reddish deposits that must have had a striking appearance when newly laid down. Securing appropriate soils added time and effort to the construction process, but had a visual impact out of all proportion to a mound's size.

Adding more earth to an existing mound was an effective way to achieve an impressive platform with the least effort. But size was not the only consideration: enlarging an earlier platform also established a physical connection with the past as a means of legitimizing the positions of the living.

Few clues remain to indicate what prompted the renewal of mound surfaces or the replacement of structures.[6] It is nevertheless possible to say something about what took place at one: Beaverdam Creek in northeastern Georgia. A platform mound was built over two large structures, one built after the other, both of which were surrounded by low earthen embankments. When the first building was torn down, a man's body decorated with many ornaments, including those of copper and marine shell, was carefully laid out on the embankment. The earthen ridge for the second structure was put directly over the corpse, so only a short time elapsed between the funeral and new building construction. Perhaps the first building was destroyed upon the man's death—just such a custom was described during the historic period in the lower Mississippi River valley. If that was indeed the case, the successor to the deceased man at Beaverdam Creek found a way to confirm his or her descent, legitimize the succession, bury a predecessor, and build a more impressive structure, all in one go.

Building big mounds—especially those at Cahokia—is sometimes assumed to have required vast numbers of people and strong coercive measures to motivate reluctant laborers. It is easy to come to such a conclusion after a tiring trudge up Cahokia's Monks Mound [**Plate 14**], which is 100 feet (30.5 meters) tall, on a hot and humid midsummer's day. But first impressions can be deceiving. The labor needed to build Cahokia's mounds was well within the capabilities of the local population, assuming that the work was spread out over several centuries.[7] A community numbering no more than a few thousand people would have been able to construct the mounds if one laborer from each household worked for less than two weeks each year.

Far less earth was moved at other sites, but populations were smaller as well, so there were fewer potential laborers. Estimates of the effort required for mound construction at Moundville, another big Mississippian site in west-central Alabama, also show the task was well within what the site's inhabitants could handle, especially if people from the surrounding area were called in to help the effort.[8] Looking elsewhere solely at the amount of earth moved, it appears that many of the Mississippian mounds, perhaps the majority of them, would have each required the effort of only several dozen people working for no more than a few weeks.

Focusing on mound size alone, of course, is deceptive because selecting special soils and finishing mounds off with wooden structures increased labor requirements. But separate construction episodes show that for many mounds the work was not done all at once. Despite the many uncertainties in estimating the effort needed to build the mounds, the work was rarely, if ever, so demanding that it interfered with essential household activities.

Cahokia

Far more earth was moved to make the mounds at Cahokia than anywhere else in eastern North America.[9] The site is located on the Mississippi River floodplain where long fingers of well-drained fertile soil once extended through shallow lakes, vegetation-choked swamps, and frequently inundated boggy ground. There were more than one hundred mounds at Cahokia, far more than at any other Mississippian site. The biggest of them, Monks Mound, dwarfs the largest mounds built anywhere else in the Eastern Woodlands [**Figure 81**].

Time has not treated Cahokia well. Many of its mounds have been plowed down or leveled by urban sprawl, with much of this destruction taking place alongside Highway 40, a particularly seedy strip that runs right through the heart of the site. For a while, the best (safest) place for excavators to enjoy hard-earned drinks at the end of a hot day's work was in a house of ill-repute, which no longer exists. Fortunately, much of Cahokia, including Monks Mound, is now preserved as a park by the state of Illinois, which has gradually expanded over the years.   ▶

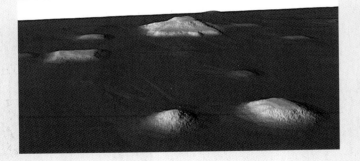

Figure 81 Cahokia's main plaza was surrounded by mounds; the largest, Monks Mound—seen in the background—marks the northern edge of the plaza. This computer-generated image was made from topographic data collected in 1966.

Figure 82 The southern end of Cahokia's central group of mounds is defined by a pair of mounds. The twin mounds are among the largest at the site, although they are dwarfed by Monks Mound at the northern edge of the large plaza.

About half of the earth moved to build mounds was put into Monks Mound, which is about 100 feet (30.5 meters) high and covers 13.8 acres (5.6 hectares). It contains approximately 814,000 cubic yards (622,000 cubic meters) of soil, has four terraces, and big wooden buildings once stood on its flat surfaces. The site's inhabitants also leveled the area to the south of Monks Mound to make an immense plaza [**Figure 82**].

Large wooden structures used for special purposes were erected in some parts of the site, including circles of big posts called woodhenges. Posts near the circles' centers marked spots where observers could use the outer ring posts to track the sun's progress throughout the year. While the woodhenges marked the passing of the seasons, they would no doubt have had more ritual than practical significance since people knew perfectly well when to plant and harvest their crops.

The most heavily occupied part of Cahokia was a natural levee along the southern side of an old river channel. Evidence of occupation tends to drop off toward lower-lying ground. The size of the site is difficult to measure because at least some habitation materials are scattered across most of the high spots in this part of the floodplain. The mounds usually said to be part of the site are distributed across an area of about 3.9 square miles (10 square kilometers). But the boundaries of this area, and all other estimates of the site's size, are to some extent arbitrary.

The core of the site consisted of mounds arranged around a large rectangular plaza. Monks Mound was located at the northern end of this open area, the most prestigious position closest to the abandoned river channel, underscoring the critical importance of wet places. The mounds and plaza were surrounded for a century or so by a stout palisade reinforced by bastions, which was replaced on several occasions. Many more mounds, several plazas, and residential areas were distributed around the walled precinct.

It is not known when the first mounds were built, but it is thought that work had started on Monks Mound by the tenth century CE. Mound-building certainly picked up during the eleventh century. At its most heavily occupied point early in the Mississippian period, anywhere from 3,000 to as many as two or even three times that number of people lived at the site (see p. 131). That was a large population by the standards of its time and place. But by the start of the fourteenth century, Cahokia had fallen into noticeable decline. Its population had dropped, and places where public architecture once stood had reverted to residential use. Old mounds were even being used for ordinary burials. By then, these mounds had lost much or all of their former significance. Mound-building continued into the fourteenth century, although it had tapered off from earlier times. The site and the surrounding floodplain were largely deserted by about 1400 CE. The marked decline in the area's inhabitants was part of a broader process of population redistribution and reduction in the Midwest (see Midwestern Mississippian Disappearance, p. 152).

Living on Mounds

It has long been recognized that important people in Mississippian societies were not only buried in mounds but also used them in various ways in life. In fact, a century ago they were described as the "dwelling-sites for chiefs" by Clarence B. Moore, who burrowed into some of them while cruising southeastern rivers in a steamboat aptly called the *Gopher* [**Figure 83**].[10] His imagination outstripped his evidence, but since that time it has, in fact, been amply demonstrated that flat-topped mounds often supported buildings used by leading members of Mississippian societies.

Figure 83 Clarence B. Moore conducted excavations in a large flat-topped mound at Citico, Tennessee, before it was destroyed by road construction. Here, the mound is shown a half-century earlier, as it appeared during the Civil War. Cannons fired in celebration of Robert E. Lee's surrender to Ulysses S. Grant collapsed a tunnel that had been dug into the mound to see what it contained and to store vegetables.

Rectangular earthen platforms literally raised the houses of the highest-ranked people above those of lesser folk. Buildings perched on mounds were an effective and constant reminder of the elevated social status of those who used them. But not all mounds supported the houses of chiefs and their close kinsfolk. Such structures as sweat lodges and council houses used for socially and ritually significant occasions were also built on them. The events that took place in and around these buildings served to knit societies together.

Debris-laden deposits have sometimes been identified in or alongside mounds.[11] Much of what these dumps contain came from meals eaten by people who lived on or near the mounds. At Annis in western Kentucky, one such deposit included deer bones cracked to extract marrow as well as bone fragments with worn edges, referred to as "pot polish," from being boiled in rough-surfaced ceramic jars. Apparently, highly ranked people at Annis were not especially well off because they had to do whatever possible to obtain all the nutritional value from the food available to them. Elsewhere, however, the trash associated with mounds indicates that important members of Mississippian societies, at least occasionally, ate somewhat better food than ordinary people. Middens associated with two mounds at Moundville contained many deer bones, especially those associated with the meatier parts of the body. At Beaverdam Creek, deer bones indicate similarly good cuts of meat, and they were found along with broken pottery and other food remains consistent with everyday refuse.

It is hard to separate the food eaten daily by important people from what they, and others, consumed in feasts on special occasions. When key figures in these societies orchestrated such events, presumably the most desirable foods were served to impress guests, in much the same way as what took place in historic times (see p. 97).

Burial in Mounds

Some mounds supported structures that held the bones of prominent ancestors. Often the buildings are referred to as temples because they contained valued objects and were a focus of attention that bolstered the positions of leading members of Mississippian societies. Multiple as well as single burials, frequently accompanied by fine objects fashioned from such precious materials as marine shell and copper from distant sources, have also been found when excavating mounds.

One burial containing the bones of multiple people was discovered in the Wilson, or Junkyard, mound near Cahokia when it was hurriedly excavated in the 1950s to make way for the Indian Mound motel.[12] As so often happens, the new building was named after something its construction had destroyed. The excavators uncovered a 14 × 18-foot (4.3 × 5.5-meter) area with the remains of more than 180 people [**Figure 84**]. Most of the bones were stacked in neat piles, each one containing parts from more than one person. Bones were scratched where stone tools had been used to cut away soft tissue. Not all of them were cut, so probably only desiccated tissue had to be scraped off. Scattered around the stacks of bones were thousands of marine-shell beads, as well as many entire whelk shells. Few other artifacts were found, although they included personal ornaments, such as earspools. It appears, therefore, as if the members of this group were for the most part treated similarly.

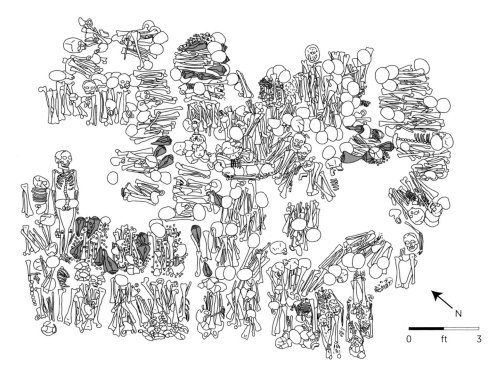

N

0 ft 3

Figure 84 Piles of bones, mostly from adults, were stacked alongside one another in the Wilson mound in Illinois. A vast number of marine-shell disk beads and many whelk shells (shaded) were distributed among the bones.

A periodic emptying of mortuary houses and their replacement with new buildings is well documented at the Harlan site in northeastern Oklahoma.[13] A burial mound consisted of three overlapping cones of earth that held the remains of more than 190 people. Many of these individuals were represented by disarticulated bones, and grave goods were scattered indiscriminately among them. The preservation of bones was not always the same, so it is probable the skeletons had accumulated over lengthy periods. Beneath and within two other mounds were the remnants of several buildings. They are thought to have originally held bones that had been cleaned out and buried elsewhere, quite possibly in the burial mound. A post in a tunnel-like entrance to at least one of the buildings prevented easy access to its interior. Such barriers would have helped keep children and animals out of the charnel houses. Similar structures in the lower Mississippi River valley dating to the historic period were equipped with doors for that very purpose.

Only a small fraction of the total population—mostly people of high rank—were interred in mounds. Visible burial places served as readily understood reminders of the legitimacy of the prestigious positions held by people who could claim a relationship to illustrious ancestors. Genealogical histories need not have been accurate, only widely accepted as being true. With the passage of time, some ancestors could have been promoted to legendary status and others omitted in orally transmitted stories, the content and emphasis of which would have been freely edited and embellished to suit the purposes of the living.

The clearest indication of the weight given to connections with ancestors, real or not, comes from a hollow chamber known as the Great Mortuary in the Craig Mound at Spiro [**Figure 85**] (see box opposite).[14] Grave goods and bones, possibly from ancestors, were dug up, moved to the Craig Mound, and buried with several people who had died recently. The body parts must have originated in artifact-rich contexts, presumably also mounds, judging from the number and diverse styles of the objects with the bones. While the people who built the Great Mortuary knew they could find human remains and impressive artifacts in mounds, they would have had no idea about which bones belonged to specific individuals. Forensic experts today have a hard time doing just that. The bones of large animals were even picked up, presumably mistakenly, along with those from humans. A special effort was made to collect skulls, or at least parts of them. They were among the easiest to recognize as being from humans, quite apart from whatever symbolic significance they possessed. The overall arrangement of skeletal remains and artifacts reinforced the importance of the buried group as a collective entity, not the social positions and roles of specific individuals. After the mortuary was sealed shut, cedar poles were erected to mark its location as dirt was laid down to enlarge the mound. A connection to the Great Mortuary, including ties to ancestors, was consequently maintained long after all traces of it, other than the upright poles, had disappeared from view.

Figure 85 Excavations were undertaken in the Craig Mound to clean up what remained after the Great Mortuary was looted in the 1930s.

Spiro's Craig Mound

The Craig Mound was one of eleven mounds at Spiro, located along the Arkansas River in east-central Oklahoma. It contained one of the finest-known examples of a mortuary deposit for high-ranking people, the Great Mortuary, although it was badly damaged by looters in the 1930s.[15] When digging for artifacts to sell, the pot hunters encountered a hollow chamber that they subsequently enlarged. Fortunately, they were stopped before destroying all of what they had discovered. Careful excavations subsequently clarified what was originally in the Craig Mound, and our present understanding stems largely from James Brown's meticulous compilation of field notes, photographs, and collections.

The Great Mortuary dates to around 1400 CE. It has received considerable attention because it contained an extraordinary number of well-preserved grave goods in a cavity that had never completely filled with soil. Here, a rectangular floor, bordered by low earthen ridges, was located on an earthen platform covering earlier burials. The floor, badly damaged by the looters, was covered by split cane and appears to have meas-

Figure 86 One of the best-known artifacts from the Craig Mound's Great Mortuary is a red cedar mask featuring carved deer antlers and ear spools. Shell inserts accentuated the eyes and mouth. Height 11.5 in. (29.2 cm).

ured about 37 × 55 feet (11.3 × 16.8 meters). Broken artifacts and disarticulated bones were placed on it, as were baskets and cedar litters arranged in several rows. The litters and baskets held more disarticulated bones and fine artifacts, sometimes great quantities of them, which had been removed from other locations. A number of intact bodies were also laid out on the floor, presumably belonging to people initially buried there. Items found amid the bones included, among others, engraved marine-shell cups and tens of thousands of shell beads [**Figure 86**]. The entire mortuary layout, including the positioning of such key objects as figurines and huge pipes, appears to represent the participants' conception of their cosmos. Posts arranged in a circle were erected on the floor and were in turn covered with earth. Rotting and settling eventually resulted in the cavity that attracted so much attention when the Great Mortuary was discovered.

After the closing of the Great Mortuary, the mound was raised upward by the addition of more soil. The Great Mortuary's position was marked by cedar poles planted over it, and they maintained continuity between the burial feature and the mound's surface for about two generations. Eventually a mantle of soil was added that signaled the closing of the cemetery.

Another well-known example of a mound that was used for more than simply burying important people is Cahokia's Mound 72.[16] Here, several small piles of earth were enlarged and joined together by the later addition of still more soil. A final capping layer signaled the closing of the burial area, which by this time had developed into a low, linear mound. Many people were interred there, some of whom must have held high positions in this society. The remains of several individuals, mostly adults, were associated with thousands of marine-shell beads, and a short distance away from them in the mound were a few more people with many fine objects.

Numerous sacrificial victims were also interred in Mound 72. The majority of them were crowded into five rectangular pits; together these graves held more than 150 individuals. The victims were mostly adults, with females being more common in three graves and males in one. Poor bone preservation limited what could be said about the skeletons in the last pit. In one grave, bodies were tossed in haphazardly, and a stone arrowhead was lodged in a lower vertebra of one of them. Elsewhere in the mound, four men were neatly laid out alongside one another. They were missing their heads and hands—both figured prominently in the iconography of that time—so they probably lost their lives during a ceremony that took place at, or around, the mound.

Cahokia was not the only place where humans were sacrificed.[17] Stylistically distinctive pots replaced the heads of four people buried together at Dickson Mounds in west-central Illinois. Such practices continued up to about 300 years ago in the lower Mississippi River valley, when adults and children were recorded as being killed upon the deaths of prominent people (see pp. 170–71).

Customs and Beliefs

The critical roles of highly ranked people and the naturalness of the social order, and everyone's place within it, were reinforced through the use and display of highly valued objects often found in mounds and associated mortuary features. Striking similarities among these artifacts and what was depicted on them indicate that customs and beliefs were widely, although variably, shared by local populations. That is not at all surprising because the members of different groups interacted with one another, their societies went through similar developmental trajectories, and people experienced much the same opportunities, constraints, and concerns in their daily lives.

Many of these objects, along with what was depicted on them, are said to have been part of a Southern Cult or Southeastern Ceremonial Complex.[18] But despite what the words cult or complex might imply, it was not a tightly integrated, uniformly understood, and universally held vision of the natural and supernatural worlds. The specific images on marine-shell and copper items have uneven geographical and temporal distributions, and the ways the subject matter was depicted and how the individual elements of larger compositions were combined vary greatly.

Socially and ritually charged items, especially elaborate images on copper plates or marine-shell cups and gorgets, probably conveyed somewhat different messages to people according to their roles in their communities [**Figures 87** and **88**]. Artistic

Figure 87 (Far right) An engraved marine-shell gorget from Castalian Springs, Tennessee, depicts woodpecker heads, a cross and circle, and other designs. Diameter 3.3 in. (8.4 cm).

Figure 88 (Right) Long- and short-nosed god masks worn on the ears have been found at a number of sites. This marine-shell mask is from Yokem in Illinois. Height 1.6 in. (4.1 cm).

works that function at two levels—one related to immediate appearances and the other necessitating sufficient contextual knowledge—are common worldwide. A superficial appreciation of what was intended could be grasped by anybody. It was essentially a literal reading of what was shown, and it was often directly relevant to daily life. The deeper meanings of what these objects represented, in all their intricate detail, could be understood only by those who were fully conversant with the group's origin myths and so on.

Elaborate items from contexts associated with the burial of people of conse-quence tend to emphasize a few themes, with war and ancestors prominent among them. Many large marine shells and copper plates were decorated with men in bird-of-prey costumes or bird-man composites [**Plate 15**].[19] Some of the figures brandished maces and clutched severed heads [**Figure 89**]. Opinion is divided over whether actual people or supernatural beings are shown, although the latter is more probable. A number of these figures, including the bird-men, probably represent a mythical being variously described in historic-period tales from northern Midwest and Plains groups.[20]

Regardless of whether these depictions were real people, ancestors who had acquired legendary status, or mythical heroes, a reference to bold and decisive action is unambiguous. Resolute and inspiring leadership was critical for chiefs who had to be ever watchful of rivals at home and enemies

Figure 89 This marine-shell gorget from Castalian Springs, Tennessee, shows an elaborately dressed warrior or mythical hero wielding a mace in one hand and holding a head in the other. He has a shell-bead necklace, and such beads are commonly found at Mississippian sites. When worn, the gorget would have been rotated to the left because the suspension holes are on the right side. Diameter 3.8 in. (9.7 cm).

elsewhere. References to everyday experience in portrayals of events involving supernatural beings made myths, and any embedded lessons, that much more real to those who heard them.

Mortuary features associated with mounds in major settlements, especially buildings placed on mound summits, provided a readily understood connection to the past. Some of the artifacts placed with the dead were direct references to ancestors, such as carved wooden figures in Spiro's Great Mortuary [**Plate 16**].[21] Similar effigies were noted in early historic descriptions of charnel houses, and stone figures have been found in midwestern and southeastern sites, including several in mounds [**Figure 90** and **Plate 19**]. A long ancestral pedigree—or the construction of one, similar to what happened at Spiro—provided legitimacy to the positions of chiefs and their immediate kin.

Items from mounds show that people from leading kin groups were involved in a rich ceremonial life.[22] Rattles and scarifiers (sharp objects used for incising skin) were presumably used in various rituals and on special occasions much as they were in the historic period. The rattles included some from a large mound at Mitchell, a site near Cahokia, where realistic turtle carapaces and plastrons (the underside) were fashioned from thin copper sheets. A copper-covered wooden turtle rattle was also found in the Craig Mound at Spiro. Other Spiro rattles included representations of human heads, carved out of cedar and covered by copper.

Sandstone palettes from Moundville, many of them decorated, are a good example of how people of different social positions participated in similar rituals [**Figure 91**].[23] The palettes were used for grinding pigments, usually red and white, and they have

Figure 90 Stone figures occasionally have been found in the important parts of sites, especially mounds. This one was found in 1874 at Ware, Illinois, when soil was removed from a large mound to build a road that crossed Running Lake, a slough that extends for many miles through the Mississippi River floodplain in southwestern Illinois. Height 11.2 in. (28.4 cm).

Figure 91 This stone palette from Moundville, Alabama, shows a human hand encircled by two rattlesnakes. Diameter 12.6 in. (32 cm).

often been found in graves. Although not restricted to a particular segment of society, those from mounds tend to be larger than the ones from other contexts. Highly ranked individuals apparently possessed the showiest ceremonial paraphernalia, even if they used the objects in much the same way as people of lesser importance.

Occasionally, ordinary people were buried with ritually significant objects, including bird wings, scarifiers, rattles, and crystals.[24] Some of these items, such as bird-wing fans, probably marked individuals who had a special role in their community, or were related to such a person. In fact, English explorers in late sixteenth-century coastal North Carolina saw "coniurers or iuglers which vse strange gestures" who "fasten a small black birde aboue one of their ears as a badge of their office."[25] During the historic period throughout the Southeast, crystals were used for divination purposes when setting out to hunt, going to war, or healing the sick. Personal rituals practiced by common people had a long history, and they existed alongside whatever beliefs served to prop up the positions of the principal kin groups. A wide distribution of such objects is consistent with broadly shared perceptions about the natural and supernatural worlds and how to deal with them, even if the specifics of customs and beliefs were not always the same.

The centrality of the quest for food is revealed by artifacts used for special purposes. A figurine carved of reddish Missouri flint clay from a site near Cahokia underscores a deep concern with growing crops and, more generally, fertility.[26] This squatting woman grasps a hoe that rests on a chimeric serpent with carnivore's teeth [**Figure 92**]. The snake's tail divides and becomes squash vines, with one winding its way up the woman's back. It is possible that this statue, as well as others from the Cahokia area, depicted a mythical female figure still recognized in stories passed down to the present day. Many Mississippian groups occasionally made pots fashioned after animals, and they were typically buried with common people.

Figure 92 This figurine carved from Missouri flint clay was found during the excavation in 1979–80 of BBB Motor, a small site near Cahokia. The woman is stroking the back of a serpent with her hoe; a stone blade is shown lashed to the handle. Height 7.9 in. (20 cm).

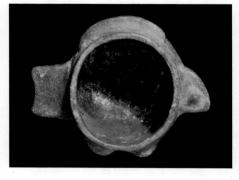

Figure 93 A ceramic bowl in the shape of a fish—its head to the right and tail to the left—was found in the 1931 excavation of the Guy Smith site in Illinois. Length 5.1 in. [12.9 cm].

While the precise meaning of these pots has long been forgotten, wetland species, including fish [**Figure 93**], ducks, beavers, frogs [**Figure 94**], and snapping turtles, figure prominently among the animals depicted on them. The critical role of rivers and wetlands in everyday life was highlighted by the items used for important occasions, including funerals.

People of high and low rank were often buried with the same kinds of artifacts, including arrows and discoidals (pill-shaped polished stones rolled across specially prepared fields as targets for poles thrown during the popular game of chunkey) [**Figure 95**].[27] The presence of these items acknowledged the significance all people, regardless of their position, attached to hunting, heading to war, and participating in competitive games.

Artifacts associated with burials of the most important people were often more elaborate than those for everyone else, and many were fashioned from materials, such as copper, that were difficult to obtain. Nevertheless, what they signified was a part of the lives of all segments of these societies. Certain rituals and socially significant practices, such as those involving rattles and scarifiers, were seemingly appropriated and elaborated by highly ranked people for their own benefit, but they remained firmly rooted in widely shared beliefs and customs. In this regard, distinctions between members of important lineages and common people were more a matter of degree than of kind.

Figure 94 Pottery occasionally depicted animals, often those that inhabit wetlands, such as this bowl from Arkansas that is shaped like a frog. Length 11.5 in. [29.2 cm].

Figure 95 This stone pipe from eastern Oklahoma depicts a chunkey player wearing ear spools and holding a discoidal. Height 8.5 in. (21.6 cm).

Where They Lived

Houses and Other Features

The remains of residential buildings can offer considerable information about daily life. Regional differences in house size, shape, and construction reflected local cultural traditions.[28] Variation in structure size within any particular site was undoubtedly related to the social position of a household, as well as its composition as marriages took place, children were born, and family members died.

All of the structures were supported by frameworks of upright poles firmly embedded in individually dug holes or in narrow trenches. In the central Mississippi River valley, the wall trench (a trench within which upright posts were put) [**Figure 96**] was an innovation that followed the widespread availability of hoes with large stone blades. It is far easier to excavate a narrow trench with such a hoe than to dig many separate postholes with mussel-shell scoops or digging sticks.[29] The walls of buildings sometimes consisted of bundles of thatch lashed to horizontal branches woven around the vertical posts. Elsewhere, wattle-and-daub—mud thickly

Figure 96 Trenches, some with partially excavated postmolds where upright posts once stood, mark the position of house walls. Many such buildings were found at Jonathan Creek, Kentucky, when it was excavated from 1940 to early 1942. Two palisades, one with a bastion, are indicated by diagonal rows of postmolds, one of which crosses a corner of the structure. The building and palisade, therefore, were not in use at the same time.

Figure 97 Wattle and daub, commonly used by Mississippian people to build their houses, consisted of mud plastered on a framework of horizontal sticks woven between sturdy upright posts. This reconstruction at Angel mounds in Indiana shows how walls were often built.

plastered against post-and-branch frameworks—was common [**Figure 97**]. House floors were often dug into the ground, and the resulting loose dirt was mounded up against the outside of the walls. This construction technique produced the low "hut rings" noticed in the nineteenth century, which for the most part have now been plowed away.[30] Extra wall trenches or rows of postmolds show that the walls of buildings were occasionally replaced, and houses were usually enlarged when doing so.

In many settlements, food was stored in pits, often dug within houses or near them [**Figure 98**].[31] The floors and walls of the pits were presumably lined, but there is little left to show how that was done. In the Cahokia area, for example, limestone slabs have been found on some pit floors, and in one a thin layer of charred grass remained in place. But this storage practice was not common everywhere, such as in eastern Tennessee. In settlements there, much of the extra food must have been put in granaries above ground.

Some pits were used when cooking food. An earth oven discovered at a central Illinois River valley site is one example where a fire was lit within the pit, but here about a hundred closely packed maize cobs were burned by mistake.[32] This cooking mishap must have caused dismay since that much food, ruined all at once, presumably was intended for an important event involving many households. Excavators have also found many hearths and scattered postmolds for light frameworks including drying racks and canopies. Smudge pits—small pits full of carbonized corncobs and twigs—were used to make thick smoke, sometimes within buildings. Thatch-covered roofs and walls soon crawl with insects, and smoke helps get rid of them.

Artifacts have occasionally been found in structures and pits where they had been tucked away for safekeeping.[33] In the Cahokia area, such objects have been found in mound centers as well as in outlying sites. Many of these were much-valued tools, such as the large stone blades of hoes. They were squeezed between building wall posts and covered by a little earth, or placed on the bottom of storage pits. Such items have been

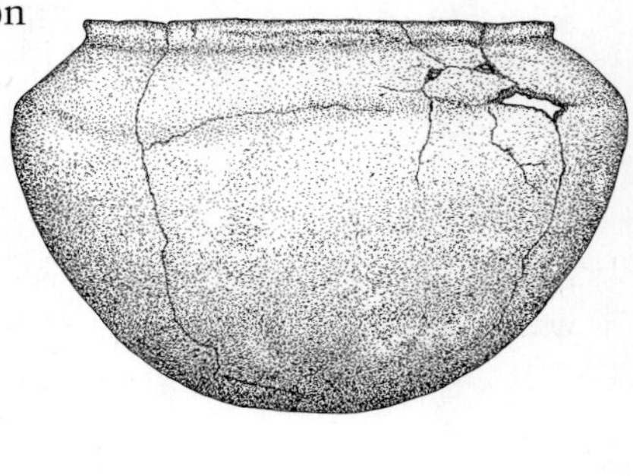

Figure 98 This pottery jar was found in a pit barely bigger than the vessel, which was dug into a house floor at the Julien site, Illinois. Its contents decayed long ago, leaving only the container behind. Diameter 14 in. (35.5 cm).

discovered elsewhere as well. For example, at a northeastern Arkansas site a long, narrow chert biface, referred to as a sword because of its shape, had been tucked away in a building's wall trench near the floor level. It cannot be known why these cached items were not recovered. Perhaps some tragedy overtook the people who hid these valued possessions before they could return for them or tell someone where they were located.

Mound Centers

The principal Mississippian sites were distinguished by the presence of mounds and plazas. Usually one plaza was ringed by wooden buildings and mounds that supported residential, charnel, and council houses. The plazas, mounds, and important buildings were in turn surrounded by dwellings for ordinary folk. Their houses were typically smaller than those of the chiefs and other prominent people, but they had similar layouts. At Cahokia, the main plaza was accompanied by smaller ones located elsewhere within the settlement.[34] Ceremonies were presumably held in these open areas and on the mounds that flanked them, similar to what occurred in historic-period Creek towns. There, community-wide festivities took place when entertaining visiting dignitaries, as noted by William Bartram, who attended a feast in a late eighteenth-century town (see p. 97). Evidence for such events at Cahokia has been found in the form of a massive debris deposit in a large pit near Monks Mound. Feasts attended by many people were a means of knitting the society together through shared experience, while they promoted the social standing of those who organized these memorable occasions.

Plazas were not empty.[35] There were mounds in plazas at Moundville and Cahokia, with the one at Moundville being almost the largest at the site [**Plate 17**]. The butt end of an enormous bald cypress post was found in the plaza at the Mitchell site [**Figure 99**]. This post was once impressive; at its base it was more than

Figure 99 What remained of a massive bald cypress post was deeply embedded in a pit when the Mitchell site in Illinois was excavated in the early 1960s, before the construction of an interstate highway. Many centuries ago, the post had snapped off at ground level when tipped at an angle as it was being taken down. Today, bald cypress grows in southernmost Illinois, but not as far north as the St. Louis area where Mitchell is located.

3 feet (1 meter) in diameter. It had broken near the ground when the post was tipped at an angle in a failed attempt to remove it centuries ago. Large, centrally located posts were probably rather common at such sites. They were replaced when necessary, as indicated by several post pits in the plaza at Town Creek in western North Carolina. Presumably the mounds and large posts within plazas were closely associated with socially and ritually important events. Quite aside from whatever else happened during these occasions, they must have reinforced the community's identity and distinctiveness from its counterparts elsewhere.

The mounds at Moundville (see Moundville, below), one of the biggest Mississippian towns, are especially interesting because of their distribution according to size and what has been found in them.[36] The largest was located on the river end of the plaza, and the amount of earth used in mound construction generally diminished with increasing distance from the river. Mounds bordering the plaza tended to alternate between those that were, relatively speaking, big and small. The latter contained a few burials, but no evidence for permanent charnel structures. Excavated debris indicates that the mounds were where ritually or socially significant objects, including those from non-local materials, were made. But those activities were unevenly distributed among the mounds. Vernon Knight has suggested that the mounds around Moundville's plaza were used by ranked kin groups, all of which were involved in the production of symbolically meaningful objects. The layout of physical space was linked to the different roles of social groups and the relations among them.

Moundville

Moundville, overlooking the Black Warrior River in west-central Alabama, is one of the largest Mississippian sites.[37] Simply viewing the mounds ringing a huge plaza conveys an impression of its former greatness. The site has benefited from considerable archaeological attention, including excavations during the Great Depression when a road was put through it [**Figure 100**].

The mounds and plaza were accompanied by extensive habitation areas that are today marked by debris and building remnants covering around 185 acres (75 hectares) [**Figure 101**]. About twenty-nine large and small mounds have been identified, although one is said to have been a natural rise. Most of the mounds fronted the plaza, but several of them were located either beyond or within it. The biggest one, which is 56.8 feet (17.3 meters) high, was located at the river side of the plaza. This open area was largely devoid of debris, and low spots were filled to make a level surface, showing that it was specially prepared and maintained as a public space integral to the community's identity.

A palisade surrounded the mounds, plaza, and residential areas. This wall, complete with bastions, was replaced at least six times. The palisade protected the three exposed sides of the site; the steep and heavily eroded fourth side overlooks the river.

Figure 100 A sequence of wall-trench structures were exposed in this excavation, which took place in 1939 before a road was built through Moundville, Alabama.

Figure 101 Large and small mounds surrounded Moundville's plaza. When visiting the site, one can get a good view of it by following the road alongside the mounds.

Moundville was occupied for several centuries. In fact, the site and the society centered on it were rather long lived relative to most others. Mound-building there began as early as the late eleventh century CE or shortly thereafter. It picked up in the thirteenth century, by which time the overall configuration of the site was established. During the peak of occupation, there were perhaps as many as a thousand people there. By the late fourteenth century, some mounds had been abandoned while others were still being enlarged. Mound use continued through the sixteenth century, although activity at the site and the symbolism of its mounds was dwindling. If the route of de Soto's expedition has been correctly reconstructed, the Spaniards encountered only a weak chiefdom that included Moundville as well as other settlements. Within another century, the site was completely deserted, and the surrounding area depopulated. Except for the mounds and whatever else could survive the passage of time, all signs of the once-powerful chiefdom had disappeared.

Much the same has been said about Cahokia.[38] There, too, the use of space and special architecture, notably mounds, reflected the nature of a sociopolitical system segmented into lineages with different responsibilities related to the society's well-being. In that sense, these Mississippian groups were structurally similar to historic-period southeastern and midwestern tribes.

Many mound centers were rather compact.[39] Thick middens with sharply defined edges have been found where a palisade constrained a settlement's growth. Examples of such sites include those near the St. Francis River, a tributary of the Mississippi in northeastern Arkansas [**Figure 102**]. Archaeologists who visited these sites in the mid-twentieth century described rectangular areas that rose up above the

Figure 102 The Vernon Paul site, an immense pile of earth and debris, was once easily visible in the flat Mississippi River bottomland of northeastern Arkansas.

surrounding floodplain. Slight depressions where plazas were located could be seen in the middle of the higher deposits of debris and soil thrown up from surrounding defensive ditches. When occupied, stinking piles of refuse must have turned these settlements into public health nightmares.

The inhabitants of other mound centers spread themselves out across considerable areas.[40] Cahokia is an example of such a settlement (see Cahokia, pp. 113–15). Yet even here the core of the site is easily identifiable because mounds, including massive Monks Mound, ringed an enormous plaza. The most heavily used parts of Cahokia, those along the banks of an abandoned river channel, grade into a sparser occupation of the immediately surrounding floodplain.

Topographic features, as well as the locations and orientations of earlier public and domestic architecture, influenced the layouts of mound centers.[41] Furthermore, precisely how space was used could change over time. The development of such sites as Cahokia and Moundville was accompanied by the imposition of a fixed site plan, including a large plaza and mounds, on areas that were already in use. So, at least occasionally, there was a purposeful, perhaps even forced, restructuring of a settlement's configuration to suit the needs of highly ranked people.

Large sites were inhabited by anything from a few hundred to several thousand people, although settlements approaching the upper end of this range were rare.[42] Even the biggest one, Cahokia, was perhaps inhabited by as few as 3,000 people during its peak of occupation, based on structures distributed throughout the site. It was unlikely to have been occupied by a population more than two or three times that size. Other estimates for Cahokia range up to about 40,000 people. The upper end of the estimate range is a triumph of unbridled enthusiasm over solid evidence and common sense. It even exceeds the sizes of the biggest cities in the first United States census in 1790. Lower figures of from 10,000 up to around 20,000 people are commonly used for the peak period of Cahokia's occupation. But even those numbers are probably wide of the mark.

Using counts of buildings, archaeologists have estimated the number of Cahokia's inhabitants using different starting values, among them structure longevity and occupancy. The results vary accordingly. But the main reason for a big discrepancy in the number of Cahokia's inhabitants has to do with sampling. Large estimates—those of 10,000 or more—are based on only a few excavations undertaken in heavily occupied parts of the site, a badly biased sample. The estimate in the low to middle thousands favored here was generated from a greater number of excavations that, collectively, are more representative of the occupation of the site as a whole.

Many other people lived in the Mississippi River floodplain near Cahokia, and in the surrounding uplands. Several miles to the west of Cahokia, nearer the river and within present-day East St. Louis, was another large settlement with mounds. There, recent large excavations have exposed the remnants of numerous buildings.[43] Thousands of people lived in this settlement when Cahokia experienced its peak in population. When added to Cahokia's inhabitants, along with others from big and small sites throughout the general area, this segment of the Mississippi Valley was by far the most heavily populated place north of Mexico during the pre-contact period.

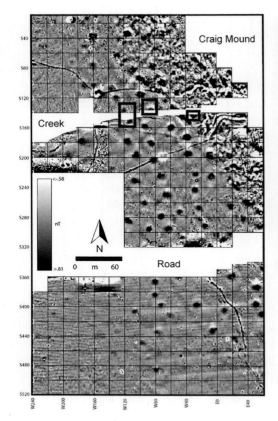

Figure 104 Remote sensing provides archaeologists with a new tool for identifying previously unrecognized architectural features, including those at sites that are otherwise well known. Here, such work is being undertaken at Spiro, where the Craig Mound can be seen in the background.

Figure 103 A remote-sensing map shows temporary structures (dark marks) near the Craig Mound at Spiro, Oklahoma. The presence of these structures was not recognized until this work was recently undertaken, despite the area being in the middle of the site.

Locally important sites with mounds presumably attracted people from the surrounding area for periodic events that solidified a common community identity. Yet evidence for occasional gatherings of people is difficult to find. At Spiro, however, remote-sensing work by Scott Hammerstedt and colleagues has identified many soil disturbances corresponding to temporary structures near the Craig Mound [**Figures 103** and **104**].[44] Excavations have produced postmolds and some stone tools, but little else. The buildings do not appear to overlap one another, suggesting that they were contemporaneous, or nearly so. Interestingly, this part of the site was previously thought to have been devoid of occupation. The unexpected discovery serves as yet another example of the use—albeit of a short-term and special-function nature—of otherwise open areas within major Mississippian sites.

Small Settlements

Innumerable settlements of one kind or another were scattered around mound centers.[45] The locations, internal configurations, and permanence of these small settlements represented a balance among labor demands, available resources, and defensive needs. In some places, houses were clustered together in an orderly fashion, sometimes around small plazas, producing compact settlements for several dozen to a few hundred people. They include the Snodgrass site in southeastern Missouri [**Figure 105**] where a ditch, which was part of a defensive work, surrounded closely spaced houses. At the King site in northwestern Georgia, houses were arranged around an open area where a central post and a large public structure were located. Here, as in many other small Mississippian communities, the general arrangement replicated what was found at the principal sites.

Elsewhere, scattered single-family houses were the norm. Buildings spread over large stretches of land do not necessarily mean that a local community organization was absent. Archaeologists, however, have a hard time recognizing such settlement layouts because excavations are often small. Fortunately, near Cahokia excavations have exposed areas ranging up to about two dozen acres, and this work uncovered the remnants of widely spaced farmsteads distributed across floodplain ridges. The families that occupied these buildings appear to have been part of dispersed communities centered on small clusters of buildings, including sweat lodges, which were also excavated. Sweat lodges were cramped structures heated by hot rocks or hearths, and they were widely used during both the prehistoric and historic periods. Several centuries ago, the indigenous people of Virginia, for instance, took "great delight in Sweating," and would "use this to refresh themselves, after they have been fatigu'd with Hunting, Travel, or the like, or else when they are troubl'd with Agues, Aches, or Pains in their Limbs."[46] Upon leaving, the experience was often capped off with a cold dip in a nearby stream. Whatever transpired at the special-function buildings in Cahokia's outlying settlements, including the sweat lodges, it presumably promoted close relations among households with shared social and economic interests.

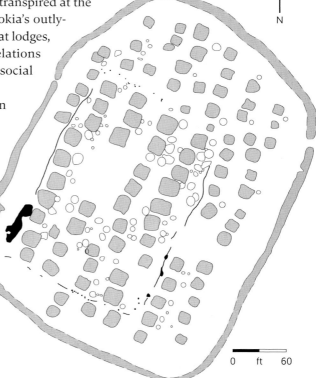

N

Far to the south of Cahokia, in what is today western Arkansas, northern Louisiana, and eastern Oklahoma and Texas, the occupants of settlements also tended to be rather dispersed.[47] Early historic-period Caddo people, for example, lived in houses scattered among

Figure 105 The Snodgrass village in Missouri was excavated in the late 1960s and early 1970s. An outer defensive ditch surrounded houses (shaded), pits (white ovals), and an inner wall (black line).

0   ft   60

fields, groves of trees, and patches of shrubby growth and grass. Settlements up to several miles long encompassed buildings and mounds that served as focal points for their communities. This arrangement of living space was centuries old, as shown by the remains of structures found in archaeological investigations. In its general form, the dispersal of houses resembled outlying settlements around Cahokia and in some other parts of the southern Eastern Woodlands.

Permanently occupied settlements were surrounded by widely scattered camps used when hunting, fishing, or collecting wild plants. Isolated arrowheads, mostly simple triangles chipped out of chert, show that hunters often sought out such game as deer, which were in short supply near large sites. Yet it seems that most people spent much of their lives close to their villages.

The picture of a rather sedentary life is reinforced by the chipped stone tools and debris from such sites as those around Cahokia.[48] Here, most tools were made by simply grabbing a convenient chert core (rock from which tools are fashioned) and knocking off just enough flakes required for the task at hand. Little or no effort was spent shaping flakes or preparing cutting edges. Carefully fashioning tools, keeping them for lengthy periods, and sharpening dull edges were not important, probably because people spent so much of their time close to home where heavy cores were stored for use whenever needed. A local production of most tools is not only indicated by debris (mainly irregularly shaped flakes). At Julien, an outlying community near Cahokia, a special-function building has been excavated that was remarkable for its size and the features within it, including a pit containing several tens of arrowheads, many of them barely modified flakes. The points look as if they were made by inexperienced people, perhaps children who simply picked up odd flakes when learning to work chert into serviceable tools.

Stone hoes, including widely traded Mill Creek chert hoes in the Midwest, represent a notable exception to the general pattern of quickly produced and then discarded tools [**Figure 106**]. When broken, the hoes were reworked to make still serviceable, albeit smaller, ones. The effort involved in obtaining the chipped stone hoes and taking care of them is consistent with a more intensive use of land at this time. They would have been much appreciated when preparing and weeding fields used for several consecutive years.

Figure 106 Several Mill Creek chert hoes that had been carefully placed on the bottom of a storage pit were discovered during the excavation in 1979 of Julien, Illinois. Broken and complete hoes, such as those shown here, can be found in such caches, an indication of their value to the inhabitants of the Cahokia area.

What They Ate

It was once widely believed that maize, squash, and beans came to the Eastern Woodlands as a group from Mesoamerica, and reigned supreme in late prehistoric times because together they provided the basis of a reasonably healthy diet. It was also thought that chiefdoms could not have arisen without the resource stability that only these plants could have provided. But, like so many seemingly good ideas, they foundered on the rocky reefs of reality. Squash was grown several thousand years before the other two plants appeared; beans were introduced several centuries after the shift to maize. Although beans became an important part of diets in many places, they were rarely, if ever, eaten by some people, including those at Cahokia.[49] That underscores the local variation that existed in diets throughout the Mississippian world, and beyond.

The move to maize was accompanied by changes in workload and oral health.[50] In northwestern Alabama, the bones of Mississippian women show they were more robust than their hunter-gatherer predecessors, particularly in their arm strength. Women would have worked in fields, but probably also pounded maize in large wooden mortars for hours on end, much as their historic-period descendants did [**Figure 107**]. Similar increases in workload, however, did not occur everywhere, because once again we see considerable diversity within broadly defined ways of life. Turning to tooth decay, it increased with the addition of significant amounts of maize to the diet—that is, the introduction of sticky food rich in carbohydrates. Cavities in tooth crowns and at the gum line led to frequent abscesses that drained into the oral cavity. Molars were especially prone to decay, and often fell out at an early age. Calculus, or tartar, also built up on everyone's teeth, sometimes great amounts of it. The extent of decay varied among populations because the specific composition of diets and their abrasiveness, affecting the rate of tooth wear, also differed.

Even after maize had become a dietary staple, several native plants continued to be grown, especially in the midcontinent (as in earlier times, they tended to be less important in the Deep South). As late as the early eighteenth century CE, people in the lower Mississippi River valley were seen scattering the seeds of an unidentified native plant on sandbars scoured by the river.[51] The plants grew without further attention in fertile alluvial soil, and that was true of bottomlands elsewhere as well.

While maize was of central importance in many diets, it was not eaten in large quantities, or at all, in some places.[52] In the lower Mississippi River valley, it did not become a dietary staple until as late as the thirteenth century CE, several hundred years after the

Figure 107 Each day, women in many Mississippian communities probably pounded maize in large wooden mortars, much like those used during the historic period. This drawing is based on a photograph of a Hitchiti woman in Oklahoma.

first appearance of mound centers. A late switch to maize was presumably related to exceedingly rich natural settings that for a long while provided a sufficiently stable and plentiful supply of food to support a population that was, for its time, relatively large. Maize was also consumed only in limited quantities, or avoided altogether, in much of peninsular Florida. One such group was the historic-period Calusa, who were able to take advantage of shallow-water coastal resources that were abundant, dependable, and concentrated in southwestern Florida. These characteristics of wild foods mimicked those of crops in fields.

Despite the importance of various crops, wild plants and animals were consumed by all Mississippian groups. In the major valleys, wetlands continued to be an important and reliable source of food.[53] Fish, in particular, were an inexhaustible resource, even in such heavily occupied places as the Mississippi River bottomland around Cahokia.

The mix of resources from wetlands, forests, and fields gave subsistence practices a resiliency that enabled people, within reason, to swap one food for another. But even large stretches of fertile soils and productive wetlands were subject to droughts and floods, some of which would have been devastating to the people who experienced them. Severe shortages are precisely what the Cahokia-area population would have faced had the devastating flood of 1993 occurred many hundreds of years earlier. That event took place during late summer instead of in the spring, which is when the floods usually happen. Had it occurred in prehistoric times, crops and stored food would have been destroyed on all but the highest ground. A late-season flood would have also interfered with fishing. This was best in shallow pools that normally dry up during the steamy summer months, not in vast sheets of floodwater.

People in the most densely occupied places depleted the animal populations near their settlements, most importantly deer.[54] With their high reproductive rate and preference for the broken vegetation cover around villages, deer would have been resistant to overhunting. Nevertheless, people had a local impact on deer numbers under the right circumstances. One of the better-known examples of the effect of intensive hunting comes from the Lewis and Clark expedition in the opening years of the nineteenth century. It was difficult to get enough meat along the Missouri River where hunters from large permanent villages were active. Easy hunting only resumed when the expedition once again passed through infrequently used land that was claimed and fought over by competing tribes. Around Cahokia, one of the most heavily populated areas in the Eastern Woodlands, deer must have been in short supply. That was unlike the situation in more sparsely occupied places, such as the narrow valleys of southeastern Kentucky. Excavations at Croley-Evans, a site with one mound along the Cumberland River, yielded an abundance of bones from deer, but few from fish. Fishing along the Cumberland was not nearly as good as it was in the wide Mississippi floodplain near Cahokia, whereas hunting pressure on game was far less. People's diets, therefore, varied accordingly.

Despite a mixed diet derived from what was grown in fields and obtained when foraging for wild plants, hunting, and fishing, people still had to cope with seasonal fluctuations in the amount and quality of their food. They experienced a yearly cycle much the same as in early seventeenth-century Virginia where people were said to have had "bodies [that] alter with their dyet, even as the deere and wilde beasts they seem fat and leane, and strong and weake."[55] An uneven seasonal availability of food, and presumably illnesses that accompany undernutrition, would have contributed to growth disruptions in tooth enamel, which is formed during childhood.[56] Such developmental upsets visible on teeth are common in skeletons throughout the southern Eastern Woodlands, regardless of where people lived during this period of time.

People of High and Low Rank

Leading Members of Society

Social relations in Mississippian times were based on kinship. That was as true of the highest-ranking members of chiefdoms as it was for common people.

Upon their deaths, highly ranked individuals were often treated as members of groups that presumably were defined by birth or marriage. That is indicated by their being buried together in mortuary features, including charnel houses, that contained the remains of many people. Yet group affiliation was not the entire story. Mostly adult bones were found in the Harlan, Spiro, and Wilson mounds.[57] Apparently access to these important burial contexts depended in part on the person's age, even though belonging to a select social group was also important.

People filling the highest social positions needed to have acceptable pedigrees, but they also had to be vigorous and decisive leaders. Artifacts emphasizing warlike themes indicate the importance of being perceived as successful in war.[58] Clusters of arrowheads that were similarly aligned, as well as sorted by shape and raw material, were uncovered in Cahokia's Mound 72 [**Figure 108**, see p. 138]. The points must have been attached to arrows held in quivers that decayed long ago. Fine stone points also have been found at other sites in mortuary settings associated with important members of Mississippian societies. Stone ax and mace imitations of actual weapons were buried with people of consequence, as were marine-shell cups and copper plates depicting menacing warriors, mythical heroes, or bird-man figures.

But the most important people did more than conduct war. They had to be persuasive and respected. Judging from what happened during the historic period, leaders were constrained by a need to consult with key members of their societies and to reach consensus, or at least the semblance of it, on weighty matters. They could not push too much without risking the alienation of powerful factions, which might result in the chiefdom fracturing along existing geographical and social divisions. Leading figures almost certainly played a part in settling disputes that would probably develop when greater numbers of people began living in close proximity to one another. More formalized means of dealing with intractable problems that were tricky to resolve locally would have become quite important when individual households and larger descent groups found it difficult to move away from sources of conflict. It was in a chief's self-interest to dampen tensions before they spiraled out of control.

Figure 108 Many well-made arrowheads sorted by raw material and shape were found in 1967 when excavating Cahokia's Mound 72.

Similar to their historic-period counterparts, chiefs probably did whatever they could to maintain full granaries with food donated by ordinary people.[59] This was probably used to help maintain their own households; to entertain visitors, such as emissaries from neighboring groups; and to distribute widely during special events. Because yields were unpredictable, prudent households—those that survived over the long run—had to adopt strategies that normally yielded modest surpluses. Each household held onto much of the surplus it produced, as indicated by large storage pits in many sites, but possessed only limited means of keeping food for much more than a single year. In good times, giving some of it away to chiefs was essentially painless because ordinary people could not otherwise use the surplus they produced. All that leading members of these societies had to do was to figure out how to lay their hands on this extra food. They presumably did so through appeals to fulfill time-honored obligations backed by threats of ritual sanctions and the more palpable menace of many warriors.

A judicious deployment of the food that chiefs had available could have blunted the sharp edge of occasional shortages. While it is difficult, if not impossible, to demonstrate that food in the distant past was given to families in times of need, some historic-period southeastern groups did distribute it in this manner.[60] Local crises presented ambitious leaders with a chance to augment their reputations through visible acts of generosity. It would be surprising if they overlooked such golden opportunities.

Chiefs and their close kinsfolk possessed a disproportionate share of the finest objects available, consistent with being points of contact with their counterparts in neighboring societies. Symbolically significant gifts were probably exchanged when sealing alliances, making peace, and fulfilling tribute obligations, much like what took place in historic times. Some of these valued goods then trickled downward through social hierarchies, ending up in the hands of ordinary folk. By selectively doling out gifts, highly ranked members of these societies could have shored up their positions by putting people into their debt. Such largesse was probably combined with carefully staged events that included feasts, for which there is direct evidence in some deposits. But while individuals of low rank possessed such items as marine shell beads, they tended to be fewer, smaller, and of poorer quality than those belonging to the most prominent people.

Much has been made of the role of strong chiefs and other influential people in these chiefdoms, and rightly so. Their very existence imparted a certain order and stability to these societies. Yet the consensual aspect of their decision-making and leadership, and along with it very real limits on the scope of what they could actually do, cannot be overlooked. There was surely considerable variation in the ability of individual chiefs to command obedience, perhaps better expressed as their inability to do so. Even for Moundville, one of the most impressive Mississippian sites, Vernon Knight has argued that the sociopolitical system was more decentralized than it was focused on a single all-powerful chief.[61] His interpretation comes from the most comprehensive study of the size, arrangement, and contents of Moundville's mounds undertaken to date. They appear to have been used by groups that, while ordered relative to one another, were similarly structured and had complementary roles in community-related affairs. Decision-making was probably more distributed, even consensual, than it was concentrated in the hands of a principal chief who exercised supreme control over what took place in this society. Key members of highly ranked lineages presumably had more say in some aspects of public life than they had in others, along the lines of the distribution of different political and ritual roles in historic-period tribes.

Ordinary People

While a few high-ranking individuals were very much in evidence in the midwestern and southeastern chiefdoms, most people never held positions of any real consequence.[62] Houses excavated within any local area, as well as the materials they contained, tended to resemble one another. Yet even within small settlements, there are signs of status differences. In the dispersed communities surrounding Cahokia, a few houses were built adjacent to ritually significant buildings, notably sweat lodges. The houses were perhaps occupied by people who played a major role in the ritual and social activities that took place in the special-function buildings. In southeastern Missouri, houses that were somewhat larger than the others at the Snodgrass site were built in the innermost part of this compact village. The centrally located houses might have been occupied by influential families, but there is no other evidence indicating they enjoyed much, if anything, in the way of genuine material advantages.

Ordinary people were usually buried in simple graves near their houses or within separate cemeteries, although there was regional variation in precisely how bodies were handled and graves constructed.[63] For example, shallow graves lined with stone slabs are common in Tennessee, Kentucky, and nearby parts of adjoining

Figure 109 Graves lined with slabs of stone were common from southern Illinois to Tennessee. This particular stone-box grave was found in a heavily forested part of southeastern Missouri. Often such shallow graves, along with much other evidence of life in the past, were destroyed long ago by agricultural activities or urban development.

states [**Figure 109**]. The organization of cemeteries, such as a grouping of graves in clusters or rows, indicate some form of family or lineage affiliation was important when deciding where a grave should be dug. In her worldwide survey of mortuary practices, Lynne Goldstein has pointed out that formally arranged cemeteries are often used by villagers to mark rights of access to essential resources, principally land. So the prehistoric burial grounds are consistent with a situation where survival depended on a local kin group's investments in fields and stores of food.

The objects placed in graves were usually rather plain ornaments, pots, and everyday tools [**Figure 110**].[64] Their distribution among people often varied according to age and sex. Tool kits used for flint knapping, for example, were usually buried with men.

A few people were buried with more precious items than their fellow community members possessed, such as marine-shell beads, which sometimes numbered a thousand or more. These individuals were perhaps village headmen or elders who earned their positions through special kin connections, unusual abilities, or simply survival to old age. Whoever they were, they were not otherwise distinguishable from everyone else buried in these cemeteries. That is, the appearance of the graves was the same, as was the way bodies were arranged in them.

The overall impression one gets from habitation and mortuary sites is that ordinary people did pretty much what everyone else of their age

Figure 110 This bowl, representing an owl, was found during the excavation in 1980 of the East St. Louis Stone Quarry cemetery in Illinois during interstate highway construction. Depicting animals on pottery used for special purposes, such as funerary offerings, underscored the importance people placed on a detailed knowledge of their natural surroundings, often infused with now mainly obscure supernatural meaning.

and sex were also doing. Despite occasional claims to the contrary, there is no evidence indicating that some people supported themselves by producing certain kinds of goods that they exchanged for the food and other items they needed to survive.[65] Members of common households, not full-time specialists, were involved in the production of, for instance, salt in Illinois and Arkansas, as well as utilitarian Mill Creek hoes in Illinois. Nor does it appear that specialists made the objects used for displays of wealth or as insignia of high rank.

If evidence for craft specialists who supported themselves by what they produced can be found anywhere, it ought to be at Cahokia. Much attention has focused on fine goods, especially marine-shell beads. The beads, however, are often so irregular that no special skills or equipment would have been needed to make them [**Figure 111**].[66] The chert microdrills used when drilling holes in beads were easy to produce, and they were made by the residents of both mound centers and outlying small sites.

In the Cahokia area, a household's bead-making capacity appears to have been determined by its ability to acquire the shell, and that depended on its social standing. Many microdrills have been picked up from fields near Monks Mound, consistent with high-status families with the most access to shell also making the most beads. There would have been plenty of time to work on the beads during seasons, especially the winter, when there were few competing demands on time. Perhaps the finest beads—they are symmetrical, highly polished, and found in matched sets—were made by particularly talented people who gained a local reputation for their abilities and so earned a place to live in a prestigious part of the site. Influential people in the Cahokia area could have sponsored the production of beads, especially the best ones, when they were needed for ritually and socially important events. But even the most able bead-makers probably spent the bulk of their time on basic subsistence-related tasks, just like ordinary households.

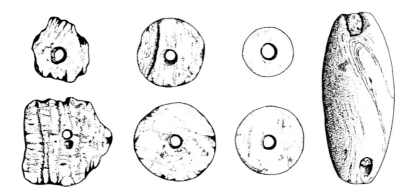

Figure 111 Six whelk-shell disk beads from the Wilson mound near Cahokia are shown arranged, from left to right, by the quality of workmanship. The two middle beads are typical of the majority found in the Cahokia area. On the right is a large whelk columella bead from Cahokia's Mound 72, which has holes that were mistakenly drilled off center. Filling the holes with carefully fitted shell plugs is consistent with the great value placed on marine-shell beads in the continental interior, particularly those made from large columellae (central columns of whelk shells). The columella bead is 1.8 in. (4.6 cm) long.

Figure 112 A hunchback, a deformity possibly caused by tuberculosis, is shown in this pottery bottle from Arkansas. The individual's body is so emaciated that the clavicles stand out clearly. Height 7.7 in. (19.5 cm).

Social Rank and Health

It is not certain that any advantages important people enjoyed in housing, access to high-value ornaments, and so on had a noticeable effect on their health.[67] The evidence that exists does not clearly and consistently indicate that highly ranked people, as a rule, ate markedly better food or had fewer illnesses than other members of their communities. The stable carbon isotope signatures of skeletons from Moundville show that people throughout the social hierarchy had about the same proportion of maize in their diets. The prevalence and severity of the diseases they suffered from were also about the same. These illnesses included two communicable infections that produced skeletal lesions that resemble those of modern tuberculosis and the treponematoses [**Figure 112**]. The treponematoses include venereal syphilis and yaws, among others, although the precise form of the pre-Columbian infection is unlikely to have been identical to one of the several treponemal diseases clinically recognized today.

The inhabitants of Mississippian chiefdoms were not the only people in the Eastern Woodlands to suffer from these diseases. In fact, one early eighteenth-century account described a "Burning of the Limbs, which tortures them grievously, at which time their Legs are so hot, that they employ the young People continually to pour Water down them."[68] They probably had a treponemal infection that we know from skeletons affected lower limb bones, especially tibiae, fibulae, and the distal femora.

Chiefs and their close kinsfolk presumably benefited during hard times from the stores of food they had amassed. In at least some communities, they even ate meals that differed somewhat from everyone else, notably in the parts of deer consumed.[69] But clear-cut and consistent signs of such advantages translating to a health benefit on a regular basis are not found in skeletons. Leading figures in these chiefdoms were perfectly capable of distinguishing themselves from everyone else by how they dressed, where they lived, and the way they were buried. That even extended to what they ate, at least on ceremonial occasions. Yet in terms of their physical well-being, they were little different from ordinary members of their societies. Here we see the very real limits of chiefly power—it tended to be more show than substance.

Turning to the Eastern Woodlands as a whole, because of uneven sampling, incomplete understandings of local social and environmental settings, and differences in the ways data are reported, it is hard to pinpoint what lay behind variation in disease experience during the late prehistoric period. But when looking at existing information, and accepting it at face value, it appears that the conditions of daily life at a local level—for example, intergroup conflict or vulnerability to food shortfalls— had a great influence on how healthy most people were most of the time. That was more important than how late prehistoric societies might be categorized in terms of their overall size, sociopolitical organization, or cultural affiliation.

Friends and Foes

In the Mississippian period, a long-range exchange of goods increased significantly from what had occurred just a few centuries earlier. Objects moved across great distances by passing through innumerable hands, presumably as gifts accompanying social transactions among both chiefs and ordinary households.[70] Jon Muller has shown that the quantity of artifacts declines as the distance from where they originated increases. That is as true for marine-shell gorgets as it is for utilitarian Mill Creek chert hoes. The fit between distance and artifact abundance is not perfect, but then neither are the data, which are incomplete and, worse, biased. Nevertheless, the overall pattern is consistent with a down-the-line exchange where some items were passed on to people in the next community, but others were not. Even the appearance of some items from distant places shows that they were in circulation for a long time. The surfaces of whelk-shell pendants from the Dickson Mounds, Schild, and De Frenne cemeteries, all in Illinois, were smoothed from prolonged handling [**Figure 113**]. Many years, perhaps even several generations, elapsed before these particular seashells ended up being buried in the continental interior.

Yet another indication of how precious objects crossed long distances is the appearance of marine-shell beads at Cahokia and nearby sites.[71] It is not uncommon to find whelk-shell beads with the small holes and narrow interconnected tracks typical of shells that wash up onto beaches. These beads are consistent with a sequence of exchanges where the poorest material, including beach-scavenged shell, had the greatest chance of moving the farthest. People deep in the continental interior,

Figure 113 Small whelk-shell pendants found at sites in the Midwest are often smoothed and polished from long use. These heavily worn pendants are from Dickson Mounds, Illinois.

at the end of many separate transactions, had to be pleased with whatever they could lay their hands on, even if it was not the best material in circulation at that time.

Many items from distant sources must have been passed from one chief to the next. They hoarded large numbers of the finest and most highly prized objects that often served as symbols of high rank. But however much archaeologists focus their attention on non-local raw materials and the artifacts made from them, exchanges of these items were probably incidental to the real purpose of the dealings chiefs had with one another. Some form of contact had to be maintained if allies were to be secured in times of need and, during war, to resume peaceful relations with enemies. Such interactions were probably accompanied by gifts, including symbolically meaningful objects that were valued because they had long histories attached to them.

While chiefs and their close kinsfolk played a big part in exchanges of highly prized goods, they were never able to secure total control over their distribution. Even when Cahokia's once-preeminent position had deteriorated, there was no noticeable decline in non-local artifacts at the small settlements in its vicinity.[72] The simplest explanation is that many of these objects were exchanged among ordinary people, eventually crossing long distances. But the kinds of materials did change, indicating that alliance networks across the region were not the same. Continued access to items from far-off places—despite a marked erosion of chiefly authority and prerogatives, with waning influence over exchange networks—is not at all surprising. After all, valued objects moved across long distances for thousands of years before there were any chiefs to tell people what to do, and they continued to be traded in the historic period well after chiefdoms had vanished.

Mesoamerican Contacts?

There has been much speculation about ties between the civilizations of Mesoamerica (Mexico and nearby Central American countries) and the southeastern part of North America where Mississippian societies were located. Until recently, there was no solid evidence for any such connection. But now a scraper made from Mesoamerican obsidian has turned up in a collection of objects from Spiro's Great Mortuary [**Figure 114**].[73] Because of this find, it is natural to ask what it might mean in terms of contact with Mesoamerica. The answer is not much.

One small tool falls far short of demonstrating direct contact with Mesoamerica. What is more extraordinary than the discovery of a single scraper is the absence of anything else like it in the entire Eastern Woodlands. Elsewhere in the world, including other parts of North America, a few odd artifacts are known to have crossed vast distances through innumerable hands, perhaps taking generations to do so. Spiro is exactly where we might expect to find such an object. It was positioned on the western fringe of the Eastern Woodlands, and the site's inhabitants had contact with people in the southern Plains who communicated with groups in the arid Southwest. They, in turn, had at least fleeting ties to Mesoamerica. Moreover, a scraper ending up in Spiro's Great Mortuary is perfectly consistent with the workings of Mississippian chiefdoms. Precious

Figure 115 This excavation in 2003 exposed a palisade trench at Annis in Kentucky. The wall surrounded a platform mound and residential structures.

Exchange had its opposite in warfare, which broke out with regularity from Late Woodland times onward. By the eleventh century CE, palisades were increasingly being built around settlements, and they would remain common from that point onward [**Figure 115**].[75] They were made of vertical posts, now detectable as long lines of large postmolds or trenches, around which pliable branches must have been woven. Mud was thickly plastered over some of these walls, such as at Aztalan in south-central Wisconsin. Nineteenth-century visitors there found great quantities of burned daub, mistakenly called brick, littering low ridges where walls had once stood. Mississippian palisades were often reinforced with bastions at roughly 98-foot (30-meter) intervals, well within overlapping bow fire, and were further strengthened by embankments and ditches. The defensive works at Angel in southwestern Indiana

Figure 114 The Great Mortuary was located within the Craig Mound, which was reconstructed after being excavated. It is one of several mounds at the Spiro site in Oklahoma.

and unusual objects—in this instance, a scraper prized for its novelty—tended to gravitate toward chiefs. Much the same happened during the sixteenth century when Spanish artifacts often ended up in locally important sites where influential people lived.[74]

show the lengths to which people had to go to protect themselves. A strong palisade with regularly spaced bastions had been erected on a low embankment, and a short distance in front of it was an additional, but smaller, wall. Attackers who climbed over the first wall were forced to cross an open area to reach the main palisade, which could only have been accomplished with a great loss of life from the defenders' arrows.

Walls were permanent fixtures around many sites. Wooden palisades were repaired or replaced as necessary, and new ones were erected as settlements expanded or contracted over time. Their maintenance indicates that the possibility of attack by a strong and determined foe could last for decades, if not generations. Sequential palisades at Jonathan Creek in western Kentucky differed in post size and depth, bastion configuration and placement, and overall upkeep as indicated by repaired wall segments [**Figure 116**].[76] When tending to their defensive needs, the Jonathan Creek villagers apparently took into account the available labor pool and the immediacy of the threat.

Fighting mostly consisted of small-scale raids and ambushes that resulted in the deaths of only a few people at a time. That is the impression one gets from cemeteries where graves hold only single victims or small groups of them. But large war parties must also have been a threat, as shown by strong defenses at many sites [**Plate 18**]. Once warriors managed to gain entry into an enemy's principal town,

Figure 116 Jonathan Creek, Kentucky, was excavated in the early 1940s by young men enrolled in the Civilian Conservation Corps. They removed plow-disturbed soil from an enormous area, mostly by hand, and in so doing identified building remnants in the subsoil. Partly excavated postmolds belonging to palisades and houses are shown here. Work at the site stopped shortly after the entry of the United States into World War II when the men found employment in the armed services and war-related industries.

they did whatever possible to despoil the structure that held the remains of the chief's ancestors.[77] That is what took place in the sixteenth century CE when Hernando de Soto's allies broke off an attack to defile one such building. Doing so struck at the core of a chief's aura of legitimacy and power because being unable to protect revered ancestors' bones was a sure sign of feeble leadership.

Organization and Distribution

The term chief, as used here, should not be taken to mean that all important roles, political as well as ritual, were bundled together in the same person. In fact, that is unlikely to have been the situation in most, if not all, Mississippian chiefdoms. In these kin-based societies, the principal members of powerful lineages probably enjoyed leadership roles in various political or ritual affairs. As already mentioned, that seems to have been true at Moundville and Cahokia, and it is consistent with the diversity in markers of high status associated with burials in noteworthy contexts, especially those in mounds.

For archaeologists focusing on Mississippian groups, one of the most vexing issues centers on determining precisely how these societies were organized, especially the biggest ones. What follows is a deliberately simplified view of their structural variation, with chiefdoms divided into two categories: simple and complex. When thinking about these models, it must be recognized that the office of chief, treated below as a single position for sake of clarity, was a more complicated combination of key people who had at least some say over various political and ritual matters. That would have been true even when one person tended to dominate societal affairs through his or her preeminent position.

Chiefdom Organization

In many chiefdoms, seemingly the majority of them, there was only one level of decision-making, the chief, above what were probably largely consensual agreements made within and among local villages. These simple chiefdoms, consisting of a number of separate settlements, are recognized archaeologically by the presence of a single center—the seat of a locally influential chief—surrounded by sites that were generally smaller, occupied for shorter periods of time, and lacked mounds. The principal sites had public architecture that typically included mounds, but they were often not much grander than ordinary villages and their general layouts were similar.

Other chiefdoms had two levels of decision-making above local communities. Archaeologically speaking, they are distinguished from simple chiefdoms by having two or more contemporaneous major centers, each surrounded by its own group of smaller settlements. Occasionally a principal site, such as Cahokia, dwarfed outlying mound centers. A chief resided in each of the main sites, although one outranked the others. The complex chiefdoms must have been knit together through relationships among leading people, the strength and permanence of which depended primarily on the effectiveness of the principal chief.

Even the largest of these societies, Cahokia, resembled an aggregation of simple chiefdoms with one being ascendant over the others.[78] These chiefdoms can be visualized as a series of similarly structured, economically self-sufficient, and politically quasi-autonomous districts, each led by a locally important chief residing in his or her own mound center. One of the chiefs was more influential than the others, a preeminence that might extend to that individual's descendants. The ability of these leaders to inspire, persuade, threaten, or command obedience, as circumstances dictated, undoubtedly waxed and waned over time. They had to handle deftly any opportunities or problems related to local resource availability, especially a lack of food during hard times; access to widely exchanged objects of social and ritual significance; factional competition within communities, including the machinations of potential rivals; and uncertain intergroup relations that often resulted in outright warfare.

If this picture of complex chiefdoms is anywhere near the mark, then their rise and fall involved little more than the addition or subtraction of structurally similar groups, each headed by its own chief. The formation of such complex chiefdoms through the coalescence of formerly separate parts could be rapid, as seems to have been the case at Cahokia.[79] Lesser chiefs backed by their own factions would have been always watchful for opportunities to advance their positions relative to their peers, sometimes to the detriment of the principal chief. De Soto's men had direct experience of this jockeying for position on their trek across the Southeast in the mid-sixteenth century.

Even the biggest and most powerful chiefdoms suffered from inherent instability. At Cahokia, there was a lengthy period when a stout palisade studded with bastions, which was replaced on several occasions, surrounded the central group of mounds. No nearby society at that time represented a credible threat to Cahokia, given the great disparities that existed in warrior mobilization potential. Danger more probably sprang from within.

Chiefdom Distribution

Chiefdoms were mostly scattered along rivers, where edible plants and animals were plentiful and soils were fertile. There were, of course, exceptions. They include the Florida Calusa, who were contacted by Spaniards in the opening years of the sixteenth century.[80] This group was fortunate to live in an exceedingly rich coastal environment that was as productive and reliable a source of food as the river valleys that snaked their way through the continental interior. Yet these coastal resources were unevenly distributed, resembling the situation along interior rivers, providing highly ranked people with opportunities to maneuver for their own advantage.

Our best estimates for the sizes of the pockets of population where resources were abundant show that they extended along rivers for as little as 6 miles to something in excess of ten times that distance (10 to 100 kilometers).[81] Most of these concentrations of sites are in the bottom end of that range. The largest ones were located where there were unusually rich and continuous distributions of resources, as well as communication routes through interconnected bodies of water, notably the central to lower Mississippi River valley.

Estimating how many people lived in these site concentrations is difficult.[82] For the most part, it seems these areas were inhabited by no more than several thousand people, occasionally a few tens of thousands. The largest populations, with the society centered on Cahokia being a possible exception, did not exceed the biggest of the historically known tribes. But the latter, which also tended to number in the low tens of thousands, were spread out over much larger areas.

Sparsely occupied land, both prime valley segments and less productive uplands, separated the population concentrations. These areas harbored abundant game, yet hunters must have often avoided them. During the historic period, long-standing animosities between neighboring societies could make them extremely dangerous places.[83] That was also true earlier as well, judging from the many palisaded settlements and skeletons from grievously injured and horrifyingly mutilated people that have been found.

As might be expected, social boundaries defining separate groups of people, who often had uneasy relations with one another to begin with, were barriers to gene flow. Dawnie Steadman's measurements of skulls from west-central Illinois show that the Mississippians were more divided up into regional populations than their immediate predecessors.[84] The skeletal data are fully compatible with archaeological evidence for a patchy distribution of groups with definite limits on the nature and extent of contact with one another.

The positions of settlement clusters and the most powerful sites changed over time.[85] For example, the midwestern Mississippian occupation, extending as far south as the Ohio and Mississippi river confluence region, had dropped to the level of archaeological invisibility by the fifteenth century CE. Some of this decline might appear to have been greater than it actually was because people moved from river bottomlands into the surrounding uplands. Sites are difficult to detect in large expanses of hilly terrain creased by small streams. Yet a redistribution of people was certainly not the entire story. There were actually fewer people by the fifteenth century, although by how many is not known. The Savannah River valley was another example. It was abandoned about a century before de Soto's expedition cut its way through the Southeast. By the time the Spaniards arrived, this area was a tangled and uninhabited wilderness.

The Rise and Fall of Chiefdoms

The Mississippian world was highly volatile. When some chiefdoms were developing, others were collapsing. Some of them remained in place for several hundred years, although usually it was closer to a few generations. Looking at the entirety of the Mississippian period, the most powerful societies and heavily populated areas can be envisioned as blinking on and off like twinkling Christmas-tree lights. Although the general picture of what happened is clear, much work remains to be done to bring it into sharp focus. The details take considerable effort to work out because what happened in one place was not the same as what occurred in another.

Chiefdom Emergence

Opinion is divided over what lay behind the emergence of Mississippian chiefdoms, but several clues point us in the right direction. They include a change in population distribution and density; the character of natural landscapes, especially the risk of catastrophic food shortfalls; a shift in technology, including the move to maize agriculture; and a descent to unprecedented levels of violence.

By the end of the first millennium CE, warfare had become firmly embedded in the fabric of everyday life, and things took a turn for the worse in the eleventh century. People seeking safety gravitated toward one another, presenting capable and charismatic war leaders with new opportunities to recruit followers, and in doing so augmenting and solidifying their positions. At the very least, a reputation for ferocity was central to chiefly power, and success in combat was a means of social advancement for other people. That is shown by warlike themes depicted on Mississippian artifacts and the comments of early European explorers [**Plate 20**]. Such a reputation also helped chiefs deal with disaffected members of their own societies.

Deteriorating intergroup relations coupled with higher local population densities meant that people put correspondingly greater pressure on local resources while they enjoyed fewer options for switching to alternative foods during hard times. Even the richest parts of the Eastern Woodlands were susceptible to periodic food shortages, some of which must have led to outright famine. Given this situation, it is not surprising that favorable locations were critical for chiefs to achieve long-term success. Local resource productivity and stability provided leaders with opportunities to promote and maintain their positions, partly by putting others in their debt by providing food when harvests failed or critical wild plants and animals were in short supply. That is nowhere clearer than in the Mississippi River floodplain near Cahokia, where major mound centers were positioned only where there was a good mix of fertile soil, permanent wetlands, and seasonally inundated ground.[86] All were needed to support many people in both good and bad years. In less desirable places, mounds, if they occurred at all, were low heaps of soil that were easily built by small numbers of people in short order. Debris near these unimpressive mounds tends to be sparse, consistent with light or short occupations.

Chiefdom Spread

Chiefdoms spread rapidly across the southern Eastern Woodlands once they had emerged late in the first millennium CE. Their presence in a large geographical area only a few centuries after their initial appearance makes sense if conflicts were as pervasive as indicated by victims and palisades [**Figure 117**].

The organizational advantages of chiefdoms over less centralized tribal societies, especially when conducting war, may not have provided much of a competitive edge, but it was apparently enough. New chiefdoms developed and old ones expanded through the coalescence of formerly discrete groups of people. Not to forge alliances with one's neighbors risked being displaced by numerically superior foes or swept up into the orbits of aggressively expanding chiefdoms. If prehistoric chiefs were anything like their historic-period counterparts, they enlisted the aid of neighboring

Figure 117 Discoveries made in the early 1980s during excavations at Rucker's Bottom, Georgia, were the inspiration for this depiction of a palisaded settlement. Walls were often built by Mississippian people to defend their homes against marauding enemies.

groups whenever possible in times of need.[87] Doing so expanded the influence of particularly charismatic and determined leaders.

Formerly quasi-autonomous groups advantaged by banding together to withstand external threats would account for much of the expansion of chiefdoms across the southern Eastern Woodlands. Yet in the Mississippian world there was always a tension between desires for local autonomy and safety in numbers, the first pushing communities apart and the second pulling them together.[88] The balance between competing aims must have shifted as conditions changed over time, contributing to variation among Mississippian societies.

Population movement also played a part in the relatively quick spread of this form of sociopolitical organization across a huge geographical region. Throughout prehistory, groups moved from one place to another, either by choice or necessity. Such movement was certainly constrained by resource-rich places being occupied or claimed by other groups. Nevertheless, a jostling of populations, however dimly seen through site locations, continued from the Late Woodland through Mississippian periods. Some of that movement probably involved the losers of disputes that broke out in weakly knit chiefdoms. These people would have been tempted to move away, provided they were strong enough to carve out a place for themselves elsewhere.

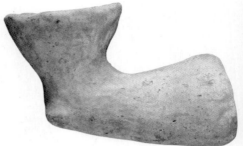

Figure 118 This ceramic pipe was found on the surface of Common Field, Missouri, along with many other artifacts, two years after the site was scoured by floodwaters when a Mississippi River levee burst during the devastating flood in 1973. Sites are damaged by erosion as well as through human activities. Maximum length (diagonal) 3 in. (7.6 cm).

Chiefdom Dissolution

The growth of complex chiefdoms, once begun, was made possible by a disparity in the capacity to wage war, with societal size and organization often proving decisive. Outward expansion was eventually halted by limits on the paramount chief's ability to project his or her authority over long distances and to maintain control over a society that retained much of its original segmented structure. A principal chief's influence over lesser chiefs, all of whom enjoyed the support of their own followers, could be expected to diminish as distance from the major center increased. It is probable that these societies were prone to disintegration at their edges where the preeminent chief's authority was the weakest. Cahokia's collapse, for example, was accompanied by the rise of one or more rivals at the periphery of its former sphere of influence, notably the Common Field site along the Mississippi River in southeastern Missouri [**Figure 118**].[89]

The self-sufficient nature of each district made it possible for ambitious sub-chiefs to break away or to usurp the highest position should favorable circumstances present themselves. Signs of discontent and feeble leadership would be apparent long before the final vestiges of chiefly authority faded away. Cahokia's final abandonment, for instance, was preceded by an extended period of population decline in the mound center and surrounding area.[90]

Even in the best of circumstances, chiefs inevitably experienced reversals of one kind or another. Their positions were surely tested during times of repeated shortages, especially if coupled with losses at the hands of their enemies. In such situations, the demands on ordinary people that had become codified through long practice could become increasingly onerous, prompting a lack of cooperation or even outright resistance. Precisely this problem—in this instance caused by repeated droughts, as indicated by tree-ring sequences—contributed to a fifteenth-century CE collapse of chiefdoms along the Savannah River.[91]

Midwestern Mississippian Disappearance

Mississippian societies that had expanded northward in the eleventh century CE during the Medieval Warm Period fell apart during a time of unrest that was related, directly or indirectly, to a deterioration in climatic conditions.[92] Not only was it generally colder during the long transition to the Little Ice Age, but an area encompassing the largest of the sites in the vicinity of the Ohio and Mississippi river confluence was experiencing widespread drought conditions by the thirteenth century. By that century's end, formerly strong midwestern chiefdoms were showing signs of weakness, and populations were beginning to decline. Once-powerful societies had all but vanished by the early fifteenth century. By that time, river valleys were occupied by less organizationally complex descendant societies or new culturally distinct groups. Many places were abandoned altogether.

Archaeologists first noticed the widespread disappearance of heavily populated societies in the Mississippi and Ohio river confluence area, accordingly named the Vacant Quarter.[93] Societal changes and, especially, depopulation are now recognized as general phenomena extending across much of the midcontinent. Mississippian chiefdoms were affected, but so too were tribal-scale societies, such as those referred to as Oneota, covered in the next chapter.

Rather than point to colder or dryer conditions as the primary culprits behind societal and population change, it is better to focus on unpredictability in food production. The fourteenth century, when midwestern chiefdoms experienced problems that led to their final dissolution, was characterized by relatively great swings in northern hemisphere surface temperature.[94] Climatic volatility would have played havoc with household decisions based on past experience about what had to be done to get enough to eat, and when to do it. Concerns over subsistence security were undoubtedly aggravated by the limited capacity of households to produce surpluses even in good years, and to store food for lean times. For the Mississippian chiefdoms, a higher frequency of back-to-back shortfalls surely eroded the authority of leading figures.

Conflicts accompanying movements of people pressed onward by hard times would have added to the difficulties midwestern chiefs faced when struggling with greater uncertainty in harvests.[95] From the perspective of the people involved, it made little difference whether their difficulties stemmed from poor harvests or marauding enemies. During this period, groups were engaged in desperate fighting, and they replaced one another in at least some places. That movement is seen most clearly by the appearance, around 1300 CE, of people classified as Oneota in the central Illinois River valley, where Mississippian chiefdoms had been present for over two centuries. Plant and animal remains excavated from thirteenth-century Mississippian sites in this area are consistent with conflict-related reductions in food-acquisition options. The Oneota group that moved into the valley shortly thereafter suffered greatly from both attacks and illnesses, many of which had developed into chronic debilitating conditions. The interaction between infection and malnutrition no doubt contributed to the poor health experienced by the Oneota newcomers.

While what caused the widespread disappearance of the major midwestern Mississippian chiefdoms has yet to be fully explained, their dissolution surely came about through the combined effects of natural and social forces. Both were important, but the latter probably played the bigger role. Only a handful of generations would pass before the downstream effects of climatic change, intergroup conflict, and the movement of increasingly desperate groups, all of which were jockeying for survival, exceeded the capacity of chiefs to resist the challenges they faced.

Chapter 7

Northern Villagers: Late Prehistory

By the beginning of the second millennium CE, and extending to European contact, agricultural villagers were scattered from the prairie and forest transition eastward through the Midwest and into the northeastern and mid-Atlantic states. Culturally distinctive groups are known by names that include, among others, Oneota in Minnesota, Iowa, Wisconsin, and Illinois; Fort Ancient in Ohio, Kentucky, and West Virginia; Monongahela in Pennsylvania, Maryland, and West Virginia; and Owasco and Iroquois in Ontario, New York, and Pennsylvania.

Distinctions in artifacts [**Figure 119**] and architecture, real as they might be, should not obscure the fact that life was not all that much different for sedentary villagers in the northern Eastern Woodlands. These people relied heavily on maize, lived in permanent villages, and settlements tended to be clumped together. People fearful of their enemies often surrounded their villages with wooden palisades. Relations between groups, often bad to begin with, had worsened by the fourteenth century CE as climatic conditions deteriorated, with widespread drought and what was to become a long slide into the Little Ice Age.

These societies are often classified as tribes, although the use of such a term does not imply that they were all the same. Constellations of villages were loosely held together by shared interests and social institutions that fostered cooperation among members of separate settlements. Evidence for permanent inherited leadership positions is notably lacking. Decisions affecting the communities were presumably made through

Figure 119 A hunter traipsing across central Pennsylvania's Tussey Mountain in 1938 found this pottery jar in a small cavity in a rock slide. It had been tucked away hundreds of years earlier, and then hidden with more rocks. Height 10.4 in. (26.4 cm).

consensus, as they are in all such tribal societies. Some people undoubtedly had a disproportionate say in community affairs, including senior members of lineages or especially capable or charismatic individuals. Their influence would have been limited to specific contexts where they had earned the respect of their fellow villagers. Despite such underlying structural similarities, there was substantial variation in precisely how groups were organized and functioned in the northern Eastern Woodlands, a subject of considerable archaeological attention.

Exceptions to this general pattern include societies with hereditary leaders that had developed no later than the early sixteenth century CE in the mid-Atlantic states, and they lasted to the early seventeenth century.[1] The best known of these groups were associated with the Powhatan of tidewater Virginia, who came to ruin shortly after the English colony at Jamestown was founded in 1607 CE. In terms of artifacts and architecture, these chiefdoms had roots extending deep into earlier societies in the mid-Atlantic region, not to Mississippian groups. The origin of the mid-Atlantic chiefdoms coincided with greater tensions among communities. In this instance, hostilities were related to competition that ultimately stemmed from population movement that accompanied worsening climatic conditions.

When looking at the entire Eastern Woodlands, a distinction drawn between northern tribes and southern Mississippian chiefdoms is convenient, but it masks considerable overlap between these societies in terms of settlement size and everyday life. The use of such categories as tribe and chiefdom as a shorthand to capture some of the variation among societies should not obscure the many features they shared.

Regardless of how they might be classified according to their cultural affiliation or social organization, northern villagers and their southern Mississippian counterparts interacted with one another.[2] Midwestern Oneota and Fort Ancient groups, for instance, obtained objects from Mississippian peoples, and these items sometimes ended up far from their points of origin. Contact also included the transmission of ideas and, to some extent, shared beliefs. For example, there were some similarities in mortuary practices, such as pots and mussel-shell spoons [**Figure 120**] from food offerings placed with the dead by the members of culturally distinct groups in Illinois. There is also evidence from architecture and artifacts for single communities consisting of people from different cultural backgrounds, notably in Fort Ancient settlements in the middle Ohio River valley.

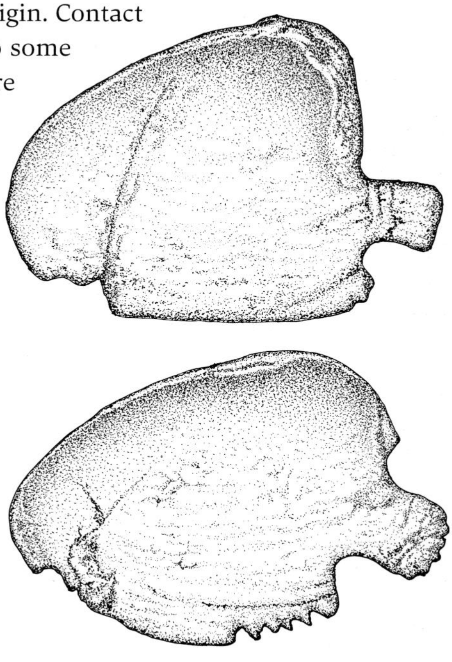

Figure 120 Some mussel-shell spoons were intact shells, whereas others were modified in various ways. These two spoons, in the shape of fish, were found with burials at the Gentleman Farm site in northern Illinois; one was found inside a pot. Length of longest spoon 4.6 in. (11.7 cm).

Burial in Mounds

Compared to the inhabitants of the southern chiefdoms, the northern villagers spent little effort building mounds. Effigy mounds in the upper Midwest, discussed in Chapter 5 (p. 94 ff.), continued to be built, with some perhaps dating as late as 1200 CE. Other mounds in the Midwest are usually rather small piles of earth, and clear signs of social ranking tend to be lacking among the people buried in them.[3] These mounds include several low ones in the Grand River group in central Wisconsin, where excavators found only a few burials and even fewer grave offerings, notably pottery. At the Gentleman Farm mound in northern Illinois, there was likewise only a modest array of artifacts, again predominantly pottery but also personal ornaments and tools. Extensive ash deposits from graveside rituals at the site highlight continuity in beliefs between prehistoric and more recent times, as some historic-period groups in the upper Midwest also lit fires near graves.

One Oneota mound from about 1300 CE, Norris Farms No. 36 in west-central Illinois (see box opposite), is particularly well documented.[4] A little more than 2 feet of dirt was piled up on a high bluff overlooking the Illinois River floodplain. The mound was so low that the natural contours of the steeply sloping ridge crest were barely modified. The cemetery grew as new graves were added, mostly on the side that faced the valley.

People at Norris Farms were frequently buried with personal ornaments, everyday tools, and pottery. Some artifacts occurred more often with certain age and sex groups. Yet nobody really stood out from the rest. Personal characteristics, family circumstances, and individual choices must have influenced what was placed in the graves. But so too did ritual concerns, as shown by an adult's severed hands carefully laid next to a child. At that time, hands were depicted on Mississippian artifacts used on ceremonial occasions (see **Figure 91**, p. 123), underscoring similarities in the beliefs of widely distributed people of different cultural backgrounds.[5]

Infant mortality at Norris Farms was high, and just over half of the people born in the community died before they reached maturity.[6] In that respect, these villagers were typical of preindustrial populations. As the Iroquois saying goes, "An infant's life is as the thinness of a maple leaf."[7] Turning to adults, it is commonly said today that few people in the small-scale societies known from archaeological materials lived into their fifties and beyond. But that misperception has its origin in flawed skeletal age-estimation procedures where the true ages of old adults are systematically underestimated. At Norris Farms, about one-third of the people who made it to their late teenage years lived to be fifty years old or older, with some surviving well beyond that age. That was similar to what took place in other late prehistoric populations where there is reasonably accurate information on adult ages.[8]

Many Norris Farms adults died at the hands of their enemies. The age distribution of the casualties of repeated attacks is consistent with what the late eighteenth-century inhabitants of the western Great Lakes region experienced. The latter were said to "begin to bear arms at the age of fifteen, and lay them aside when they arrive at the age of sixty."[9] Apparently adults of any age could die violently in intergroup conflicts in both the distant past and the contact period.

Violent Death at Norris Farms No. 36

The Norris Farms No. 36 cemetery provides us with a good picture of late prehistoric warfare.[10] Many of the more than 260 people buried in this completely excavated mound were killed by their enemies, including one-third of all men and women over the age of fifteen years. The number of victims must have been higher than indicated by the skeletal evidence because fatal wounds do not always result in recognizable damage to bone.

People had been shot with arrows and smacked with clubs mounted with stone ax heads [**Figure 121**]. They were also often scalped, decapitated, or dismembered. Scavenging animals, including wolves, coyotes, or dogs, fed on the exposed corpses. After the remains—intact bodies, partially decayed pieces of them, or scattered bones—were discovered by other villagers, they were returned to the cemetery for burial.

No more than a few victims were placed in single graves. When several individuals were buried together, their skeletons were often in the same state of disarticulation, indicating that similar amounts of time had passed between death and burial. Therefore it appears that small groups of people were sometimes attacked and died together. Victims often suffered from debilitating conditions, including diseases that affected bone, unhealed fractures, or permanently dislocated joints, all of which diminished their ability to escape or protect themselves. The situation within the community was desperate enough that people with disabilities had to be engaged in physically demanding tasks that involved travel well beyond the safety of their village.

Considering the extent of carnivore damage and disarticulation in some skeletons, it is probable that many people were killed in rarely frequented spots, perhaps while foraging for food. Others were attacked closer to home, perhaps in their fields or when getting water, judging from the presence of complete skeletons without signs of scavenger damage. A few survivors with healed injuries— they had been scalped, beaten, or shot with arrows—show that people occasionally managed to struggle home before succumbing to blood loss and exposure. These severely injured people lived for many months, or even years, after their ordeals.

The Norris Farms villagers suffered truly appalling losses. Nobody was spared the emotional anguish, disruptions in family life, and interruptions in essential survival tasks brought about by sudden and unpredictable deaths. Warfare certainly threatened this community's very existence.

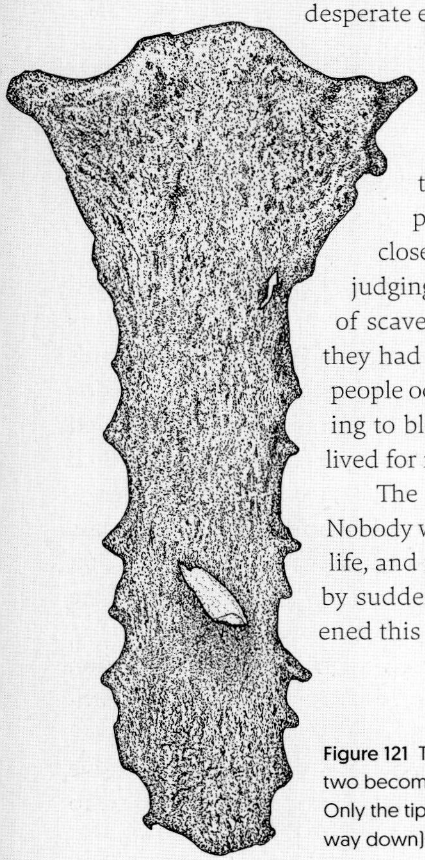

Figure 121 This sternum is from a man who had been shot with arrows, with two becoming lodged in the back of this bone after passing through his body. Only the tip of the upper stone arrowhead remains (right side, one-third of the way down); the lower point sticks out of the bone.

Other mounds built at this time include one in Virginia excavated by Thomas Jefferson.[11] His mound was about 40 feet wide and 7.5 feet high (12.2 × 2.3 meters), and it contained many jumbled bones. They had been moved from their initial burial place, as shown by their disorderly arrangement and the use of skulls as handy containers for small bones. The skeletal remains were encountered at different levels in the mound, so it was not built all at once. Both adults and children were found, although Jefferson felt there were too few of the latter, presumably because he was all too aware of the high childhood mortality of his day. He reasonably attributed the shortage of children to poor bone preservation.

More mounds have been discovered in the piedmont and mountainous parts of Virginia since Jefferson's time, but there were never many of them.[12] Some of them held the remains of numerous people. At the Rapidan Mound, mostly disarticulated bones were heaped together in different layers, and they are thought to have come from at least a thousand people of all ages.

Additional piles of bones without accompanying mounds have also been discovered. They were part of a widespread practice of communal burial in ossuaries (graves containing skeletal remains from many people) by late prehistoric and early historic groups from the mid-Atlantic states into New England and across the Great Lakes region.[13] Bones were periodically removed from their initial places of interment, cleaned, and then packed tightly together in a pit, often accompanied by some artifacts. Intact skeletons, which also occur, were presumably from individuals who had died shortly before the loose bones were acquired for collective burial. People of all ages and both sexes were treated in this manner. This way of handling the dead reinforced a sense of community, continuity across generations, and attachment to a particular place.

Enclosures

Enclosures marked by embankments, sometimes with ditches, were occasionally built in the Great Lakes region.[14] Many embankments were intended for ceremonial events that met various social needs, if we follow the same reasoning used on the much more numerous Middle Woodland enclosures. Indeed, normal habitation debris is often mostly absent, such as at the Mikado site in northeastern Michigan. The earthen embankment here had a number of openings that would have greatly reduced its effectiveness as a defensive barrier. Several such gaps were also present in other earthen rings, for example at Rifle River, again in northeastern Michigan, where everyday debris is sparse. Michigan's enclosures tend to be situated in areas of local environmental diversity, and nearby rivers, although narrow, permitted the passage of canoes. This positioning suggests the existence of social mechanisms that facilitated the acquisition and movement of food during times of need in a setting where resource uncertainty, always a concern, worsened as the centuries wore on.

Other embankments and ditches appear to have been defensive structures, especially those that encircled compact residential areas loaded with refuse. Settlements protected by wooden palisades, some accompanied by shallow ditches and low embankments, were common in these troubled times. There is no reason, of course, why enclosures always had to serve the same purpose. After all, they were built over several centuries by culturally dissimilar groups to meet different local needs.

The Shift to Crops

About a millennium ago, maize began to be incorporated as a significant part of diets that were otherwise based principally on wild plants and animals.[15] Maize was not adopted everywhere, but it was nonetheless consumed in great quantities by many people from the northern Midwest into the Northeast and mid-Atlantic region. The transition to a heavy reliance on maize took place, on average, a few centuries later than it did in the southern Midwest and Southeast. The dietary shift is identifiable in charred plant remains carefully sifted from village refuse and the stable carbon isotope composition of human bones. Tooth decay and subsequent loss were also common in many groups, similar to what happened elsewhere whenever great amounts of maize were eaten. Only later, after about 1300 CE, were beans added to diets. These two plants, along with squash, which had a long history of use, eventually became dietary mainstays for many people. They were the "three sisters" of the Iroquois. The plants were grown together, and in some places low corn hills or ridged fields have been identified, many in Michigan and Wisconsin [**Figure 122**]. A seventeenth-century description of New England farming practices provides an impression of their appearance: "The Indians…at every Corn-hill, plant with the Corn a kind of French or Turkey-Beans: The Stalks of the Corn serving instead of Poles for the Beans to climb up with. And in the vacant places between the Hills they will Plant Squashes and Pompions; loading the Ground with as much as it will bear."[16]

Figure 122 Corn hills in Waukesha, Wisconsin, are shown in this early twentieth-century photograph of the Carroll College (now University) campus.

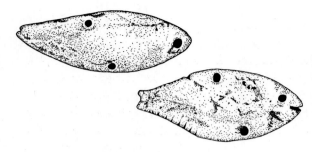

Figure 123 Shell fishing lures, such as these examples from the Oneota Norris Farms No. 36 site in Illinois, were used in the upper Midwest. These lures measure 2.9 and 3.1 inches long (7.4 and 7.9 cm).

Everywhere, people also fished [**Figure 123**], hunted large and small mammals and birds, and gathered wild plants, especially nuts. Patchworks of active and abandoned fields along with swaths of old and second-growth forests around villages were ideal habitats for deer. But even the numbers of deer could be greatly reduced by relentless hunting near settlements, forcing people into long trips to get their food. The earliest English settlers in tidewater Virginia, for instance, found that deer were difficult to find in settled areas relative to unoccupied places.[17] The same was true two centuries later when the Lewis and Clark expedition encountered pockets of game scarcity near villages as they traveled from the Plains to the Pacific Ocean along otherwise resource-rich river valleys.

The inhabitants of coastal areas were especially fortunate because they could easily catch fish, including those that swam in vast numbers up rivers to spawn. One example of how these resources influenced settlement choices is the distribution of early seventeenth-century sites in Virginia's tidewater, such as those belonging to the Powhatan. The sites tended to be situated near the best places for aquatic foods.[18] Once again, river or wetland resources had as much, if not more, influence on precisely where to establish settlements as the requirements for growing crops.

Village Life

Settlement excavations often uncover signs of houses, pits, hearths, and postmolds. Storage pits would have been similar to those of seventeenth-century New England: "The Natives commonly Thresh it [maize] as they gather it, dry it well on Mats in the Sun, and then bestow it in holes in the Ground (which are their Barns) well lined with withered Grass and Matts, and then covered with the like, and over all with earth."[19] The walls of houses, regardless of their size or shape, typically consisted of rows of vertical poles supporting frameworks covered by thatch or bark. Often, the circular to rectangular houses were so small that only single families, which consisted of parents, children, and perhaps a few relatives, could have lived in them. But some buildings were bigger and played a critical part in community affairs, as with a few Fort Ancient villages that rivaled the biggest Mississippian buildings.[20] The size and prominent position of these structures within villages, which were presumably related to the number of people who took part in key events, highlights the fuzzy overlap in societies that archaeologists put in separate categories, such as Fort Ancient and Mississippian.

Longhouses

Making its appearance at this time was a new kind of residential structure: the multi-family longhouse [**Figure 124**]. Buildings that were similar to the ones used by the seventeenth-century Iroquois and Huron had a several-hundred-year history in Ontario and New York.[21] Related families, each with its own space, belongings, and hearth, occupied the historic-period longhouses. Many of the prehistoric buildings also have hearths running down their middle, a clear indication that several families lived in them as well. Wall poles could not have lasted more than several years before they rotted, so it is not surprising that superimposed rows of postmolds are found where walls had been repaired or replaced. Such work often lengthened or shortened houses to accommodate changes in the number of people who occupied them.

When much of a settlement is excavated, sometimes at least one longhouse is found that is much bigger than the rest. This presumably housed a village leader.[22] In the historic period, such structures served as both residences and places where important social functions took place. But they were otherwise similar to other buildings in these communities. The amount of storage space relative to the number of occupants shows that important families were no better off than their neighbors. Apparently a disproportionate say in village affairs, to the extent it took place, did not translate into greater access to essential goods. That is, it did not result in a clear archaeological signature indicative of an improvement in the well-being of the most influential households.

Longhouses were also built in some Oneota villages in Iowa, Illinois, and Wisconsin, although the artifacts found at these sites, especially pottery, were stylistically distinct from those in Iroquois settlements.[23] The presence of longhouses does not necessarily signify particularly close or amicable relations among the various widely

Figure 124 Iroquois and Huron longhouses looked something like this reconstruction at the Lawson site in Ontario. But here the walls are a bit too high, and the roof is not sufficiently curved.

distributed groups that used them. In fact, the descendants of these people probably spoke completely different languages. But it seems that roughly similar social and economic demands at this time favored living arrangements within communities that reinforced close ties and working relations among related families.

Village Layout

Houses in many villages from the Midwest eastward to the mid-Atlantic region [**Figure 125**] were arranged in a circle or oval around an open area.[24] Compact residential areas promoted a sense of community, facilitated cooperation among households in everyday chores, and provided an additional margin of safety from marauding enemies. Central posts were erected in public spaces within some villages, much as they were in Mississippian communities. Small mounds were even associated with a few Fort Ancient villages. Little is known about them, although they contained burials and other features. Elsewhere, houses within villages were jumbled together, particularly in the Iroquois area where longhouses were often built close to one another and then tightly encircled by palisades.

Within any particular region, most of the contemporaneous villages were roughly the same size and had similar layouts. Together they formed multi-community groups that were socially and politically separable from similar clusters of villages elsewhere. But the great disparity in site size and configuration within a given society that was so typical of the southern chiefdoms was lacking.

Compact villages have naturally received the most archaeological attention—they are the easiest to identify. But these settlements were not the only ones that existed. Some sites consisted of no more than a few houses. There were also scattered short-term camps used by small groups of people for special purposes, such as when hunting or fishing.

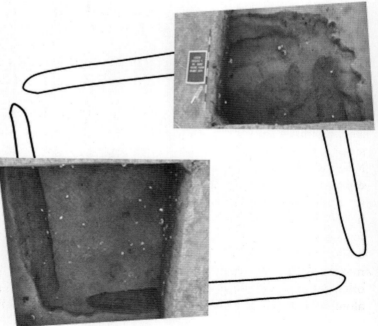

Figure 125 In this composite bird's-eye view of a partially excavated residential structure at the Fort Ancient Guard site in southeastern Indiana, one can see the progress from excavations (bottom left and top right) to maps (black lines) of buildings. Archaeologists combine the outlines of structures, pits, hearths, and other evidence of human activities to depict entire settlement layouts.

Figure 126 Palisades often surrounded villages inhabited by the immediate predecessors of the historic-period Iroquois and Huron in New York and Ontario. This reconstructed wall at Lawson in Ontario provides an impression of what they might have looked like. During the last several centuries of the pre-contact period, people increasingly had to adopt measures to protect themselves from their enemies.

As social relations in many places deteriorated in the several centuries following 1000 CE, people increasingly found it prudent to live behind fortifications.[25] Often, palisades appear as if they were thrown up when needed, with little advance planning. They were no larger than necessary to surround most, and typically all, of a village's houses. They were also sometimes accompanied by low embankments. For the most part, these ridges seem to have been no more than just enough soil piled up to help keep wall posts upright. Village refuse soon filled depressions where dirt had been scooped out to help support the posts. These ridges and ditches did not strengthen defensive barriers, unlike those at some large mound centers in the southern Midwest and Southeast.

Usually, the palisades were little more than screens that prevented enemies from slipping unnoticed into villages [**Figure 126**]. They were not stout enough to withstand attacks by large parties of determined warriors. The village walls in Ontario and New York tended to be stronger, indicating that serious fighting often broke out there, especially later in time. Here, substantial defensive barriers are indicated by multiple rows or thick bands of postmolds found in excavations. It is possible to estimate the height of one of these palisades—at Kelso in central New York—from angled soil stains for poles that had once crossed one another.[26] When standing, the poles intersected one another at 12 feet (3.7 meters), and their free ends must have stuck up higher, making the wall even harder to climb over. The protection provided by palisades was often enhanced by situating villages on easily defended hilltops and running walls along steep slopes, particularly in the hilly parts of the Northeast.

Iroquois villages were usually occupied for no more than a single generation, often much less, and this also appears to be true of many settlements elsewhere.[27] No matter how good a particular spot might have been, large game near villages was soon depleted, treks to gather firewood lengthened, and smelly garbage accumulated. At some point, the inconveniences of everyday life outweighed resistance to moving elsewhere, building new houses, and clearing more land for fields. People were forever repairing and replacing houses, as well as preparing additional fields, so this work could just as easily be done in a new location.

Villages of this period were typically inhabited by no more than a few hundred people, and often much less.[28] In a study of ossuary skeletons from Maryland, Douglas Ubelaker found that his estimated community size, just over 200 people, was consistent with John Smith's early seventeenth-century eyewitness counts of warriors in villages around the lower Potomac River.

Settlements from the Great Lakes and middle Ohio River valley into the Northeast and mid-Atlantic states began to get bigger between the late thirteenth and fifteenth centuries. Some of the later sites were occupied by up to a thousand or more people. These settlements exceeded the populations of all but the largest Mississippian mound centers.

Increases in village size occurred at the same time as relations among groups deteriorated, as shown by more palisades. People were unlikely to congregate in large settlements unless there was a compelling reason to do so. More villagers meant heavier demands on nearby game and firewood, longer walks to fields, and fewer alternatives when harvests failed. Still, the inconveniences of living in a big village were no match for worries over safety, and villages grew accordingly.

The influence of village size on settlement longevity has been nicely shown in a study of the sixteenth- and seventeenth-century Iroquois.[29] Village populations had a greater effect on settlement duration than any environmental feature examined, including soil conditions and proximity to streams and trails. Many people were associated with shorter occupations, presumably because they placed greater demands on local resources.

With larger settlements came a need for people who exercised some say over community affairs, even if it was strictly limited to specific situations. One such individual has possibly been identified at Sunwatch, a Fort Ancient site in Ohio.[30] He was buried with a well-worn small whelk-shell pendant, repurposed as a head ornament. The shell's smooth surface, polished from long use, resembled those of similar pendants from the Mississippian Dickson Mounds, Schild, and De Frenne sites in Illinois. All of these pendants must have been in circulation for lengthy periods before being buried. At Sunwatch, the whelk-shell pendant was worn in an unconventional manner on the man's head, as if it had lost much, or all, of its original meaning. This man was also the tallest known from the village. His imposing physical presence could have contributed to his prominence in the community, an assumption consistent with his possession of a highly prized and rare object.

These communities must have periodically split along kin lines, and formed through the joining of groups that each consisted of related people. That "fission–fusion"

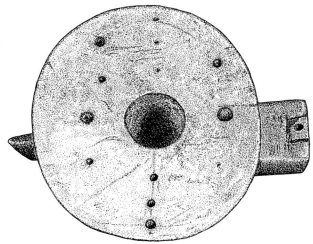

Figure 127 Disk pipes characteristic of Oneota communities are common in southern Wisconsin and northeastern Iowa but were exchanged widely across the midcontinent. This pipe from Wisconsin is 3 inches (7.6 cm) long, and it would have had a wooden pipe stem attached to it.

process almost certainly had a long history extending back to the earliest inhabitants of the Eastern Woodlands.[31]

In the Midwest, and quite possibly elsewhere as well, communities from the late thirteenth century onward took in people of diverse origins, perhaps as single individuals up to entire families and even larger groups.[32] Archaeologically, that is seen in Oneota and Fort Ancient sites where locally anomalous forms of architecture and artifacts are found in contexts consistent with the actual movement of people, as opposed to simple exchanges of objects from one person to the next [**Figure 127**]. Coalitions of culturally distinct people within single settlements appear to have been relatively common when conflicts increased and populations declined across much of the Midwest.[33] The overall picture is one of local groups that experienced relentless and crippling attacks doing whatever they could to maintain their strength. They incorporated people whenever they could, sometimes from distinctly different cultural traditions, perhaps even including former enemies.

Clusters of Settlements and Conflict

People were concentrated in rich natural settings, as they had been for millennia. It is also known that, during the several centuries prior to the arrival of Europeans, clusters of closely affiliated villages were separated by long expanses of unoccupied land.[34] These pockets of population did not remain fixed over time. Relatively short movements would have been prompted by problems stemming from a prolonged use of areas immediately surrounding settlements. But people also migrated over long distances, often when pushed onward by attacks from their enemies.

The leading edges of population expansions could be associated with devastating violence. The Norris Farms villagers, for example, were part of a southward Oneota push into Illinois around 1300 CE. At least one-third of the adults in this community were killed in a series of ambushes. Such losses had lasting effects, compromising the capacity to produce sufficient food and jeopardizing the lives of surviving family members. Essential tasks in normally self-sufficient households were certainly disrupted by sudden deaths, and the threat of attack probably curtailed foraging trips by small and vulnerable work parties.

Any interference in acquiring enough to eat was a serious matter. A precarious existence meant that concerted attacks, especially during a bad year, could push people into outright starvation. That happened in the mid-seventeenth century when the Huron, according to Jesuits who were trying to convert them to Christianity, were forced from their homes by their Iroquois enemies. Many of the refugees—"dying skeletons eking out a miserable life, feeding even on the excrements and refuse of nature"—perished from hunger and disease over a long, hard winter.[35]

A jostling of groups for advantageous positions took on new urgency in the fourteenth century. A deteriorating climate resulted in dryer conditions in some places and colder temperatures with the long slide into the Little Ice Age, increasing resource insecurity partly through shorter growing seasons.[36] The worst effects were felt where

The towne of Pomeiock and true forme of their howses, couered and enclosed some wth matts, and some wth barcks of trees. All compassed abowt wth smale poles stock thick together in steedd of a wall.

Figure 128 A late sixteenth-century watercolor by John White shows the coastal North Carolina village of Pomeiooc. Buildings encircled an open public area, and were in turn surrounded by a palisade. This general village layout had a several-hundred-year duration in the mid-Atlantic region.

the cultivation of maize had been pushed to its northernmost (coolest) limits, so the risk of crop failure was already high. Movement spurred on by hard times, especially in the midcontinent, had a domino-like effect as increasingly desperate groups successively bumped into one another. Conflicts spread accordingly, as shown by palisaded villages [**Figure 128**] that became more widespread over time.

Not until the fifteenth century did defensive walls become a common feature of settlements in the mid-Atlantic piedmont and coastal plain. New kinds of pottery in the Potomac River drainage indicate a downstream movement of people at about that time. When Jamestown was established early in the seventeenth century, the Powhatan and their allies were not only fighting their enemies to the west but were also holding off more northerly people. One such heavily armed raiding party was even encountered in 1608 CE by an English exploring party in the upper reaches of the Chesapeake Bay.[37]

In these troubled times, distinct groups of people would have found it advantageous to forge alliances for defense. Such political arrangements leave little tangible evidence of their existence, so they are difficult to detect from archaeological materials alone. Of the historic-period alliances, the best known was the long-lasting, but loosely knit, League of the Iroquois [**Figure 129**].[38] It had reached its Five Nations form by 1600 CE. Close ties among some of its member groups, however, date a century or more earlier, so it developed over a lengthy period, not as an outcome of a single event. One of the main reasons behind the league's formation was to quell fighting among linguistically related groups distributed across upstate New York. Its existence put the Iroquois in a good position, numerically speaking, for the turbulent times that followed the early seventeenth-century establishment of permanent French, Dutch, and English colonies.

Figure 129 This Iroquois pipe depicting a human head is from Otstungo in New York. The face is 2.8 inches [7 cm] high.

Chapter 8

A Trail of Tears: Native American and European Contact

In the sixteenth century CE, Europeans began to explore, and shortly after settle, the coastlines of eastern North America in ever-increasing numbers. In the tumultuous centuries that followed, native societies were thoroughly transformed as they were swept up in competing European interests, were pushed off long-occupied land, and new plants, animals, and microorganisms were introduced. One of the most widely known tragedies was the Trail of Tears, a forced relocation of several southeastern groups that took place early in the nineteenth century. But it was only part of a long and calamitous history of cultural change, population loss, and displacement.

Only where contact between indigenous groups and the European newcomers was early and continuous is it possible to move easily from knowledge about long prehistoric sequences to the tribes named in written sources, many of which can be traced to the present day. For the most part, this occurs in areas located along the Atlantic and Gulf coasts, such as those inhabited by the Powhatan in Virginia and the Calusa in Florida. There are fewer examples of seamless connections between the archaeological and historical records in the continental interior, although they include the well-known Iroquois and their bitter enemies the Huron. There is often uncertainty about precisely who the earliest Europeans encountered and how they were related to other such groups. Uncertainty also arises from changes in group location and composition that took place between initial, and frequently fleeting, contacts and later sustained interactions accompanied by fuller descriptions of ways of life and tribal affiliations.

Early Contact

The world of native groups was forever changed following the arrival of adventurers, settlers, and missionaries from across the Atlantic, starting in the sixteenth century CE. Europeans were soon vying for ascendency in what for them was initially an unknown land. Generally speaking, Spanish efforts focused on what is today Florida and nearby areas. English, French, and Dutch attention was oriented toward the mid-Atlantic and more northerly coastlines, as well as the St. Lawrence River. By the end of the sixteenth century, a Spanish presence was firmly established, whereas enduring English and French settlement would only take place at the beginning of the seventeenth century.

Sixteenth-century Spaniards were the first to penetrate deeply into the interior, with Hernando de Soto's mid-century expedition being the most well known. His men started in Florida, traveled through the southern Appalachians, and then headed west to reach land beyond the Mississippi River. Some of his beleaguered men, but not de Soto who died along the way, finally reached Mexico without the riches they had so eagerly sought.

Early Spanish adventurers, who were generally ill-provisioned, actively sought out native settlements to secure food for themselves. Two of these sites have yielded secure evidence of lengthy stays by members of Spanish expeditions into the interior. The discoveries are truly remarkable considering the vast area involved, the innumerable changes in the land that have taken place over the past few centuries, and the difficulty of tying modern locations to vague sixteenth-century descriptions. De Soto's first winter encampment, where his men stayed for several months in 1539–40, has been found within what is today Tallahassee, Florida.[1] Known as the Governor Martin site, excavations yielded Spanish pottery, glass beads, and metal items including chain mail, nails, and coins. The other site is a small fort in western North Carolina built about a quarter century later.[2] It was one of several forts established to claim land far from the coast, and it was garrisoned for less than two years by men under the direction of Juan Pardo. Now called the Berry site, archaeologists have found Spanish artifacts and the remains of food indicating that the soldiers were largely provisioned by the native people who lived nearby. Several buildings where the Spaniards had lived were located close to the fort. The structures had burned, presumably during an uprising that ended Spanish efforts to establish themselves in this mountainous area.

Other places that were probably on or near the routes of Spanish expeditions have also been identified, including Etowah in Georgia.[3] It is difficult, however, to establish unambiguously a Spanish presence at such sites. The items they left behind were exchanged, hence dispersed, among native groups. But by the end of the sixteenth century, Spaniards were well established in the Southeast, especially in present-day Florida. It was not an easy process, with failed attempts even along the coast where provisioning by sea was possible. Part of the problem stemmed from droughts—as now identified through bald-cypress tree-ring sequences—which affected Spaniards and indigenous groups alike.[4]

English, French, and Dutch settlement in the early seventeenth century followed decades of coastal explorations. A notable late-sixteenth-century English failure to establish a permanent settlement took place on a North Carolina barrier island.[5] The Roanoke settlers, now referred to as the "Lost Colony," disappeared before they could be reprovisioned from England. They had the misfortune of experiencing an utterly unfamiliar land during the worst multi-year drought in many hundreds of years, as also indicated by bald-cypress tree rings. Two decades later, colonists at

Jamestown in southeastern Virginia similarly faced difficulties partly attributable to excessively dry conditions. While their settlement was ultimately successful, it too nearly came to ruin.

After an uncertain start, the newcomers managed to establish themselves in colonies that grew with each passing year. By the mid-seventeenth century, Europeans were firmly ensconced on the coast, and their presence had a noticeable effect on neighboring native groups and those deep in the continental interior.

The Last Mounds

Only after the original inhabitants had been pushed off most of their land, by the nineteenth century, did there develop a widespread interest in the antiquities of the Eastern Woodlands. Mounds, being hard to miss, naturally attracted the most attention. But it was all too easy to believe that the ancestors of then-decimated native groups had nothing to do with them. The few examples of mound use mentioned in early Euroamerican sources made little impression on popular opinion.

Members of the de Soto expedition had actually seen mounds used as platforms for structures. They even erected a large cross on a mound—it was probably the big one at Parkin [**Figure 130**] in northeastern Arkansas—at the request of a chief to break a drought.[6] Good fortune intervened, and it rained. The Spaniards' reputation was enhanced at a point when they sorely needed all the help they could get.

Up to the early eighteenth century, the Natchez of southwestern Mississippi continued to bury chiefs and other important people in mounds, similar to what took place

Figure 130 A large mound at Parkin in Arkansas is probably where Hernando de Soto erected a wooden cross when he was passing through the Mississippi River valley during the mid-sixteenth century.

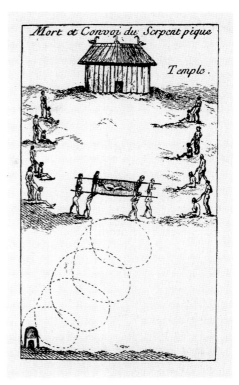

Figure 131 In this early eighteenth-century drawing of the burial of an important man among the Natchez in Mississippi, people are shown being killed as the funeral procession makes its way to a charnel structure on top of a mound.

in earlier Mississpian societies throughout the southern Eastern Woodlands. Antoine Simon le Page du Pratz saw what occurred upon the death of the chief's brother, who also happened to be his friend.[7] A litter was used to carry the body to a mortuary structure on a mound, while several people were strangled [**Figure 131**]. The building's wattle-and-daub walls, supported by rot-resistant cypress posts, were said to have been about 10 feet (3 meters) high. Three large wooden birds, facing east, were perched on the roof. The entire episode—burial in a structure on top of a mound and human sacrifices—has an unmistakably Mississippian flavor. But the days of this society were numbered, like so many others across the Eastern Woodlands.[8]

A late use of mounds is also indicated by artifacts of European origin.[9] In the Southeast, they include objects dating to the sixteenth century that were presumably given away or lost by members of Spanish expeditions. At the early sixteenth-century Tatham mound in central Florida, mound use is even indicated by two skeletons of people whose arms were cut off with swords or axes wielded by the practiced hands of soldiers. European objects, including silver ornaments and copper kettles—they date to a century or more later in time and are often of French origin—have also been found in mounds in the upper Midwest. These discoveries were made long ago, so it is sometimes unclear whether the individuals buried with these items were members of groups that built the mounds. Yet there can be no doubt that graves were dug into mounds that already existed. They include an early nineteenth-century grave house consisting of crossed sticks—in the upper Midwest, small structures over individual burials had a long history—built on the back of a turtle mound in Waukesha, Wisconsin. By choosing such a location, a connection was established to a significant spot, in this instance an effigy mound that was already several centuries old.

European Tools and Ornaments

Soon after Europeans arrived in North America, their tools and ornaments began to make their way deep into the continental interior, far beyond places where the newcomers traveled or settled [**Figure 132**, see p. 172]. That was the beginning of a change in everyday items that eventually had a profound impact on the lives of native people.

Figure 132 Spanish bells, referred to now as Clarksdale bells, have been found at contact-period sites, including this one from Little Egypt in Georgia. It could very well have been carried by the mid-sixteenth century de Soto expedition, which passed through the general area. Diameter 1.1 in. (2.8 cm).

In the Southeast, new objects, such as glass beads and metal chisels, date as early as the mid-sixteenth century at sites far in the interior where they were obtained through direct contact with Spanish expeditions.[10] Many of these items were subsequently passed from one person to the next, so the places where they ended up were not necessarily visited by the Spaniards. From that point onward, objects of Euroamerican origin were widely exchanged, with the amount and nature of these goods changing over time.

By the late sixteenth century, European-derived objects had reached the middle Ohio River valley.[11] Not long thereafter they made it to northern Illinois, and by the mid-seventeenth century, before the first French expeditions down the Mississippi and Illinois rivers, they were no longer rarities there. Much of the early material that penetrated deep into the Midwest was metal scrap repurposed into various objects, notably ornaments. They include tinkling cones, bits of metal fashioned into elongated cones that were attached to clothing [**Figure 133**]. Many of these items probably originated with Basque fishermen who had established an early presence far to the northeast in the Gulf of St. Lawrence and nearby shores. The objects had passed through many hands before finally ending up in the Midwest.

As early as the sixteenth century, European copper kettles, or large pieces of them, were being placed in native graves, mostly in the Canadian Maritimes but elsewhere as well.[12] Their use in such contexts is consistent with at least some of the new items, including kettles, being prized for their social and ritual significance, perhaps even more than their functional value. Groups farther inland, including those as distant as the midcontinent, for the most part had to be satisfied with whatever might come their way through long-established exchange networks. Sixteenth-century contact between midwestern groups and people to the south is indicated by a small Clarksdale bell, thought to be from a Spanish source, found at a Fort Ancient site.

A connection between the Midwest and Northeast is also indicated by an unusual form of native-made pottery where a pedestal was attached to what is otherwise a small but normal-looking vessel.[13] There are not many of these chalice-like vessels, but they have been found from eastern Pennsylvania to southern Ohio and southern Ontario [**Figure 134**]. Dating to the sixteenth and seventeenth centuries, they were perhaps inspired by European chalices. If so,

Figure 133 Tinkling cones were commonly made from metal scrap, such as these specimens from the Mohawk Valley, New York. The longest cone is 2.6 inches (6.6 cm).

Figure 134 Pots of native design on pedestals have occasionally been found at contact-period sites in the Northeast and Midwest, such as this vessel from a Susquehannock village in southeastern Pennsylvania. Diameter c. 4 in. (10.2 cm).

they presumably had some ritual importance in the indigenous groups that made and used them.

The chalice-like vessels and far more numerous pieces of metal and glass beads indicate that, for at least several generations during the early contact period, villagers in the Midwest enjoyed stronger connections with people in the Northeast than they did with those in the South. Directional trends in contacts among different native groups, seen archaeologically by an uneven distribution of non-local objects, would change throughout the contact period in response to social, political, and economic circumstances.

By the eighteenth and early nineteenth centuries, many European-derived items were in circulation throughout the Eastern Woodlands, and they often show up on archaeological sites. The extent to which they were adopted, often replacing their traditional counterparts, varied greatly from one native group to the next.[14] But by the end of this period, Euroamerican metal, glass, and ceramic objects were in common use.

The relative abundance of trade goods differed according to a group's proximity to the sources of those items, along with the nature of ever-changing relationships among Native American and Euroamerican societies. Native groups were not just passive recipients of new items and associated changes in ways of life, with steadily increasing numbers of Euroamerican objects simply being added over time. Acceptance of different objects was influenced by varied histories of accommodation and resistance to the pressures that were being faced, as well as perceptions about how the goods could, or even should, be integrated into indigenous economic and social systems.

Despite a widespread replacement of many traditional items, they continued to be made and used for domestic purposes throughout the nineteenth century. For example, tribally distinctive ceramic vessels were still being produced after southeastern groups had moved to Indian Territory, now Oklahoma, in the early nineteenth century.[15] Fragments of locally made pottery vessels are found in archaeological excavations, alongside those of Euroamerican origin, including bowls, plates, cups, and saucers.

New Plants and Animals

Contact between Europeans and Native Americans initiated an exchange of plants and animals that profoundly altered ways of life on both sides of the Atlantic. The movement of species, intentional or not, is, of course, very much part of our world today.

The earliest known human-assisted transatlantic movement of a species was an introduction of an American clam to northern European waters.[16] Several specimens have been dated to the medieval period, well before Columbus's journeys. Homeward-bound Viking seafarers, who had landed on the shores of North America within the clam's range, must have inadvertently transported viable larvae in sufficient numbers to establish local populations that later spread widely.

From the sixteenth century onward, many plants and animals were introduced to eastern North America. Archaeological remains, however, indicate only a few of them were soon incorporated into native diets, notably peaches and watermelons.[17] The former, brought across the Atlantic by Spaniards, were already being grown deep in the southeastern interior by the late sixteenth century. In the early eighteenth century, native groups in North Carolina were said to "claim [peaches] as their own, and affirm, they had it growing amongst them, before any *Europeans* came to *America*".[18] Watermelons, also a sixteenth-century Spanish introduction, had even made it as far as the Midwest by the late seventeenth century. Many other plants, however, did not fit as comfortably into existing ways of life, so they were not as readily incorporated into native diets. Livestock were also slow to be adopted. Presumably that had to do with the traditional importance attached to plant cultivation, and the damage domesticated animals could cause to fields coupled with the labor needed to care for them.

Dogs, which were such a prominent part of human life for thousands of years, were replaced by their European counterparts.[19] The original dogs left little in the way of a genetic signature in today's breeds. So it appears that native dogs were also casualties of Old and New World contact, despite once being widely and plentifully distributed.

Depopulation and Culture Change

The contact period witnessed a catastrophic decline in the Native American population. Losses were so great that European settlers could view the Eastern Woodlands as an underutilized, even pristine, wilderness. A bountiful land seemed to be providentially opened to burgeoning populations at home in Europe and in the new colonies. The resulting demographic imbalance led inexorably to the eventual displacement of native groups from land they had long occupied.

Diseases introduced by Europeans caused an enormous loss of life. The greatest killers, those of primary concern here, were such highly contagious diseases as measles, smallpox, and influenza, which quickly result in severe symptoms that can end in death. These diseases, transmitted directly from one person to the next, must have spread erratically from their points of introduction, with the history of any particular outbreak determined by innumerable chance events. For the pathogens to move from one spatially discrete group to another, people from separate communities had to come into contact with one another at precisely the right time. During any single epidemic, some communities would have suffered horribly whereas others were spared, leaving behind a patchwork of affected and unaffected groups.

Outbreaks of disease, no matter how terrible, were not the entire story. Wars, enslavement expeditions, forced dislocation, heavy demands on labor, and mistreatment, all directly or indirectly related to the Euroamerican expansion into the continent, also claimed their share of lives.[20] These misfortunes, which proved so disastrous for native people, began with the earliest European explorations of the Eastern Woodlands. The disruptive presence of newcomers intent on pursuing their own political and economic objectives served to reignite long-standing animosities that were all too well remembered by indigenous groups. Early Spanish incursions into the interior [**Figures 135** (below) and **136**, see p. 176] provided community leaders with irresistible opportunities to maneuver for advantageous positions, upsetting long-established relations among neighboring groups. Many of the resulting outbreaks of violence involved Spaniards who found it expedient to ally themselves with some communities when they attacked others. It was a pattern that would become all too common in the years ahead.

Yet many of the greatest declines in native populations were almost certainly attributable to newly introduced diseases and the social disruptions that followed in their wake. The relative contributions to excess mortality of disease and attendant turmoil are hard to measure, and undoubtedly varied from one situation to another. Nevertheless, as early as the late sixteenth century, English settlers at Roanoke found

Figure 135 Recent excavations at the Berry site in mountainous North Carolina have revealed direct evidence of a mid-sixteenth century Spanish presence in the region. Artifacts from Juan Pardo's expeditions have been found at the site, as has the footprint of a short-lived fort (part is shown here) built in a village that was already in existence when the Spaniards arrived.

Figure 136 One of several buildings at the Berry site that contained an abundance of Spanish items is shown being excavated. It and others nearby were burned down, presumably when Pardo's men were killed in an uprising that effectively ended Spanish efforts to settle the interior of the Southeast.

it remarkable that "within a few dayes after our departure from euerie such towne, the people began to die very fast, and many in short space; in some townes about twentie, in some fourtie, in some sixtie, & in one six score."[21] For the people affected, the illness was "so strange, that they neither knew what it was, nor how to cure it; the like by report of the oldest men in the countrey neuer happened before." Nobody at that time had the remotest idea about what caused infectious diseases, although the outcome was obvious to all. During the centuries that followed, the Roanoke experience would be repeated innumerable times across the continent, with the same devastating effect.

We can be reasonably sure about what happened when epidemics hit from descriptions of disease outbreaks in isolated populations elsewhere in the Americas and the Pacific Islands, including those that took place relatively recently.[22] When many members of a community fall ill in short succession, only a few of them are capable of providing even rudimentary supportive care for those who are sick, such as keeping them adequately supplied with fluids. Mortality rises rapidly as a result.

New diseases—while terrible enough—were just the start of the difficulties the Eastern Woodlands groups faced. In addition to coping with the emotional distress of losing family members and friends during an outbreak, people had to recreate viable households and other social institutions to carry on with tasks essential for survival. Failure to complete such work as planting or harvesting during the height of an epidemic would come back to haunt the survivors during lean times of the year.

While everyone was proficient in the basics of everyday life, hence allowing the reconstruction of functional households, that was not true of their grasp of oral traditions. Origin myths, community and kin-group histories, and rituals can be passed down through many generations, but their transmission is vulnerable to the sudden and unexpected deaths of the individuals who possess intimate knowledge of them. Often these people would have been elders who were particularly vulnerable to newly introduced pathogens. It would not have taken long before much cultural knowledge was lost.

Weakened and dispirited groups became targets for their traditional enemies, and there was no shortage of them to judge from conflicts that dated back many centuries. Potentially dangerous imbalances in the capacity to mobilize warriors must have commonly occurred. Numerically depleted groups suffered accordingly. The situation was aggravated further by native communities being drawn into wars that benefited European powers intent on expanding their political and economic spheres of influence.

Some native societies managed to hang on, but others disappeared altogether.[23] Strong chiefdoms across the Southeast proved to be particularly vulnerable. In the 1500s, the southeastern groups bested several Spanish attempts to explore or establish a permanent presence, de Soto's ill-fated expedition among them. But the majority of the large and powerful chiefdoms did not last more than a handful of generations after de Soto's journey. The lower Mississippi River valley chiefdoms were hit hard and relatively early. Only shattered remnants were encountered in the late 1600s when explorers once again passed through the valley. Far to the east in northwestern Georgia and eastern Tennessee, de Soto's men had been impressed by the Coosa chiefdom, which consisted of pockets of people distributed over as much as several hundred kilometers. Only a few decades later, however, other Spanish expeditions found that the chiefdom was already in decline.

The spread of such highly contagious diseases as measles would have been made easier in densely settled chiefdoms, and in those similar to Coosa where regular and formal connections were maintained among geographically separate concentrations of people. Sudden, unexplained, and uncontrollable losses of life surely eroded the authority of chiefs, even if they escaped death during the outbreaks. With so many people dying, disruptions in the normal succession to chiefly office certainly took place. Feeble leaders and questionable claims on newly vacated positions no doubt aggravated animosities among rival factions and furthered the disruption of formerly powerful groups.

The Chickasaw in northeastern Mississippi are especially interesting because they had developed into a force to be reckoned with by the eighteenth century.[24] Their ascendancy was in marked contrast to the situation only two hundred years earlier when heavily populated and strong chiefdoms were still present in the nearby Mississippi River valley. Prior to de Soto's time, people in the Chickasaw area generally lived in small, widely spaced communities. Dispersed settlement—and a more atomized society than the tightly knit river-valley chiefdoms—put these upland people at an advantage when epidemics struck by reducing the probability of pathogen transmission through intercommunity contact. They too suffered horrific losses, but fared better than the inhabitants of the Mississippi Valley to the west.

There are additional signs that the spread of such diseases as smallpox was probably interrupted in societies comprising constellations of loosely allied villages.[25] The Mohawk, Oneida, and Onondaga of New York, Huron-Petun (Wendat-Tionontaté) of Ontario, and Powhatan of Virginia survived intact until the early 1600s when the English, French, and Dutch established lasting toeholds on the continent. That is also true of groups in the hills of North Carolina, only they made it to the end of the seventeenth century before suffering crippling losses. These groups lacked the regular intergroup communication of such chiefdoms as Coosa where far-flung people were united, however tenuously and temporarily, under one political umbrella. Thus the clusters of villages that were only weakly tied together tended to remain relatively unscathed longer than tightly integrated Mississippian chiefdoms.

Culture change was accelerated by the incorporation of native groups into European economies [**Figure 137**]. In the north, Native Americans exchanged beaver pelts for European goods. In the south, they went after deer hides for that purpose, and a few groups were greatly feared for their slave raiding. Existing rivalries were accentuated as groups competed for positions near sources of guns and other valued goods.

Figure 137 Native Americans played active parts in the tremendous cultural changes that transformed their world following the European arrival. They avidly sought out new goods, while they bargained hard for the most desirable ornaments, tools, and guns. These items were often repurposed to meet their needs. Excavations of historic-period settlements accordingly yield a mix of traditional and Euroamerican objects. A Kickapoo house in central Illinois is shown here as it might have appeared in the early nineteenth century.

The disruptive effect of trade—in which Native Americans were active, not passive, participants—produced a more volatile cultural setting than had ever existed before.

Despite grievous losses, native groups long remained formidable obstacles to the westward expansion of Euroamerican settlers.[26] They did so, in part, by doing whatever was possible to remain numerically formidable. That often involved adding new members from weaker communities. The League of the Iroquois, already in place before the contact period, succeeded by dampening internal tensions and facilitating the incorporation of other people, including their defeated enemies. Turning to the Southeast, the largest societies also maintained their numbers for long periods, although their sizes fluctuated over time from disasters offset by influxes of more people. The reduction of the overall southeastern population was not accompanied by a corresponding great decline in individual village sizes, although there were fewer of them. Safety in numbers at both the community and tribal levels was essential in these troubled times. A coalescence of formerly discrete groups of people, down to individual families, is seen archaeologically in the diversity of distinctive pottery varieties at a settlement, Townsend in eastern Tennessee, occupied by the Cherokee three centuries ago. Seeking refuge by banding together during desperate times had a long history, extending at least as far back as the late pre-contact period. Wherever it occurred, communities were transformed, underscoring the complexity of what happened to the original inhabitants of the Eastern Woodlands.

Contact Population Size

While populations certainly plummeted after 1500 CE, the magnitude and timing of this loss are hotly debated. Current population estimates for the United States and Canada at the time of Columbus range from 2 to 18 million, many of whom lived in the fertile and well-watered Eastern Woodlands.[27] The lower estimate is derived from crude census information in documents that often postdate what were quite possibly great losses from epidemics and other misfortunes. The higher figure was obtained by extrapolating from speculative population density and resource productivity estimates. It was said to be supported by an estimate for the precontact Timucua of Florida, obtained by ratcheting the population upward in a series of steps corresponding to supposed sixteenth-century epidemics that were assumed to have happened frequently and spread uniformly across vast distances. There is little reason to believe, however, that such pandemics occurred repeatedly in the Eastern Woodlands during the sixteenth century.

All would agree that horrifyingly large numbers of people died when epidemics hit. What is questioned is whether the great killers, such as smallpox, spread widely and often from one group to the next during the first two centuries of the contact period. The alternative is that the transmission of these diseases was naturally limited by how people were distributed and the nature of the contacts among them. The debate has yet to be resolved to everyone's satisfaction because it focuses on the period prior to when rough census information, such as tallies of warriors, is widely available.

Archaeological work over the past few decades has shed light on this long-simmering controversy. It is now apparent that people were much more unevenly distributed across even the best land than was recognized when the high estimates were proposed.[28] In addition, much of the midcontinent had been depopulated for upward of two centuries prior to the European arrival in the sixteenth century. Communication among geographically discrete populations appears to have been irregular enough that highly contagious diseases, such as smallpox, measles, and influenza, must have often burned themselves out before they were introduced to neighboring groups. All of these findings have a bearing on the epidemic issue. Pathogens no doubt spread beyond face-to-face contact with sick Europeans, but there is no reason to believe that outbreaks of disease developed into pandemics that swept repeatedly and frequently across much or all of North America.

Dean Snow's and Gary Warrick's analyses of the numbers and sizes of Mohawk and Huron-Petun (Wendat-Tionontaté) settlements show that these populations did not decline until the early seventeenth century.[29] Site data are consistent with the appearance of destructive epidemics described by observers in various places. That is, the drop in the number of people inhabiting upstate New York and southern Ontario took place a century later than when the sharp decline should have occurred if the biggest population estimates based on enormous sixteenth-century losses are anywhere near correct.

That leaves us with the question of how many people actually lived in what would eventually become the United States and Canada. It is reasonable to conclude that this vast area was inhabited by more than two million people in 1500 CE.[30] But it is unlikely there were any more than two or three times that number.

Removal

During the early nineteenth century, the remaining Native American tribes were for the most part pushed out of the eastern states. But some groups hung on tenaciously up to the present day. They included, among others, the Iroquois in New York, the Cherokee in North Carolina, and the Chippewa and Menominee in Wisconsin. But most of the original inhabitants of the Eastern Woodlands had by then either disappeared or were in the process of moving beyond the Mississippi River, leaving only scattered remnants behind. For the Euroamericans, good land was simply too valuable to be left in the hands of the original inhabitants if any way could be found to push them off it. With a growing disparity between the numbers of natives and newcomers, the former did not possess the means to protect their homes, nor could they effectively protest the injustice of repeatedly broken treaties and the resulting loss of land.

Of the forced removals from the eastern states, one of the saddest became known as the "Trail of Tears" [**Figure 138**].[31] Following the passage of the Indian Removal Act in 1830, the members of several tribes were driven from their ancestral homes and made to march westward all the way to Indian Territory, present-day Oklahoma,

Figure 138 Many people perished from hardship during their forced removal from the Southeast to Indian Territory, now Oklahoma, in the early nineteenth century. This arduous and heartbreaking journey has become known as the Trail of Tears.

which only achieved statehood in 1907. Thousands died along the way from exhaustion and disease.

Only late in the nineteenth century did the plight of Native Americans begin to become a matter of widespread concern. By that time, the struggle for the continent was mostly over. The last remnants of the groups that formerly occupied the Eastern Woodlands had been shunted to the poorest land where they often suffered terribly from disease and privation. Their prospects looked bleak.

Yet, despite horrific population losses, the downward spiral in numbers was finally reversed just over a century ago.[32] Today, these people survive as rightfully proud descendants of long cultural traditions that stretch back to a time when they were the sole inhabitants of eastern North America. Mounds that still dot the land are only the most visible of their ancestors' many notable achievements.

Notes to the Text

ABBREVIATIONS
GLO General Land Office
ISA Illinois State Archives
ISM Illinois State Museum
NAA National Anthropological Archives, Smithsonian
     Institution
NMNH National Museum of Natural History, Smithsonian
     Institution
UMMA University of Michigan Museum of Anthropology
WPA Works Progress Administration
WSWMA William S. Webb Museum of Anthropology,
     University of Kentucky

PREFACE
1 The names used in classification systems often provide
   clues about where artifacts came from and their
   characteristics. But occasionally they refer to something
   else entirely, such as LuLu Linear Punctated, a type of
   pottery named after LuLu White, who ran a popular
   brothel in Storyville, New Orleans's red-light district,
   a little more than a century ago.

CHAPTER 1
1 Delcourt and Delcourt 2004: 84–86, 94–95, 162–69;
   Krech 1999: 101–22; Munoz et al. 2014: 2200.
2 Black and Abrams 2001: 2576–77, 2583–84;
   Foster et al. 2004: 32, 36, 42; Munoz et al. 2014: 2200–1.
3 Tanner 1987: 20–21.
4 Styles 1994: 48; white-tailed deer (Odocoileus virginianus).
5 Limp and Reidhead 1979: 72.
6 Goosefoot (Chenopodium berlandieri).
7 Beverley 1947 [1705]: 146.
8 Lawson 1966 [1709]: 170.
9 Jefferson 1954 [1787]: 97–102.
10 Brackenridge 1818: 154, 158.
11 Fowke 1898: 380.
12 Thomas 1894; Bureau of Ethnology was later changed to
    Bureau of American Ethnology.
13 Cole and Deuel 1937: 2.
14 Thomas 1894: 20.
15 Hoffman 1835: 67–68.
16 Anonymous 1869b: 4.
17 Anonymous 1869a: 4.
18 Marietta's Conus is not the only such centerpiece of
    a modern cemetery. Mounds have also been used for
    burial by Euroamericans, including temporary interments
    of Union casualties after the battle of Shiloh in 1862
    (Anderson and Cornelison 2013: 54, 63). The continued use
    of places deemed sacred by culturally dissimilar peoples is
    not at all unusual, with noteworthy examples being Jelling
    in Denmark and the temple complex on Luxor's corniche
    in Egypt.
19 Putnam 1887: 188; Willoughby 1919: 163.
20 Jefferson 1954 [1787]: 98.
21 Brown 1996: 41–52; La Vere 2007: 39–54, 168–80;
    Phillips and Brown 1978: 3–5.
22 Krause 2014: 97–105; Lyon 1996: 63–190; Milner and
    Smith 1986: 10–13.
23 Committee on Basic Needs in American Archaeology, 22 Jan.
    1945: 1–2, Johnson Papers, NAA; Krause 2014: 105–111.
24 McManamon 2014: 232–49.
25 Phillips et al. 1951. When describing pottery, the authors
    of this monumental work, P. Phillips, J. A. Ford, and
    J. B. Griffin, could not resist slipping in a reference to
    themselves as the "3 lugs" (146).
26 WPA Quarterly Report, July–September 1940: 22,
    WSWMA.

CHAPTER 2
1 Clark et al. 2009: 710–11; Meltzer 1993: 30.
2 Guthrie 2001: 550–60, 566–68.
3 Auerbach 2012: 530–32; Goebel et al. 2008: 1497–98;
   Llamas et al. 2016: 3; Moreno-Mayar et al. 2018: 206;
   Potter et al. 2017: 37–38; Waters 2019: 1.
4 Auerbach 2012: 530–32; Jantz and Spradley 2014: 479–87.
5 Mandryk et al. 2001: 302–8; Mann and Hamilton 1995:
   457–65; Waters 2019: 3–4, 7.

6 Goebel et al. 2008: 1499.
7 Dillehay 1997; Dillehay and Pino 1997: 48; Meltzer 1997:
   754, 2013:4–5; Meltzer et al. 1997: 662. For examples of
   early sites other than Monte Verde, see Davis et al. (2019),
   Dillehay et al. (2017), Waters et al. (2018), and Williams
   et al. (2018).
8 Alley et al. 2003: 2007–8; Gonzales and Grimm: 2009: 237;
   Rasmussen et al. 2014: 17–18, 25; Yu 2000: 1737–41.
9 Carr and Adovasio 2012: 276–81; Graham 1986: 139–41;
   Graham and Lundelius 1984: 224–26, 231, 234; Graham
   et al. 1996: 1601–2; Jackson et al. 2000: 503; Jacobson et
   al. 1987: 280, 286; Meltzer 2015: 37; Semken Jr. et al. 2010:
   248-53.
10 Anderson 1990: 164; 1996: 30; Meltzer 1997: 754; Miller
    et al. 2014: 210.
11 Adovasio et al. 1990; Clausen et al. 1979: 609, 611;
    Dunbar 2006: 411–12; Goebel et al. 2008: 1500;
    Meltzer 1993: 72–75; Waters 2019: 4.
12 Anderson 1990: 170–71, 1996: 31, 34–36, 50; Anderson
    and Gillam 2000: 59; Morse and Morse 1983: 80.
13 Carr and Adovasio 2012: 276; Fairbridge 1992: 15, 17;
    Goodyear 1999: 468–69; Meltzer 1993: 29; Stright 1990:
    439–46.
14 O'Steen 1996; Wiant 1993.
15 Birmingham and Eisenberg 2000: 72; Broster and Norton
    1996: 296; Dincauze 1993: 45–47; Freeman et al. 1996:
    402; Futato 1996: 308–10; Goodyear 1999: 434; Meltzer
    1988: 8–10; Robinson et al. 2009: 428, 440; Tankersley and
    Morrow 1993: 122–26.
16 Alroy 2001: 1895; Martin 1973; Mosimann and Martin 1975.
17 Boulanger and Lyman 2014: 41–43; Grayson and Meltzer
    2015: 188–89; Griffin 1967: 176; Meltzer 1988: 3–4, 2015:
    36–44; Webster 1981.
18 Graham et al. 1981: 1115–16.
19 Dunbar 2006: 410–11, 422–23; Dunbar and Webb 1996:
    333–50; Goodyear 1999: 444–45; Meltzer 1988: 29;
    2015: 40; Webb et al. 1984: 388; Pleistocene bison (Bison
    antiquus).
20 Cannon and Meltzer 2009: 8–11, 13–14; Carr and Adovasio
    2012: 277–79, 291–92; Clausen et al. 1979: 609; Graham
    1986: 135–37; Meltzer 1988: 6–8, 25; 1993: 122; Meltzer
    and Smith 1986: 12–13; Robinson et al. 2009: 438; Speth
    et al. 2013: 112; Storck and Spiess 1994: 134–37.
21 Amick 2015: 133–34; Carr and Adovasio 2012: 289–90;
    Curran 1999: 8; Ellis 2011: 393–94; Meltzer 1988: 26–33,
    1989: 11, 33; Robinson et al. 2009: 427; Speth et al. 2013:
    112, 129–30; Shott 1989: 224; Tankersley 1990: 283–84.
22 Kay 2012: 245–46; Meltzer 1988: 26–33; Meltzer and Smith
    1986: 13; Morse and Morse 1983: 72–75; Tankersley 1990:
    275, 294.
23 Carr and Adovasio 2012: 290, 306; McGahey 1996: 378;
    O'Steen 1996: 104–5; Tankersley 1990: 294.
24 Anderson et al. 2011: 577–78; Holliday and Meltzer 2010:
    584.
25 Bentley et al. 1993: 273–74; Campbell and Wood 1988: 56.
26 Ahler 1991: 5; Chapman and Adovasio 1977: 620, 624;
    Daniel 1998: 29–37; Driskell 1996: 322–26; Fowler 1959:
    24; Jefferies 1996a: 42–46; 2008: 107; Kimball 1996:
    177–83; Mitchie 1996: 266; Morey and Wiant 1992: 225;
    O'Steen 1996: 101; Sassaman 1996: 73–75; Smith 1986:
    16–17.
27 Leathlobhair et al. 2018: 81, 84; Leonard et al. 2002: 1614;
    McMillan 1970: 1247; Morey and Wiant 1992: 227; Perri
    et al. 2019: 73–75.
28 Ahler 1991: 6; Jefferies 2008: 113–14.
29 Jefferies 2008: 111–13; Kay 2012: 237; Meltzer and Smith
    1986: 16–17; Smith 1986: 11–13.

CHAPTER 3
1 Webb 1939: 14.
2 Baker et al. 1992: 380, 384–86; Dahl-Jensen et al. 1998:
   270; Delcourt et al. 1999: 25–27; Wright 1992: 129.
3 Delcourt et al. 1999: 19; Guccione et al. 1988: 77–78;
   Schuldenrein 1996: 8–9, 26; Smith 1986: 22, 25; 2011:
   476–77.
4 Blanton 1996: 201; DePratter and Howard 1981: 1292–94;
   Dunford 1999: 43–46; Fairbridge 1992: 17; Schuldenrein

1996: 7; Thompson and Worth 2011: 53–55. See DePratter and Thompson (2013: 152–67) and Marquardt and Walker (2012: 31–44) for the effects of shoreline changes on settlement well after the Archaic period ended.

5   Bense 1994: 75–76, 86; Cook 1976: 44, 76–77, 79–81; Jefferies 1983: 202–3, 1996a: 55, 2008:124–44, 191–214; Jefferies and Lynch 1983: 307–11; Marquardt 2005; Wiant et al. 2009: 269–70.

6   Goldstein 2004: 97–104; Smith 2009: 173; Wiant et al. 2009: 272.

7   Kistler et al. 2014: 2938–40; Newsom 2002: 203–4; Smith 1986: 28–30; 1989: 1567–68; Watson 1989: 559; squash (Cucurbita pepo) and bottle gourd (Lagenaria siceraria).

8   Sassaman 1996: 68–69, 71; 1999: 76–77; Truncer 2004: 489, 491; Webb and DeJarnette 1948: 50–55.

9   Smith 1986: 30; Sassaman 1993: 16–22.

10 Bense 1994: 82, 91; Brown 1985a: 215–16; Brown and Vierra 1983: 185; Crothers 2004: 86–87; Dye 1996: 145, 154, 158; Griffin 1967: 178–79; Jefferies 1996a: 57–58, 77, 2008: 121–24, 216–22; Jefferies and Lynch 1983: 311–14; Marquardt 1985: 72–83; Marquardt and Watson 1983: 330–31, 2005: 631–32; Milner and Jefferies 1998: 120–23; Sassaman and Ledbetter 1996: 76–79; Smith 1986: 24–27; Webb 1950: 357–59; Webb and DeJarnette 1942: 306–19; Webb and Haag 1940.

11 Milner and Jefferies 1998: 122.

12 Crothers 2004: 90; Jefferies 2008: 156; Jefferies and Lynch 1983: 319; Mensforth 1990: 89; Milner and Jefferies 1998: 121–23, 126–28; Milner et al. 2009: 117–18, 123–24; Powell 1996: 120–24.

13 Walker et al. 2005: 84–85; Webb 1946: 155–58, 1950:360–62; Webb and DeJarnette 1942: 68–69, 183, 314, 317; Webb and Haag 1940: 81–82. The cacophony that accompanied confusion and excitement when strangers arrived in a settlement, to which dogs made a mighty contribution, must have been similar to what the Long expedition in the upper Mississippi River valley experienced in 1823. Upon their approach to a village they were "assailed by a host of yelping dogs that were attended by their masters and a throng of children" (Long in Kane et al. 1978 [1823]: 147).

14 Brown and Vierra 1983: 185–89; Jefferies 1983: 199–200, 202; 2008: 151–59; Jefferies and Lynch 1983: 301–2, 315; Styles 2011: 450; Styles and Klippel 1996: 118; Webb and Haag 1940: 68–70.

15 Crothers 2004: 87, 90; Jefferies 2008: 150; Moore and Thompson 2012: 276–79; Thompson 2010: 220.

16 Emerson and McElrath 1983: 228–38; Fortier 1983: 248–51; Higgins 1990: 102–6.

17 Only rarely can children's play be identified in habitation contexts, but at one Mississippi River valley site where I worked a rodent burrow was found chock-full of chert flakes. One can imagine a young child sitting by a hole, determinedly cramming flakes down it. The flake-filled burrow, while inconsequential in itself, is a reminder that people once worked and played in the sites we excavate.

18 Dye 1996: 141; Emerson and McElrath 1983: 230–32; Jefferies 1983: 202–3.

19 Jackson and Scott 2001: 189–90, 193–95; Kidder and Ervin 2018: 523.

20 Marquardt 2010: 563–64; Russo 1996b: 178, 181–96, 2010: 152–59; Sanger et al. 2018: E7673; Smith 1986: 28; Thompson 2010: 221–24; Thompson and Worth 2011: 68–69.

21 Hill et al. 2019: 1090-91; Sanger et al. 2018: E7675-77.

22 Sanger and Thomas 2010: 54–55.

23 Thompson et al. 2013: 80, 86–93.

24 Décima and Dincauze 1998: 157–59, 165.

25 Jefferies 1983: 203–4, 1996a: 54, 70; 2008: 221.

26 Ruff 1999: 315–17.

27 Buikstra 1981: 126, 129, 131; Jefferies and Lynch 1983: 319; Milner and Jefferies 1998: 129; Milner et al. 2009: 124.

28 Moulton 1990: 169. Original spelling and Moulton's word clarification.

29 Jefferies 2008: 174.

30 Fritz 1995: 6–8; Smith 1989: 1566; 1995: 12–13; 2011: S471; Smith and Yarnell 2009: 6561; Watson 1989: 562.

31 Smith 1989: 1567–68; 1995: 196; Watson 1989: 563; erect knotweed (Polygonum erectum), marsh elder (Iva annua), maygrass (Phalaris caroliniana), little barley (Hordeum pusillum), and sunflower (Helianthus annuus).

32 Crites 1993: 147; Fritz 2000: 230–31; 2019: 21, 32; Hart and Sidell 1997: 528, 532; Petersen and Sidell 1996: 688, 693;

Smith 1989: 1567–69; 1995: 184–201; 2011: S472; 2014: 57, 67–72; Smith and Yarnell 2009: 6561.

33 Bense 1994: 76, 88; Brown 1985a: 218, 223; Jefferies 1995b: 133, 1996a: 61–62, 1996b: 232; Marquardt 1985: 78, 80–81.

34 Milner et al. 2009: 125–26.

35 Jefferies 1996b: 225–32; 1997: 470–84; 2004: 73–80, 85; 2008: 183–86, 212–14, 283–85.

36 Hill 2012: 281–89; Jefferies 1996b: 225–30, 1997: 481, 2008: 186; Johnson and Brookes 1989: 142–43; O'Gorman and Lovis 2006: 27; Pleger and Stoltman 2009: 707–12.

37 Jefferies 1996b: 233.

38 Jefferies 1996a: 46, 2008: 251–52; Mensforth 2007: 231–47, 251–55; Milner 1999: 120–22; Milner et al. 2009: 127–28; Smith 1997: 250–56.

39 Russo 1996a: 261–71, 276–81; Saunders et al. 1997: 1796–98, 2005: 632–33, 638–40, 648–50, 663.

40 Jackson and Scott 2001: 189–91; Saunders 2004: 148–53; Saunders et al. 2005: 650–53, 657–62.

41 Gibson 1996: 289–91, 2000: 80–91; Kidder 2002: 90–99; Kidder and Ervin 2018: 521–23, 526–28; Ortmann 2010: 663, 675; Ortmann and Kidder 2013: 67, 73–74, 76–77; Sherwood and Kidder 2011: 74, 76; Smith 1986: 32–34; Webb 1977: 16–19, 28–31, 40–43, 48–52.

42 Gibson 1996: 293; Kidder 2002: 90–91; Kidder and Ervin 2018: 522, 524–25; Ortmann 2010: 675; Russo 1996a: 262; Smith 1986: 29, 32.

43 Gibson 1996: 289–91; 2000: 80–91, 96–105; Kidder 2002: 95–99; Saunders et al. 2001: 76; Webb 1977: 16–19, 28–53.

44 Kidder and Ervin 2018: 527–28; Ortmann and Kidder 2013: 73–74, 76–77.

45 Gibson 1996: 301–2, 2000: 172–6; Smith 1986: 30, 32–33.

46 Kidder and Ervin 2018: 520.

47 Gibson 1996: 294–96; Russo 1996a: 266–81; 1996b: 194; 2010: 156.

48 Albertson and Charles 1988: 29–33; Charles 1996: 86–87; Charles and Buikstra 1983: 127–28, 130; Klepinger and Henning 1976: 105–9, 128–33.

49 Albertson and Charles 1988: 33–38; Charles 1996: 86; Charles and Buikstra 1983: 132; Klepinger and Henning 1976: 105–9.

Chapter 4

1   Ashley 1998: 208–13; Bense 1998: 259; Esarey 1986: 240; Smith 1986: 42.

2   Webb 1940: 51; 1941b: 228–36, Fig. 2; 1942a: 309, 332; 1942b: 427, Figs. 22, 23; 1943a: Fig. 7; 1943b: Fig. 2.

3   Milner and Jefferies 1987: 40.

4   Brown 1997: 475.

5   Webb and Baby 1957: 14–23; Webb and Snow 1945: 44–48, 70–73, 91–96, 98–102.

6   Milner and Jefferies 1987; Webb 1942b.

7   Copper breastplates are rectangular plates with rounded corners and generally two suspension holes.

8   Clay 1983: 113–16.

9   Abrams and Le Rouge 2008: 226–30; Milner and Jefferies 1987: 37–41.

10 Brown 1979: 213–15; Greber 1979: 30–36, 1983: 13–38; 2015: 89–121; Greber and Ruhl 1989: 52; Konigsberg 1985: 131.

11 Greber and Ruhl 1989: 172–78; Morgan 1952: 90, Fig. 94; Song et al. 1996: 252–62.

12 Brown 1979: 213–15, 2006: 90-94; Mills 1922: 269–79.

13 Abrams 1992: 85–90.

14 Bluff-crest mounds are wonderful places to excavate—nice views, cool breezes, and easily dug loess—as long as one keeps a sharp eye out for rattlesnakes that infest these places.

15 J. Brown 1979: 215–18; 1981: 34–36; Bullington 1988: 227–33; Griffin et al. 1970: 13–123; Leigh et al. 1988; Ruby et al. 2005: 135; Van Nest et al. 2001: 635, 636–42.

16 An upside down placement of most blocks of sod makes sense to anyone who, like myself, has carried hundreds of them. Holding chunks of sod with the grassy side downward makes them less likely to buckle and break apart, and thus be dropped. Sod blocks were simply placed on growing piles in the same way they were carried. That is no doubt why, wherever they are found, they are usually in this position (e.g. Monaghan and Peebles 2010: 943; Sherwood and Kidder 2011: 75).

17 Braun et al. 1982: 9–27; Buikstra 1976: 35, 42; Griffin et al. 1970: 13–123; Leigh 1988: 198–209; Leigh et al. 1988: 71–72, 77.

18   McKern 1931: 206–11, 242–47, 252–56, 263–67.
19   Ford 1963: 9–40.
20   McKern 1931: 210–13.
21   Walthall 1979: 200–2.
22   Jefferies 1976: 3–5, 6–18.
23   Leigh et al. 1988: 51, 56.
24   Jefferies 1976: 20; McGimsey and Wiant 1986: 534–41
25   Fowke 1928: 414, 422; Jefferies 1994: 73–82; Knight 1990: 34–49, 168–69; Lynott 2014: 155; Mainfort 1986: 15–17, 82; Milanich 1994: 174–79; Pickard 1996; Pluckhahn and Thompson 2017: 85–87, 90; Ruby et al. 2005: 140–42; Toth 1974: 11.
26   Ford and Willey 1940: 14–16, 22–30, 35–45, 122–26.
27   Milanich 1994: 173–79.
28   Jefferies 1994: 76–82; Knight 1990: 34–49, 168–69; Mainfort 1986: 15–17, 82; Pickard 1996.
29   Fowke 1928: Plt. 64; Garland and Beld 1999: 140–42; H. E. Jackson 1998: 215; Jones and Kuttruff 1998; Kellar 1979: 100–2; Lynott 2014: 146; Mainfort 1986: 7; Mainfort and Carstens 1987: 58–59; Toth 1974: 9–13.
30   Clay 1987: 46; Fenton and Jefferies 1991: 43; Fowke 1902: 220–21, 332; Griffin 1947: 190–91; Jefferies et al. 2013: 93; Squier and Davis 1848: 8–103; Thomas 1894: 450–51; Vickery 1979: 60–61; Webb 1941a: 141–42; field notes, WSWMA.
31   Webb 1941a: 142–58.
32   F. L. Cowan, personal communication, 2001; Lynott 2014: 92, 217, 240.
33   Squier and Davis 1848: 73–75.
34   Fowke 1928: 492; Griffin 1947: 190–91; Shetrone 1925:48–50; Vickery 1979: 59–60; Bohannan field notes, WSWMA.
35   Clay 1985: 12–17; 1987: 49.
36   Fowke 1902: 186, 193; Lynott 2014: 99–100, 172; Squier and Davis 1848: 8–103.
37   Connolly 1998; Essenpreis and Moseley 1984; Faulkner 1996: 7–8, 10; Jefferies 1976: 43–44; Lynott 2014: 187-209; Prufer 1997; Riordan 1996, 1998; Ruby 2009: 54.
38   Lepper 1996: 233; Riordan 1996: 248, 251–52; 1998: 81.
39   Connolly 1998: 93–95; Squier and Davis 1848: 47–103.
40   Fowke 1902: 159–62; Greber 1997: 218; H. E. Jackson 1998: 207; Jones and Kuttruff 1998: 52; Lepper 1996: 233, 1998: 126; Lynott 2014: 107, 114, 149-50, 205; Prufer 1997: 316–19, 324; Riordan 1996: 248, 252–53, 1998: 81–82.
41   Brown 2006: 172–77; Fowke 1902: 160–69; Greber 1997: 213–14; Greber and Shane 2009: 27; Jones and Kuttruff 1998: 50, 52; Lepper 1996: 232; 1998: 123; Lynott 2014: 148, 167, 172, 174.
42   Greber and Shane 2009: 27; Lynott 2014: 106–7, 165–78, 222.
43   Drooker 1997: 273; Fletcher et al. 1996: 116–23, 133; Lepper 2018: 70; Romain et al. 2017: 208–14, 218–20; Squier and Davis 1848: 96–97; Willoughby 1919: 153–60.
44   Connolly 1998: 90; Lynott 2014: 193.
45   Baby and Langlois 1979; Cowan 2006: 36–44; Lynott 2014: 119–21, 237–39.
46   Riordan 2015: 127–42.
47   Burks and Cook 2011: 676–78; Greber and Shane 2009: 31, 32, 47; Lynott 2014: 98–100, 167, 260.
48   Emerson et al. 2013: 57–59; Farnsworth et al. 2015: 35-36; Griffin 1967: 184; Lynott 2014: 256.
49   Brown 1979: 214–15; Essenpreis and Moseley 1984: 26; Greber 2015: 124; Greber and Ruhl 1989: 23, 77–78, 80, 90, 191–92, 257; Mills 1907: 64–65; Shetrone 1926: 27–29, 43, 74–76, 109, 140.
50   Jefferies 1976: 21–27; Snyder 1962 [1895]: 195; Walthall 1979: 203.
51   Greber and Ruhl 1989: 11–13, 23, 27, 77–78, 80, 90, 191–92, 257; Shetrone 1926: 27–29, 43, 74–76, 109, 140; Squier and Davis 1848: 26–29; Mound 17 is also referred to as Mound 29.
52   Carr 2005: 584; Griffin 1967: 184.
53   Carr 2005: 582-84; Lynott 2014: 256-57.
54   Milner 1999: 122.
55   Butler 1979: 151–53; Fortier 1989: 58–94; Lepper and Yerkes 1997: 180–83; Pacheco 1996: 25–28; Ruby et al. 2005: 134, 138–39, 150–52; Smith 1986: 39–41, 44; 1992: 213; Stafford 1985: 449–50; Stoltman 1979: 129–32; Weaver et al. 2011: 25–30.
56   Butler 1979: 151–52; Carr 2008: 104–6, 109–11; Pacheco and Dancey 2006: 6–7; Ruby et al. 2005: 132–35, 138–40; Smith 1986: 39, 44; 1992: 214–16, 240–43; Stafford 1985: 447, 454–55; Stoltman 1979: 131.
57   Coughlin and Seeman 1997: 240; Genheimer 1997: 295; Lepper 1996: 234; Lynott 2014: 118, 132; Pacheco 1996: 19;
Pacheco and Dancey 2006: 11.
58   Bense 1998: 257–62.
59   Griffin et al. 1970: 74–76, Plate 72.
60   Harriot 1972 [1590]: 53.
61   Buikstra 1976: 46–47; Neumann 1942: 308. Cradleboard deformation is often asymmetric, consistent with a posterior deformation of the cranial vault (plagiocephaly) that can arise today in babies from their habitual sleeping positions.
62   Smith 1989: 1567; 1995: 184.
63   Mueller 2018: 40–42, 44; 2019: 318, 329–30.
64   Chapman and Crites 1987: 353; Crawford et al. 1997: 114–15; Fritz 2019: 53–54, 68; Simon 2014: 100–1, 109–12; Smith 1989: 1570; Warrick 2008: 165; Watson 1989: 560.
65   Lovis et al: 2001: 621–22, 628–29; O'Gorman and Lovis 2006: 32–33; Styles et al. 1985: 434–35.
66   Bense 1998: 253–55; Thompson and Worth 2011: 62–63.
67   Johnston 2008: 499; Konigsberg 1985: 126, 129; Milner and Jefferies 1987: 40; Webb and Snow 1945: 247.
68   Buikstra 1976: 33–40; Bullington 1988: 237.
69   Braun et al. 1982: 9–10; Dragoo and Wray 1964: 196–98; Farnsworth et al. 2015: 4–45, 51; Fenton 1998: 33, 102, 122, 200–1; Greber and Ruhl 1989: 29–30; Griffin et al. 1970: 28; Lepper 1996: 232; Mills 1907: 58–59; Neumann and Fowler 1952: 201–2, 209–10; Shetrone 1926: 163–66; Webb and Baby 1957: 61–71.
70   Jefferies 1976: 49–50. Today a major interstate highway passes by Tunacunnhee, underscoring the area's long-standing importance as a corridor for communication through difficult terrain.
71   Mills 1907: 76; Seeman 1995: 130–32.
72   Shetrone 1951: 25.

CHAPTER 5

1   Phillips 1970: 20.
2   Birmingham and Eisenberg 2000: 110, 138; Goldstein 1995: 102–5. Mallam 1976: 2, 104–9; Salkin 2000: 533; Stoltman and Christiansen 2000: 501, 507.
3   Birmingham and Eisenberg 2000: 110, 125–28; Goldstein 1995: 105–7; Salkin 2000: 533; Stoltman and Christiansen 2000: 501–4.
4   Birmingham and Eisenberg 2000: 117; Goldstein 1995: 102, 109–10, 119–20.
5   Goldstein 1995: 102, 105, 113; Mallam 1976: 38–40; Salkin 2000: 536; Stoltman and Christiansen 2000: 512.
6   Birmingham and Eisenberg 2000: 171; Buikstra and Goldstein 1973: 3–4; Butler and Wagner 2000: 701–2; Chapman 1980: 78–137; Charles et al. 1988: 85–102; Conner 1991: 240–43; Esarey 2000: 394; Halsey 1999: 234; Howey et al. 2016: 7444; Nassaney 2000: 721; Pollock and Henderson 2000b: 628; Reeder 2000: 194, 205–6; Schroedl et al. 1990: 183; Seeman and Dancey 2000: 599–600; Smith 1986: 52.
7   Atwell 1991: 237; Charles et al. 1988: 85–102; Conner 1991: 240–43.
8   Kidder 1998: 130; Williams and Brain 1983: 333–36, 352.
9   Pluckhahn 2003: 1, 56–73, 108–9, 193; Pluckhahn et al. 2018: 332–38.
10   Rolingson 1990: 11–17; 1998: 2, 95.
11   Bartram in Waselkov and Braund 1995: 62, 246–47.
12   Rolingson 1990: 3, 5, 11–17; 1998: 2–3, 22–23, 95–100; Thomas 1894: 243.
13   Belovich and Brose 1992: 8, 14, 17–20.
14   Butler and Wagner 2000: 698; Muller 1986: 150–53; Pollack and Henderson 2000b: 621.
15   Butler and Wagner 2000: 697; Pollack and Henderson 2000b: 628, 630; Railey 1984: 29, 84–90.
16   Kelly 1990a: 87–105, 1990b: 126–35.
17   Kelly and Brown 2014: 300–2; Kidder 1992: 147, 1998: 129–30; Nassaney 2000: 718–19; Rolingson 1998: 101–4.
18   Birmingham and Eisenberg 2000: 103; Butler and Wagner 2000: 696, 702; Green 1993: 206–8; McElrath and Fortier 2000: 97, 100; Muller 1986: 128–29; Nassaney 2000: 719; Pollack and Henderson 2000b: 632; Seeman and Dancey 2000: 602; Smith 1986: 52.
19   Fritz 1990: 416–24; Johannessen 1984: 202; 1993: 59–66; Simon 2000: 42, 46, 48, 52; Smith 1989: 1570.
20   Bridges et al. 2000: 227–30.
21   Buikstra 1992: 95; Fritz 1990: 398, 408–9; Johannessen 1984: 203; 1993: 63, 66; Katzenberg et al. 1995: 344–46; Smith 1986: 51; 1989: 1570.
22   Brown et al. 1990: 265–70; Cobb 2000: 65.

23 Seeman and Dancey 2000: 589; Wymer 1997: 156–57, 159.
24 Blitz 1988: 130–31, 135; Butler and Wagner 2000: 695;
    Nassaney 2000: 715–17; Seeman 1992: 41; Seeman and
    Dancey 2000: 594; Shott 1996: 288; Styles 2011: 455–56.
25 Beverley [1705] 1947: 309.
26 Brashler *et al.* 2000: 555–56; House 1990: 19; Styles 1994:
    43; 2000: 85–90; 2011: 450–51.
27 Atwell 1991: 237; Butler and Wagner 2000: 701–2; Charles
    et al. 1988: 85–102; Esarey 2000: 394; Schroedl *et al.* 1990:
    183; Seeman and Dancey 2000: 600; Smith 1986: 52.
28 Williams and Brain 1983: 42–56, 334–35.
29 Kelly 1990b: 130; Muller 1986: 140; Nassaney 2000:
    715–16, 721; Smith 1986: 52.
30 Milner 1999: 122.
31 Kelly 1990b: 130–36; Knight and Steponaitis 1998: 11;
    Milner 1998: 174–75.
32 Rindos and Johannessen 1991: 43; B. D. Smith 1987:
    47–51.
33 Fritz 1990: 411, 1995: 9, 2000: 238–39; Kidder 1998:
    129–30; Thomas 2008: 1090–93.

CHAPTER 6

1   Brown 1996: 620–25; Drooker 2017: 25–26, 32–34.
2   Anderson 1994: 178–79, 182, 209, 212; Black 1967: 266;
    Blitz and Lorenz 2006: 48, 165–67, 202; DeJarnette and
    Wimberly 1941: 61; King 2003: 67, 76; Larson 1971: 60;
    Price and Fox 1990: 24; Smith 1969: 66; Swanton 1911:
    262–69.
3   Blitz 1993: 74–85.
4   Fowler 1997: 87; King 2003: 66–67, 75–77; Milner 1998:
    144–46; Muller 1997a: 273; Sherwood and Kidder
    2011: 82.
5   Anderson *et al.* 2013: 309–96; Brennan 2018: 208, 211;
    Krause 1990: 75–86; Monaghan and Peebles 2010: 943;
    Regnier *et al.* 2019: 302; Sherwood 2013: 483–523;
    Sherwood and Kidder 2011: 74–75. Shiloh in 1862 was
    one of the Civil War's bloodiest battles. It was where John
    Wesley Powell, who would later lead an expedition down
    the Colorado River through the Grand Canyon and become
    director of both the U. S. Geological Survey and Bureau
    of Ethnology, lost his right arm, although he continued to
    serve after his wound healed.
6   Anderson 1994: 196–99; Du Pratz 1972 [1774]: 339; Le
    Petit in Thwaites 1896–1901 vol. 68: 129; Rudolph 1984:
    35–39.
7   Milner 1998: 146–50; Muller 1986: 200–4, 1997a: 273–75.
8   Lacquement 2019: 172–76.
9   Fowler 1997; Kelly and Brown 2014: 303–15; Milner 1998:
    106–14, 121–24, 144–46; Pauketat 1998: 122–28; 2004: 76,
    78–80.
10 Moore in Morse and Morse 1998: 29. Moore was not the
    first to dig into many of his sites, such as the Citico mound
    in Tennessee where deep tunnels collapsed in 1865 from
    cannons fired in celebration of the Army of Northern
    Virginia's surrender at Appomattox (Read 1872: 402).
11 Anderson 1994: 210–11; Blitz 1993: 82; Hammerstedt
    2005: 16–17; 2013: 195, 199; Jackson and Scott 2010:
    329–47; Rudolph 1984: 38, 41; Wesler 2001: 38.
12 NMNH, ISM, and UMMA notes and collections.
13 Bell 1972: 18–19, 110, 142–45, 160–65, 179–81; J. Brown
    1981: 32–34; 1996: 23, 170–71; Du Pratz 1972 [1774]: 334.
14 Brown 1996: 53–103, 188, 319, 421; 2010: 43–46; Regnier
    et al. 2019: 307–8.
15 Brown 1996: 12–13, 53–103, 161, 166–67, 188–89, 195,
    419–21; 2010: 38–48.
16 Emerson *et al.* 2016: 410–11, 413–15; Fowler *et al.* 1999:
    3–13, 64–79.
17 Conrad 1991: 128–29; Du Pratz 1972 [1774]: 337–39;
    Le Petit in Thwaites 1896–1901 vol. 68: 131–33; Swanton
    1911: 264–67.
18 Hally 2007: 189–229; Knight 2006; Knight *et al.* 2001:
    129–31; Lankford 2004: 208; Muller 2007: 27–36.
19 Brown 1985b: 114–23; 1996: 549; Dye 2004: 194–96;
    Knight *et al.* 2001: 134–36; Phillips and Brown 1978:
    119–20, 124–30, 153.
20 Brown and Dye 2007: 279–89; Dye 2004: 195–96.
21 Brown 1996: 96, 189, 194, 531; Knight *et al.* 2001: 132.
22 Brown 1996: 532–34; Winters 1974: 38–42.
23 Steponaitis 2016: 125, 130–32; Steponaitis and Knight
    2004: 174–75.
24 Boudreaux 2007: 73; Goldstein 1980: 58, 65; Hally 2008:
    259, 261; Harn 1980: 16, 26; Hudson 1976: 166–69, 244,

343, 356–57; Marcoux 2010b: 61; Milner 1998: 136; Perino
    1971a: 18, 20, 22–24, 50, 54; Rodning and Moore 2010:
    85–87, 91–94.
25 Original spelling. Harriot 1972 [1590]: 54. Several decades
    later and not far to the north in Virginia, John Smith (2007
    [1624]: 283) described hair ornaments that included bird
    wings and entire birds, but did not mention the roles of
    the people who wore them.
26 Emerson 1997: 198–205; Fritz 2019: 105–6, 111–13, 150;
    Milner 1983: 52, 1984a: 240.
27 Brown 1996: 439–56, 534–35; Fowler *et al.* 1999: 102–10,
    129–32; Goldstein 1980: 58, 65; Hally 2008: 229–32,
    237–38; Harn 1980: 16; Marcoux 2010b: 152–58; Milner
    1998: 135; Perino 1971a: 112–13, 126–30, 1971b: 164–65.
28 Boudreaux 2007: 17–26, 2017: 210–15; Hally 2008:
    50–120; Milner 1998: 91–96.
29 Heavy Mill Creek chert hoes bite deeply into the ground,
    permitting rapid and effective digging, as demonstrated
    through the use of replica tools (Hammerstedt and Hughes
    2015: 153–54; Milner *et al.* 2010: 108–9).
30 Thomas 1894: 31.
31 Milner 1998: 97; Schroedl 1998: 88
32 Milner 1998: 92; Wilson and VanDerwarker 2015: 169–72.
33 Fortier and Finney 2007: 640–42; Milner 1998: 87; Morse
    1973: 65–66.
34 Kelly and Brown 2014: 300, 306–15; Pauketat *et al.* 2002:
    258–68; 2004: 76.
35 Boudreaux 2007: 41–42, 54–55; Fowler 1997: 24; Kelly and
    Brown 2014: 308–9; Knight 1998: 48; 2010: 2–3, 302–12;
    2016: 24–25; Porter 1974: 294–97.
36 Knight 1998: 50–52, 60; 2010: 5–7; 2016: 24–25, 32–34,
    38–41.
37 Knight 2010: 2–3; Knight and Steponaitis 1998: 2–6,
    13–24; Steponaitis 1998: 39, 43.
38 Kelly and Brown 2014: 321–22.
39 Phillips *et al.* 1951: 329–35; Stout and Lewis 1998: 152.
    When describing these Mississippi River bottomland
    sites, James B. Griffin told me that in the 1930s and 1940s
    they were well suited to "windshield surveys" because the
    middens were high enough to see from a car.
40 Fowler 1997: 193–200; Kelly and Brown 2014: 303–15;
    Milner 1998: 109–14.
41 Kelly and Brown 2014: 304; Knight and Steponaitis 1998:
    15; Milner 1998: 110–13, 156–57; Payne and Scarry 1998:
    40; Stout and Lewis 1998: 152, 154–55.
42 Milner 1998: 121–24; Muller 1997a: 213–15; Pauketat
    2004: 79, 106; Schroedl 1998: 90; Steponaitis 1998: 42–43;
    Wesler 2001: 150.
43 Brennan *et al.* 2018: 161–64; Emerson 2018: 496–97.
44 Hammerstedt *et al.* 2017: 17, 19–21, 24–26.
45 Brown 2007: 152; Hally 2008: 122–39, 152–59; Hally and
    Kelly 1998: 49–54; Kidder 1998: 147; Milner 1998: 100–2;
    Muller 1997a: 222; Price and Griffin 1979: 31–45; Smith
    1978: 488–91; Stout and Lewis 1998: 154.
46 Beverley 1947 [1705]: 218–19.
47 Early 2000: 129–30; Perttula *et al.* 2008: 98–103; Regnier
    et al. 2019: 324; Rogers 1995: 85, 91–94; Samuelsen 2010:
    265–76.
48 Milner 1984b: 40, 43–44, 105, 1998: 81–87.
49 Johannessen 1984: 207; Lopinot 1991: 170; Monaghan
    et al. 2014: 35, 37–42; Rindos and Johannessen 1991: 39;
    common bean (*Phaseolus vulgaris*).
50 Bridges *et al.* 2000: 234; Larsen 1982: 200–10; Larsen *et al.*
    1991: 182–86; Powell 1985: 327–32.
51 Du Pratz 1972 [1774]: 156–57.
52 Fritz 1990: 419–21, 1995: 8–10; Hutchinson 2004: 127–28;
    Hutchinson *et al.* 2000: 110–15, 2016: 56, 59, 61, 66–67;
    Kidder 1998: 130; Marquardt 2001: 162; Marquardt and
    Walker 2012: 29–31; Thomas 2008: 1090–93; Thompson
    et al. 2018: 30; Widmer 1988: 260–76.
53 Milner 1998: 68–69, 73–74; Smith 2009: 171–72; Styles
    2011: 450–51, 458.
54 Jefferies 1995a: 260; Laliberte and Ripple 2003: 996–99;
    Martin and Szuter 1999: 38–40; Milner 1998: 69, 72–74;
    Smith 2009: 170.
55 Smith 2007 [1624]: 285.
56 Larsen 2015: 44–57.
57 Bell 1972: 110; J. A. Brown 1981: 32–34; 1996: 188; NMNH,
    ISM, and UMMA notes and collections.
58 Brown 1975: 19–22; 1996: 436–37, 469–88; Dye 2004:
    194–203; Fowler *et al.* 1999: 102–4; 168–70; Phillips and
    Brown 1978: 108, 119, 124–30.

59 Muller 1997a: 84–85, 92, 395.
60 Bartram in Waselkov and Braund 1995: 127, 159–60.
61 Knight 2016: 25–28, 31–34, 37–41.
62 Milner 1998: 101, 138; O'Brien 2001: 158, 222–28, 295; Price and Griffin 1979: 47, 139.
63 I. W. Brown 1981: 2–14; Goldstein 1980: 97–106; Hally 2008: 214–22; Milner 1998: 135; Peebles 1971: 71–72; Sullivan 1987: 24; Webb and DeJarnette 1942: Fig. 70.
64 Cobb and Pope 1998: 4, 6, 13; Goldstein 1980: 65; Hally 2008: 222–70, 337–46; Harn 1980: 14–33; Milner 1998: 135–36; Peebles 1971: 71–72, 1983: 192; Perino 1971a: 14–57; 1971b: 164–66. One flint knapping tool kit was even buried with a man who had sufficient standing in his community to have an iron knife from the sixteenth century Juan Pardo expedition into the interior of North Carolina (Rodning et al. 2016: 309, 333).
65 Cobb 2000: 149–53, 186; Early 1993: 230–34; Milner 1998: 138–40; Muller 1997a: 301–53.
66 Milner 1998: 141–43.
67 Buikstra and Williams 1991: 162, 165, 168; Powell 1991: 176–79, 1998: 112; Schoeninger and Schurr 1998: 128–29.
68 Lawson 1966 [1709]: 223.
69 Jackson and Scott 1995: 194, 199; 2010: 326, 346–47; Rudolph 1984: 38, 41.
70 Brown et al. 1990: 268–70; Muller 1997a: 368–79; Perino 1971a: 101; ISM and NMNH collections.
71 Milner 1998: 164.
72 Milner 1998: 165.
73 Barker et al. 2002: 104–7.
74 Gentleman of Elvas in Smith 1968: 64; M.T. Smith 1987: 91–92, 102–3; 2000: 90.
75 Barrett 1933: 256–65; Black 1967: 120–228; Milner 1999: 120, 123–24.
76 Schroeder 2006: 121–28.
77 Dye and King 2007: 165–81; Garcilaso de la Vega in Varner and Varner 1951: 292–93, 438, 493.
78 Milner 1998: 158–60.
79 Milner 1998: 168, 175; Pauketat 1994: 171–72.
80 Marquardt 2001: 158, 166–68; Marquardt and Walker 2012: 29–31, 53–57; Thompson et al. 2018: 30–31; Widmer 1988: 260–76.
81 Brain 1988: 266–72; Hally 1993: 161; 2008: 535; Hally and Kelly 1998: 49; Harn 1994: 29–30; Meyers 2006: 161–67; Milner 1998: 64; D. F. Morse 1990: 78–83; P.A. Morse 1990: 123–24; Welch 1998: 134.
82 Fenton 1998: 21; Hally 2008: 537–58; Knight and Steponaitis 1998: 20; Milner 1998: 120–25; Muller 1997a: 206–21; Rountree and Turner 1998: 266.
83 Anderson 1994: 94–95; DePratter 1991: 29–34; Martin and Szuter 1999: 43–44.
84 Steadman 2001: 69–71.
85 Anderson 1994: 326–29; Blitz 1999: 588; Blitz and Lorenz 2006: 79–87; Butler 1991: 271–74; Cobb and Butler 2002: 628, 636–38; Hally and Chamblee 2019: 428–29; Hally and Rudolph 1986: 37–78; King 2003: 108–38; Mainfort 2001: 184–85; Milner 1998: 169–73; Milner and Chaplin 2010: 720–21; Smith 1986: 59; Smith 2001: 147; Williams 1980: 109.
86 Milner 1998: 157–59; Schroeder 2004: 818–20.
87 Du Pratz 1972 [1774]: 351–52.
88 Blitz 1999: 589; Brown 2007: 150–52; Milner 1998: 175–76.
89 Milner 1998: 62–63, 171, 173.
90 Emerson 2018: 497; Milner 1998: 121–25; Pauketat and Lopinot 1997: 119–20; White et al. 2018: 133.
91 Anderson 1994: 280–83; Anderson et al. 1995: 277.
92 Benson et al. 2009: 476; Bird et al. 2017: 5–9; Cobb and Butler 2002: 628, 636–38; Cook 2017: 109; Esarey and Santure 1990: 166; Mann et al. 2009: 1257–58; Milner 1998: 173; Pauketat 2004: 156–58; Pollack 2006: 310–11, 316–19; Schroeder 2004: 817; Smith 1986: 59.
93 Cobb and Butler 2002: 625–26; Milner and Chaplin 2010: 711, 716, 720; Monaghan and Peebles 2010: 950–51; Williams 1980: 109.
94 Mann et al. 2009: 1257.
95 Milner 1999: 125–26; Milner et al. 1991: 583–93; 2013: 98; Steadman 2008: 54–57; VanDerwarker and Wilson 2016: 87–97; Worne et al. 2012: 148–56.

CHAPTER 7
1 Gallivan 2003: 155–82; Potter 1993: 149–50; Rountree and Turner 1998: 273.
2 Cook 2008: 103–5, 108–9, 144–46; Milner and Schroeder 1992: 63.

3 Birmingham and Eisenberg 2000: 171–72; Brown 1967: 4, 9–14, 42; Cook 2017: 65; Drooker 1997: 87–88, 200, 279–80; Emerson 1999: 31–33; Griffin 1966: 102–4; Howey et al. 2016: 7444; Jeske 1927: 156–63; Kreisa 1993: 44–48; Krogman 1931: 415; Pollack and Henderson 2015: 300.
4 Santure 1990: 66–71; Santure and Esarey 1990: 106–10.
5 Brown and Dye 2007: 284; Dye 2004: 204; Knight 2010: 165; Lankford 2004: 212; Steponaitis and Knight 2004: 170–73.
6 Milner and Ferrell 2011: 420–21; Milner et al. 1989: 56–57; recent adult age estimate revisions.
7 Fenton 1998: 29.
8   Milner et al. 2018: 596, 609–12; Wilson 2014: 273.
9 Carver 1802: 169; Milner and Ferrell: 2011: 423.
10 Milner and Ferrell 2011: 420–29; Milner et al. 1991: 582–93; Santure 1990: 66–74.
11 Jefferson 1954 [1787]: 97–102. Another two centuries would pass before differential bone preservation and its effect on interpretations became an important part of archaeological work.
12 Dunham et al. 2003: 110–11, 119–22; Gallivan 2003: 35–40, 158; Gold 2000: 195–206; Hantman 1990: 683–84; 2001: 108.
13 Curry 1999: 10–67; Dodd et al. 1990: 353–56; Gallivan 2003: 30, 158; McManamon et al. 1986: 8–14; O'Shea 1988: 76–79; Ubelaker 1974: 8–40; 2013: 52; Ward and Davis 1999: 218; Williamson and Steiss 2003: 101–20; Williamson et al. 2003: 140–58.
14 Brose 2001: 57–58; Brown and Sasso 2001: 221–22, 224; Hinsdale 1924: 4–7, 10; Howey 2012: 78–83, 114–24; Howey et al. 2016: 7444–46; Howey and Clark 2018: 890–92; Kullen 1994: 4–14; Milner and O'Shea 1998: 185–88, 195–201; Neusius et al. 1998: 202–4, 229–30; Thomas 1894: 516–18; Zurell 1999: 244–48.
15 Brown and Sasso 2001: 217, 224; Buikstra 1992: 89–96; Emerson et al. 2005: 80–85, 92–93, 96–98; Fenton 1998: 22; Fritz 1990: 423–24; Gallagher and Sasso 1987: 141; Greenman 1957: 12, 14; Hart 1999: 63; Hart and Scarry 1999: 656; Karsten et al. 2019: 756–60; Katzenberg et al. 1995: 343–45; Little 2002: 114; Monaghan et al. 2014: 43–45; O'Gorman and Lovis 2006: 39–42; Sasso 2003; Smith 1989: 1570; Thomas 1894: 550; Warrick 2000: 437; 2008: 167, 171.
16 Winthrop 1963 [1678]: 1067.
17 Laliberte and Ripple 2003: 996–99; Martin and Szuter 1999: 38–40; Smith 2007 [1624]: 276–77, 286.
18 Rountree and Turner 1998: 275–77.
19 Winthrop 1963 [1678]: 1066.
20 Pollack and Henderson 2015: 300–11.
21 Birch and Williamson 2015: 19–20, 27–51; Dodd 1984: 204–14, 274; Fenton 1998: 23; Finlayson 1985: 125, 411, 414; Ramsden 1990: 378–79; Ritchie 1980: 305–10, 314–15; Snow 1994: 28–30, 40–46; Warrick 1984: 60, 2000: 434–54; 2008: 21–22.
22 Dodd 1984: 207; Fenton 1998: 25; Finlayson 1985: 411; Ramsden 1990: 374; Warrick 1984: 20, 42, 44; 2008: 185.
23 Alex 2000: 207–8; Birmingham and Eisenberg 2000: 167; Brown and Sasso 2001: 216; Hollinger 1995: 144–50; Markham 1991: 102, 110–11; McKusick 1973: 14–16; O'Gorman 2010: 580; Overstreet 1997: 283, 286; Rodell 2000: 390–91.
24 Brose 1994: 176; 2000: 103–7; 2001: 56–58; Cook 2008: 12, 14, 134; 2017: 65, 86–93, 169; Custer et al. 1995: 34; Drooker 1997: 122; Drooker and Cowan 2001: 91–95; Finlayson 1985: 44; Griffin 1978: 554–57; Hart 1993: 97–101; Jefferies 2018: 145–48; Means 2007: 106–44; Nass and Hart 2000: 134–40; Nass and Yerkes 1995: 66–68; Pollack and Henderson 2000a: 202–7; 2015: 300, 317; Sharp 1996: 167–69; Ward and Davis 1999: 106; Warrick 1984: 92.
25 Milner 1999: 119–20, 125.
26 Ritchie 1980: 307.
27 Fenton 1998: 23; Snow 1995: 1602.
28 Birch and Williamson 2015: 16, 19, 20, 78; Brose 1994: 176; 2001: 57; Cook 2017: 162; Curry 1999: 74–75; Custer et al. 1995: 28; Dodd et al. 1990: 357; Drooker 1997: 203; Drooker and Cowan 2001: 90; Gallivan 2003: 83; Means 2007: 109; Overstreet 1997: 283; Snow 1994: 38; 1995: 1603; Stewart 1995: 194; Ubelaker 1974: 66–69; Ward and Davis 1999: 106; Warrick 1984: 12; 2000: 447; 2008: 29, 169, 175, 186, 200.
29 Jones and Wood 2012: 2599–00.

30 Cook 2008: 50–51, 121; 2017: 181, 183.
31 Over a half-century ago, the genetic consequences of community fragmentation and formation in small kin-structured societies was referred to as a fission-fusion pattern (Neel and Salzano 1967: 556–58).
32 Bengtson and O'Gorman 2016: 26; Cook 2008: 103–5, 108–9; Drooker 1997: 328; Esarey and Conrad 1998: 44–46, 53; D. Jackson 1998: 98–99, 104.
33 Milner and Chaplin 2010: 720–21; Milner et al. 2013: 98–99.
34 Alex 2000: 168–69; Esarey and Santure 1990: 166; Milner 1999: 125–26; Milner et al. 1991: 593; O'Gorman and Lovis 2006: 38; Rodell 2000: 388; Snow 1994: 48–50; 2001: 20, 22; Warrick 1984: 65; 2000: 434–54; 2008: 103.
35 Ragueneau in Thwaites 1896–1901 vol. 35: 89–91.
36 Bird et al. 2017: 5–9; Brose 2000: 108; Cook 2017: 108–11; Milner 1999: 126; O'Gorman 2010: 579; Potter 1993: 126–38, 176–77; Rountree and Turner 1998: 279, 281; Stewart 1995: 195; Warrick 1984: 65.
37 Clark et al. 2007: 112.
38 Fenton 1998: 68–72, 130; Kuhn and Sempowski 2001: 303, 311–12; Ritchie 1980: 316–17; Snow 1994: 60, 231.

CHAPTER 8
1 Ewen and Hann 1998: 72–86.
2 Beck 2013: 73–74, 90–92; Beck et al. 2016a: 87–132, 2016b: 19–22, 2018: 580–92; Moore et al. 2017: 100, 106–112; Rodning et al. 2013: 234.
3 King 2003: 82.
4 Blanton and Thomas 2008: 803–5.
5 Stahle et al. 1998: 566.
6 Gentleman of Elvas in Smith 1968: 110; Garcilaso de la Vega in Varner and Varner 1951: 432–33.
7 Du Pratz 1972 [1774]: 333–39.
8 The Natchez Grand Village, or Fatherland site, was abandoned several years after the burial described by du Pratz. French forces during their 1730 campaign against the Natchez commandeered several buildings, apparently including the structure where the body was interred (Brown and Steponaitis 2017: 187–92, 199–200).
9 Birmingham and Eisenberg 2000: 172–73; Boudreaux 2007: 62; Hutchinson 1996: 55–56, 62; Hutchinson and Mitchem 1996: 48; Krogman 1931: 419; Langford 1930: 82–83; Latham 1855: 27, Plt. 19; Mitchem 1989: 103–9; P. A. Morse 1990: 130; M. T. Smith 1987: 91–92; Thomas 1894: 51–52, 376.
10 Beck 2013: 85–88; Beck et al. 2018: 579–81; Hally 2008: 222–23; Johnson et al. 2008: 21; Rodning 2010: 27–53; Rodning et al. 2013: 234–35, 2016: 313–39; M.T. Smith 1987: 23–53; 2000: 34–49.

11 Brown and Sasso 2001: 211; Drooker 1996: 147–74; 1997: 153–73, 283–94; Drooker and Cowan 2001: 99–102; Loewen and Delmas 2012: 221–40; Mazrim 2015: 21–27.
12 Drooker 1996: 150–52, 174; 1997: 162, 168, 171, 283; Drooker and Cowan 2001: 101; Howey 2018: 54–57; Petersen et al. 2004: 2, 41–44.
13 Drooker 1997: 82, 88; Kent 1984: 377–78; Latta 1987: 718–19, 721.
14 Johnson et al. 2008: 11–12, 19–23; Schurr 2010: 52–53; Voss and Blitz 1988: 133; Wagner 2001: 73–131; 2011: 117–218.
15 Gettys 1995: 22–34.
16 Essink and Oost 2019: 2, 5; Petersen et al. 1992: 679; soft-shell clam (Mya arenaria).
17 Blake 1981: 196; Gremillion 1993: 16–17; 2018: 113–15, 118–19; Kowalewski and Hatch 1991: 4–5; Newsom and Gahr 2011: 559–62, 565–66; Pavao-Zuckerman and Reitz 2011: 580, 582–84; Rodning 2010: 27, 46–51, 62; VanDerwarker et al. 2006: 26, 32, 35.
18 Lawson 1966 [1709]: 110 (italics in original). Heavy reliance on crops obscures their true origins, as also shown by watermelons that the early twentieth century Omaha on the Plains believed they had "grown from time immemorial" (Gilmore 1919: 120).
19 Leathlobhair et al. 2018: 84.
20 Beck 2013: 70–178; Larsen 2001: 27–28, 32–36; Larsen et al. 1992: 26–30; Rodning et al. 2013: 235–45.
21 Harriot 1972 [1590]: 28.
22 See Centerwall (1968: 78–79) for a measles epidemic among isolated villagers in tropical lowland South America that was eerily similar to historically recorded disease outbreaks.
23 Brain 1988: 272; Mainfort 2001: 188–89; Smith 2000: 34–49; 2001: 150; Williams and Brain 1983: 414–15.
24 Johnson 2000: 89–90; Johnson and Lehmann 1996: 48, 50–51.
25 Beck 2013: 127–28; Jones 2010: 400–2; Snow 1995: 1603; 1996: 164–65; Ward and Davis 1993: 413–18, 422–32; 2001: 140–41; Warrick 2008: 210, 222–23.
26 Fenton 1998: 247, 250; Marcoux 2010a: 96–107, 141; Muller 1997a: 194–96, 1997b: 355–59.
27 Dobyns 1983: 37–42, 291–95; Ubelaker 1988: 291.
28 Milner and Chaplin 2010: 711; Milner et al. 2001: 12.
29 Snow 1995: 1603, 1996: 164–65; Warrick 2008: 210, 222–23, 233.
30 Milner and Chaplin 2010: 720.
31 Thornton 1987: 114–18.
32 Thornton 2001: 137.

Further Reading

Anonymous, "An Indian Velocipede," Missouri Democrat, April 19, 1869a, p. 4.
— "The Big Mound," St. Louis Daily Times, April 16, 1869b, p. 4.
Abrams, E. M., "Archaeological Investigation of the Armitage Mound (33-At-434), The Plains, Ohio," Midcontinental Journal of Archaeology 17 (1992):79–111.
Abrams, E. M., and M. F. Le Rouge, "Political Complexity and Mound Construction Among the Early and Late Adena of the Hocking Valley, Ohio," in Transitions: Archaic and Early Woodland Research in the Ohio Country, eds. M. P. Otto and B. G. Redmond. Athens: Ohio University Press, 2008.
Adovasio, J. M., J. Donahue, and R. Stuckenrath, "The Meadowcroft Rockshelter Radiocarbon Chronology 1975–1990," American Antiquity 55 (1990):348–54.
Ahler, S., "Modoc Matting and Beads: Cultural Complexity in the Early Archaic Period," The Living Museum 53 (1991):3–6.
Albertson, D. G., and D. K. Charles, "Archaic Mortuary Component," in The Archaic and Woodland Cemeteries at the Elizabeth Site in the Lower Illinois Valley, eds. D. K. Charles, S. R. Leigh, and J. E. Buikstra. Kampsville, IL: Center for American Archeology, 1988.
Alex, L. M., Iowa's Archaeological Past. Iowa City: University of Iowa Press, 2000.

Alley, R. B., et al., "Abrupt Climate Change," Science 299 (2003):2005–10.
Alroy, J., "A Multispecies Overkill Simulation of the End-Pleistocene Megafaunal Mass Extinction," Science 292 (2001):1893–96.
Amick, D. S., "Evolving Views on the Pleistocene Colonization of North America," Quaternary International 431 (2015):125–51.
Anderson, D. G., "The Paleoindian Colonization of Eastern North America: A View from the Southeastern United States," in Early Paleoindian Economies of Eastern North America, eds. K. B. Tankersley and B. L. Isaac, Greenwich, CT: JAI Press, 1990.
— The Savannah River Chiefdoms: Political Change in the Late Prehistoric Southeast. Tuscaloosa: University of Alabama Press, 1994.
— "Models of Paleoindian and Early Archaic Settlement in the Lower Southeast," in The Paleoindian and Early Archaic Southeast, eds. D. G. Anderson and K. E. Sassaman. Tuscaloosa: University of Alabama Press, 1996.
Anderson, D. G., and J. E. Cornelison Jr., "A History of Investigations at Mound A, Shiloh: 1999-2004 and After," in Archeological Investigations at Shiloh Indian Mounds

National Historic Landmark (40HR7) 1999–2004, eds.
D. G. Anderson, J. E. Cornelison Jr., and S. C. Sherwood.
Tallahassee, FL: Southeast Archeological Center, National
Park Service, 2013.

Anderson, D. G., and J. C. Gillam, "Paleoindian Colonization
of the Americas: Implications from an Examination of
Physiography, Demography, and Artifact Distribution,"
American Antiquity 65 (2000):43–66.

Anderson, D. G., D. W. Stahle, and M. K. Cleaveland,
"Paleoclimate and the Potential Food Reserves of
Mississippian Societies: A Case Study from the Savannah
River Valley," *American Antiquity* 60 (1995):258–86.

Anderson, D. G., et al., "Multiple Lines of Evidence for Possible
Human Population Decline/Settlement Reorganization
During the Early Younger Dryas," *Quaternary International*
242 (2011):570–83.

Anderson, D. G., et al., "Mound Stages, Structures, and
Features," in *Archeological Investigations at Shiloh Indian
Mounds National Historic Landmark (40HR7) 1999–2004*,
eds. D. G. Anderson, J. E. Cornelison Jr., and S. C. Sherwood.
Tallahassee, FL: Southeast Archeological Center, National
Park Service, 2013.

Ashley, K. H., "Swift Creek Traits in Northeastern Florida," in
A World Engraved: Archaeology of the Swift Creek Culture,
eds. M. Williams and D. T. Elliott. Tuscaloosa: University of
Alabama Press, 1998.

Atwell, K., "Analysis of Burial Program," in *The Kuhlman
Mound Group and Late Woodland Mortuary Behavior
in the Mississippi River Valley of West-Central Illinois*,
eds. K. A. Atwell and M. D. Conner. Kampsville, IL: Center for
American Archaeology, 1991.

Auerbach, B. M., "Skeletal Variation Among Early Holocene
North American Humans: Implications for Origins and
Diversity in the Americas," *American Journal of Physical
Anthropology* 149 (2012):525–36.

Baby, R. S., and S. M. Langlois, "Seip Mound State Memorial:
Nonmortuary Aspects of Hopewell," in *Hopewell
Archaeology*, eds. D. S. Brose and N. B. Greber. Kent, OH:
Kent State University Press, 1979.

Baker, R. G., et al., "Patterns of Holocene Environmental
Change in the Midwestern United States," *Quaternary
Research* 37 (1992):379–89.

Barker, A. W., et al., "Mesoamerican Origin for an Obsidian
Scraper from the Precolumbian Southeastern United States,"
American Antiquity 67 (2002):103–8.

Barrett, S. A., *Ancient Aztalan*. Milwaukee, WI: Milwaukee
Public Museum, 1933.

Beck, R. A., *Chiefdoms, Collapse, and Coalescence in the Early
American South*. Cambridge: Cambridge University Press, 2013.

Beck, R. A., et al., "The Built Environment of the Berry Site
Spanish Compound," in *Fort San Juan and the Limits of
Empire*, eds. R. A. Beck, C. B. Rodning, and D. G. Moore.
Gainesville: University Press of Florida, 2016a.

— "The Politics of Provisioning: Food and Gender at
Fort San Juan de Joara, 1566-1568," *American Antiquity*
81 (2016b):3–26.

— "A Road to Zacatecas: Fort San Juan and the Defenses of
Spanish La Florida," *American Antiquity* 83 (2018):577–97.

Bell, R. E., *The Harlan Site, Ck-6, A Prehistoric Mound Centers
in Cherokee County, Eastern Oklahoma*. Oklahoma
Anthropological Society, 1972.

Belovich, S. J., and D. S. Brose, "Late Woodland Fortifications
in Northern Ohio: The Greenwood Village Site," *Kirtlandia*
47 (1992):3–23.

Bengtson, J. D., and J. A. O'Gorman, "Children, Migration and
Mortuary Representation in the Late Prehistoric Central
Illinois River Valley," *Childhood in the Past* 9 (2016):19–43.

Bense, J. A., *Archaeology of the Southeastern United States*.
San Diego, CA: Academic Press, 1994.

— "Santa Rosa-Swift Creek in Northwestern Florida," in
A World Engraved: Archaeology of the Swift Creek Culture,
eds. M. Williams and D. T. Elliott, Tuscaloosa: University
of Alabama Press, 1998.

Benson, L. V., T. R. Pauketat, and E. R. Cook, "Cahokia's Boom
and Bust in the Context of Climate Change," *American
Antiquity* 74 (2009):467–83.

Bentley, G. R., T. Goldberg, and G. Jasienska, "The Fertility of
Agricultural and Non-Agricultural Traditional Societies,"
Population Studies 47 (1993):269–81.

Beverley, R., *The History and Present State of Virginia*, ed.
L. B. Wright. Chapel Hill: University of North Carolina Press,
1947 [1705].

Birch, J., and R. F. Williamson, *The Mantle Site*. Lanham, MD:
Rowman and Littlefield, 2015.

Bird, B. W., et al., "Midcontinental Native American Population
Dynamics and Late Holocene Hydroclimate Extremes,"
Scientific Reports 7 (2017):41628. doi: 10.1038/srep41628.

Birmingham, R. A., and L. E. Eisenberg, *Indian Mounds of
Wisconsin*. Madison: University of Wisconsin Press, 2000.

Black, B. A., and M. D. Abrams, "Influences of Native Americans
and Surveyor Biases on Metes and Bounds Witness-Tree
Distribution," *Ecology* 82 (2001):2574–86.

Black, G. A., *Angel Site: An Archaeological, Historical, and
Ethnological Study*. 2 vols. Indianapolis: Indiana Historical
Society, 1967.

Blake, L. W., "Early Acceptance of Watermelon by Indians of
the United States," *Journal of Ethnobotany* 1 (1981):193–99.

Blanton, D. B., "Accounting for Submerged Mid-Holocene
Archaeological Sites in the Southeast: A Case Study from the
Chesapeake Bay Estuary, Virginia," in *Archaeology of the Mid-
Holocene Southeast*, eds. K. E. Sassaman and D. G. Anderson.
Gainesville: University Press of Florida, 1996.

Blanton, D. B. and D. H. Thomas, "Paleoclimates and Human
Responses Along the Central Georgia Coast: A Tree-Ring
Perspective," in *Native American Landscapes of St. Catherines
Island, Georgia*, ed. D. H. Thomas. New York: American
Museum of Natural History, 2008.

Blitz, J. H., "Adoption of the Bow in Prehistoric North America,"
North American Archaeologist 9 (1988):123–45.

— *Ancient Chiefdoms of the Tombigbee*. Tuscaloosa:
University of Alabama Press, 1993.

— "Mississippian Chiefdoms and the Fission-Fusion
Process," *American Antiquity* 64 (1999):577–92.

Blitz, J. H., and K. G. Lorenz, *The Chattahoochee Chiefdoms*.
Tuscaloosa: University of Alabama Press, 2006.

Boudreaux, E. A. III, *The Archaeology of Town Creek*.
Tuscaloosa: University of Alabama Press, 2007.

— "Early Mississippian in the North Carolina Piedmont," in
Mississippian Beginnings, ed. G. D. Wilson, Gainesville:
University of Florida Press, 2017.

Boulanger M. T. and R. L. Lyman, "Northeastern North
American Pleistocene Megafauna Chronologically
Overlapped Minimally with Paleoindians," *Quaternary
Science Reviews* 85 (2014):35–46.

Brackenridge, H. R., "Cantine Mounds, and the Monastery of
La Trappe," *Louisiana Gazette*, January 9, 1811, p. 3.

— "On the Population and Tumuli of the Aborigines
of North America," *Transactions of the American
Philosophical Society* 1 (1818):151–59.

Brain, J. P., *Tunica Archaeology*. Cambridge, MA: Peabody
Museum, Harvard University, 1988.

Brashler, J. G., et al., "Adaptive Strategies and Socioeconomic
Systems in Northern Great Lakes Riverine Environments:
The Late Woodland of Michigan," in *Late Woodland
Societies: Tradition and Transformation Across the
Midcontinent*, eds. T. E Emerson, D. L. McElrath, and
A. C. Fortier. Lincoln: University of Nebraska Press, 2000.

Braun, D. P., J. B. Griffin, and P. F. Titterington, *The Snyders
Mounds and Five Other Mound Groups in Calhoun County,
Illinois*. Ann Arbor: Museum of Anthropology, University
of Michigan, 1982.

Brennan, T. K., "Main Street Mound and the Mississippian
Landscape," in *Revealing Greater Cahokia, North America's
First Native City*, eds. T. E. Emerson, B. H. Koldehoff, and
T. K. Brennan. Urbana: Illinois State Archaeological Survey,
University of Illinois, 2018.

Brennan, T. K., et al., "Community Organization of the
East St. Louis Precinct," in *Revealing Greater Cahokia,
North America's First Native City*, eds. T. E. Emerson,
B. H. Koldehoff, and T. K. Brennan. Urbana: Illinois State
Archaeological Survey, University of Illinois, 2018.

Bridges, P. S., J. H. Blitz, and M. C. Solano, "Changes in Long
Bone Diaphyseal Strength with Horticultural Intensification
in West-Central Illinois," *American Journal of Physical
Anthropology* 112 (2000):217–38.

Brose, D. S., "The Woodland Period," in *Ancient Art of the
American Woodland Indians*, by D. S. Brose, J. A. Brown, and
D. W. Penney. New York: Harry N. Abrams, 1985.

— *The South Park Village Site and the Late Prehistoric
Whittlesey Tradition of Northeast Ohio*. Madison, WI:
Prehistory Press, 1994.

— "Late Prehistoric Societies of Northeastern Ohio and
Adjacent Portions of the South Shore of Lake Erie:
A Review," in *Cultures Before Contact: The Late Prehistory*

of Ohio and Surrounding Regions, ed. R. A. Genheimer. Columbus: Ohio Archaeological Council, 2000.
— "Penumbral Protohistory on Lake Erie's South Shore," in *Societies in Eclipse*, eds. D. S. Brose, C. W. Cowan, and R. C. Mainfort Jr. Washington, DC: Smithsonian Institution Press, 2001.

Broster, J. B., and M. R. Norton, "Recent Paleoindian Research in Tennessee," in *The Paleoindian and Early Archaic Southeast*, eds. D. G. Anderson and K. E. Sassaman. Tuscaloosa: University of Alabama Press, 1996.

Brown, I. W., "A Study of Stone Box Graves in Eastern North America," *Tennessee Anthropologist* 6 (1981):1–16.
— "Plaquemine Culture in the Natchez Bluffs Region of Mississippi," in *Plaquemine Archaeology*, eds. M. A. Rees and P. C. Livingood. Tuscaloosa: University of Alabama Press, 2007.

Brown, I. W., and V. P. Steponaitis, "The Grand Village of the Natchez Indians was Indeed Grand," in *Forging Southeastern Identities: Social Archaeology, Ethnohistory, and Folklore of the Mississippian to Early Historic South*, eds. G. A. Waselkov, and M. T. Smith. Tuscaloosa: University of Alabama Press, 2017.

Brown, J. A., *The Gentleman Farm Site*. Springfield: Illinois State Museum, 1967.
— "Spiro Art and its Mortuary Contexts," in *Death and the Afterlife in Pre-Columbian America,* ed. E. P. Benson. Washington, DC: Dumbarton Oaks Research Library and Collections, 1975.
— "Charnel Houses and Mortuary Crypts: Disposal of the Dead in the Middle Woodland Period," in *Hopewell Archaeology*, eds. D. S. Brose and N. B. Greber. Kent, OH: Kent State University Press, 1979.
— "The Search for Rank in Prehistoric Burials," in *The Archaeology of Death*, eds. R. Chapman, I. Kinnes, and K. Randsborg. Cambridge: Cambridge University Press, 1981.
— "Long-Term Trends to Sedentism and the Emergence of Complexity in the American Midwest," in *Prehistoric Hunter-Gatherers: The Emergence of Cultural Complexity*, eds. T.D. Price and J. A. Brown. Orlando: Academic Press, 1985a.
— "The Mississippian Period," in *Ancient Art of the American Woodland Indians*, by D.S. Brose, J. A. Brown, and D. W. Penney. New York: Harry N. Abrams, 1985b.
— *The Spiro Ceremonial Center*, 2 vols. Ann Arbor: Museum of Anthropology, University of Michigan, 1996.
— "The Archaeology of Ancient Religion in the Eastern Woodlands," *Annual Review of Anthropology* 26 (1997):465–85.
— *Mound City: The Archaeology of a Renown Ohio Hopewell Mound Center*. Lincoln, NE: Midwest Archeological Center, 2006.
— "Cosmological Layouts of Secondary Burials as Political Instruments," in *Mississippian Mortuary Practices: Beyond Hierarchy and the Representationist Perspective*, eds. L. P. Sullivan and R. C. Mainfort Jr. Gainesville: University Press of Florida, 2010.

Brown, J. A., and D. H. Dye, "Severed Heads and Sacred Scalplocks: Mississippian Iconographic Trophies," in *The Taking and Displaying of Human Body Parts as Trophies by Amerindians*, eds. R. J. Chacon and D. H. Dye. Springer: New York, 2007.

Brown, J. A., and R. F. Sasso, "Prelude to History on the Eastern Prairies," in *Societies in Eclipse*, eds. D. S. Brose, C. W. Cowan, and R. C. Mainfort Jr. Washington, DC: Smithsonian Institution Press, 2001.

Brown, J. A., and R. K. Vierra, "What Happened in the Middle Archaic? Introduction to an Ecological Approach to Koster Site Archaeology," in *Archaic Hunters and Gatherers in the American Midwest*, eds. J. L. Phillips and J. A. Brown. New York: Academic Press, 1983.

Brown, J. A., R. A. Kerber, and H. D. Winters, "Trade and the Evolution of Exchange Relations at the Beginning of the Mississippian Period," in *The Mississippian Emergence*, ed. B. D. Smith. Washington, DC: Smithsonian Institution Press, 1990.

Buikstra, J. E., *Hopewell in the Lower Illinois Valley*. Evanston, IL: Archeological Program, Northwestern University, 1976.
— "Mortuary Practices, Palaeodemography and Palaeopathology: A Case Study from the Koster Site (Illinois)," in *The Archaeology of Death*, eds. R. Chapman, I. Kinnes, and K. Randsborg, Cambridge: Cambridge University Press, 1981.

— "Diet and Disease in Late Prehistory," in *Disease and Demography in the Americas*, eds. J. W. Verano and D. H. Ubelaker. Washington, DC: Smithsonian Institution Press, 1992.

Buikstra, J. E., and L. G. Goldstein, *The Perrins Ledge Crematory*. Springfield: Illinois State Museum, 1973.

Buikstra, J. E., and S. Williams, "Tuberculosis in the Americas: Current Perspectives," in *Human Paleopathology: Current Syntheses and Future Options*, eds. D. J. Ortner and A. C. Aufderheide, Washington, DC: Smithsonian Institution Press, 1991.

Bullington, J., "Middle Woodland Mound Structure: Social Implications and Regional Context," in *The Archaic and Woodland Cemeteries at the Elizabeth Site in the Lower Illinois Valley*, eds. D. K. Charles, S. R. Leigh, and J. E. Buikstra. Kampsville, IL: Center for American Archeology, 1988.

Burks, J., and R. A. Cook, "Beyond Squier and Davis: Rediscovering Ohio's Earthworks Using Geophysical Remote Sensing," *American Antiquity* 76 (2011):667–89.

Butler, B. M., "Hopewellian Contacts in Southern Middle Tennessee," in *Hopewell Archaeology*, eds. D. S. Brose and N. B. Greber. Kent, OH: Kent State University Press, 1979.
— "Kincaid Revisited: The Mississippian Sequence in the Lower Ohio Valley," in *Cahokia and the Hinterlands: Middle Mississippian Cultures of the Midwest*, eds. T. E. Emerson and R. B. Lewis. Urbana: University of Illinois Press, 1991.

Butler, B. M., and M. J. Wagner, "Land Between the Rivers: The Late Woodland Period of Southernmost Illinois," in *Late Woodland Societies: Tradition and Transformation Across the Midcontinent*, eds. T. E. Emerson, D. L. McElrath, and A. C. Fortier. Lincoln: University of Nebraska Press, 2000.

Campbell, K. L., and J. W. Wood, "Fertility in Traditional Societies," in *Natural Human Fertility: Social and Biological Determinants*, eds. P. Diggory, M. Potts, and S. Teper. London: Macmillan, 1988.

Cannon, M. D., and D. J. Meltzer, "Explaining Variability in Early Paleoindian Foraging," *Quarternary International* 191 (2009):5–17.

Carr, C., "Rethinking Interregional Hopewellian 'Interaction,'" in *Gathering Hopewell: Society, Ritual, and Ritual Interaction*, eds. C. Carr and D. T. Case. New York: Kluwer Academic, 2005.
— "Settlements and communities," in *The Scioto Hopewell and Their Neighbors*, eds. D. T. Case and C. Carr. New York: Springer, 2008.

Carr, K. W., and J. M. Adovasio, "Shades of Gray Redux: The Paleoindian/Early Archaic 'Transition' in the Northeast," in *From the Pleistocene to the Holocene: Human Organization and Cultural Transformations in Prehistoric North America*, eds. C. B. Bousman and B. J. Vierra. College Station: Texas A&M University Press, 2012.

Carver, J., *Three Years Travels Throughout the Interior Parts of North America*. Boston: West and Greenleaf, 1802.

Centerwall, W. R., "A Recent Experience with Measles in a 'Virgin-Soil' Population," in *Biomedical Challenges Presented by the American Indian*. Washington, DC: Pan American Health Organization, 1968.

Chapman, C. H., *The Archaeology of Missouri, II*. Columbia: University of Missouri Press, 1980.

Chapman, J., and J. M. Adovasio, "Textile and Basketry Impressions from Icehouse Bottom, Tennessee," *American Antiquity* 42 (1977):620–25.

Chapman, J., and G. D. Crites, "Evidence for Early Maize (*Zea mays*) from the Icehouse Bottom Site, Tennessee," *American Antiquity* 52 (1987):352–54.

Charles, D. K., "Diachronic Regional Social Dynamics: Mortuary Sites in the Illinois Valley/American Bottom Region," in *Regional Approaches to Mortuary Analysis*, ed. L. A. Beck. New York: Plenum, 1996.

Charles, D. K., and J. E. Buikstra, "Archaic Mortuary Sites in the Central Mississippi Drainage: Distribution, Structure, and Behavioral Implications," in *Archaic Hunters and Gatherers in the American Midwest*, eds. J. L. Phillips and J. A. Brown. New York: Academic Press, 1983.

Charles, D. K., S. R. Leigh, and D. G. Albertson, "Late Woodland and Unassignable Components," in *The Archaic and Woodland Cemeteries at the Elizabeth Site in the Lower Illinois Valley*, eds. D. K. Charles, S. R. Leigh, and J. E. Buikstra. Kampsville, IL: Center for American Archeology, 1988.

Clark, P. U., *et al.*, "The Last Glacial Maximum," *Science* 325 (2009):710–14.

Clark, W. E., K. Mountford, and E. Haile, "John Smith's Second Voyage Up the Chesapeake Bay: July 24 – September 7, 1608," in *John Smith's Chesapeake Voyages 1607–1609*, eds. H. C. Rountree, W. C. Clark, and K. Mountford. Charlottesville: University of Virginia Press, 2007.

Clausen, C. J., *et al.*, "Little Salt Spring, Florida: A Unique Underwater Site," *Science* 203 (1979):609–14.

Clay R. B., "Pottery and Graveside Ritual in Kentucky Adena," *Midcontinental Journal of Archaeology* 8 (1983):109–26.
— "Peter Village 164 Years Later: 1983 Excavations," in *Woodland Period Research in Kentucky*, eds. D. Pollack, T. Sanders, and C. Hockensmith. Frankfort: Kentucky Heritage Council, 1985.
— "Circles and Ovals: Two Types of Adena Space," *Southeastern Archaeology* 6 (1987):46–56.

Cobb, C. R., *From Quarry to Cornfield*. Tuscaloosa: University of Alabama Press, 2000.

Cobb, C. R., and B. M. Butler, "The Vacant Quarter Revisited: Late Mississippian Abandonment of the Lower Ohio Valley," *American Antiquity* 67 (2002):625–41.

Cobb, C. R., and M. Pope, "Sixteenth-Century Flintknapping Kits from the King Site, Georgia," *Journal of Field Archaeology* 25 (1998):1–17.

Cole, F-C., and T. Deuel, *Rediscovering Illinois*. Chicago: University of Chicago Press, 1937.

Conner, M. D., "Summary and Conclusions," in *The Kuhlman Mound Group and Late Woodland Mortuary Behavior in the Mississippi River Valley of West-Central Illinois*, eds. K. A. Atwell and M. D. Conner. Kampsville, IL: Center for American Archaeology, 1991.

Connolly, R. P., "Architectural Grammar Rules at the Fort Ancient Hilltop Enclosure," in *Ancient Earthen Enclosures of the Eastern Woodlands*, eds. R. C. Mainfort Jr. and L. P. Sullivan. Gainesville: University Press of Florida, 1998.

Conrad, L. A., "The Middle Mississippian Cultures of the Central Illinois Valley," in *Cahokia and the Hinterlands*, eds. T. E. Emerson and R. B. Lewis. Urbana: University of Illinois Press, 1991.

Cook, R. A., *Sunwatch: Fort Ancient Development in the Mississippian World*. Tuscaloosa: University of Alabama Press, 2008.
— *Continuity and Change in the Native American Village: Multicultural Origins and Descendants of the Fort Ancient Culture*. Cambridge: Cambridge University Press, 2017.

Cook, T. G., *Koster: An Artifact Analysis of Two Archaic Phases in Westcentral Illinois*. Evanston, IL: Archeological Program, Northwestern University, 1976.

Coughlin, S., and M. F. Seeman, "Hopewell Settlements at the Liberty Earthworks, Ross County, Ohio," in *Ohio Hopewell Community Organization*, eds. W. S. Dancey and P. J. Pacheco. Kent, OH: Kent State University Press, 1997.

Cowan, F. L., "A Mobile Hopewell? Questioning Assumptions of Ohio Hopewell Sedentism," in *Recreating Hopewell*, eds. D. K. Charles and J. E. Buikstra. Gainesville: University Press of Florida, 2006.

Crawford, G. W., D. G. Smith, and V. E. Bowyer, "Dating the Entry of Corn (*Zea mays*) into the Lower Great Lakes Region," *American Antiquity* 62 (1997):112–19.

Crites, G. D., "Domesticated Sunflower in Fifth Millennium B. P. Temporal Context: New Evidence from Middle Tennessee," *American Antiquity* 58 (1993):146–48.

Crothers, G. M., "The Green River in Comparison to the Lower Mississippi Valley During the Archaic: To Build Mounds or Not to Build Mounds?," in *Signs of Power: The Rise of Cultural Complexity in the Southeast*, eds. J. L. Gibson and P. J. Carr. Tuscaloosa: University of Alabama Press, 2004.

Curran, M. L., "Exploration, Colonization, and Settling In: The Bull Brook Phase, Antecedents, and Descendants," in *The Archaeological Northeast*, eds. M. A. Levine, K. E. Sassaman, and M. S. Nassaney. Westport, CT: Bergin and Garvey, 1999.

Curry, D. C., *Feast of the Dead: Aboriginal Ossuaries in Maryland*. Crownsville: Maryland Historical Trust Press, 1999.

Custer, J. F., *et al.*, "Data Recovery Excavations at the Slackwater Site (36LA207), Lancaster County, Pennsylvania," *Pennsylvania Archaeologist* 65 (1995):19–112.

Dahl-Jensen, D., *et al.*, "Past Temperatures Directly from the Greenland Ice Sheet," *Science* 282 (1998):268–71.

Daniel, I. R. Jr., *Hardaway Revisited*. Tuscaloosa: University of Alabama Press, 1998.

Davis, L. G., *et al.*, "Late upper Paleolithic occupation at Cooper's Ferry, Idaho, USA, ~16,000 years ago," *Science* 365 (2019):861–97.

Décima, E. B., and D. F. Dincauze, "The Boston Back Bay Fish Weirs," in *Hidden Dimensions: The Cultural Significance of Wetland Archaeology*, ed. K. Bernick. Vancouver: University of British Columbia Press, 1998.

DeJarnette, D. L., and S. B. Wimberly, *The Bessemer Site*. University: Geological Survey of Alabama, 1941.

Delcourt, P. A., and H. R. Delcourt, *Prehistoric Native Americans and Ecological Change*. Cambridge: University of Cambridge Press, 2004.

Delcourt, P. A., H. R. Delcourt, and R. T. Saucier, "Late Quaternary Vegetation Dynamics in the Central Mississippi Valley," in *Arkansas Archaeology*, eds. R. C. Mainfort Jr. and M. D. Jeter. Fayetteville: University of Arkansas Press, 1999.

DePratter, C. B., *Late Prehistoric and Early Historic Chiefdoms in the Southeastern United States*. New York: Garland, 1991.

DePratter, C. B., and J. D. Howard, "Evidence for a Sea Level Lowstand Between 4500 and 2400 Years B. P. on the Southeast Coast of the United States," *Journal of Sedimentary Petrology* 51 (1981):1287–95.

DePratter, C. B., and V. D. Thompson, "Past Shorelines of the Georgia Coast," in *Life Among the Tides: Recent Archaeology on the Georgia Bight*, eds. V. D. Thompson and D. H. Thomas. New York: American Museum of Natural History, 2013.

Dillehay, T. D., *Monte Verde: A Late Pleistocene Settlement in Chile*, vol. 2. Washington, DC: Smithsonian Institution Press, 1997.

Dillehay, T. D., and M. Pino, "Radiocarbon Chronology," In *Monte Verde: A Late Pleistocene Settlement in Chile*, vol. 2, ed. T. D. Dillehay. Washington, DC: Smithsonian Institution Press, 1997.

Dillehay, T. D., *et al.*, "Simple technologies and diverse food strategies of the late Pleistocene and early Holocene at Huaca Prieta, coastal Peru," *Science Advances* 3 (2017):e1602778.

Dincauze, D. F., "Pioneering in the Pleistocene: Large Paleoindian Sites in the Northeast," in *Archaeology of Eastern North America: Papers in Honor of Stephen Williams*, ed. J. B. Stoltman. Jackson: Mississippi Department of Archives and History, 1993.

Dobyns, H. F., *Their Number Become Thinned*. Knoxville: University of Tennessee Press, 1983.

Dodd, C. F., *Ontario Iroquois Tradition Longhouses*. Ottawa: National Museum of Man, 1984.

Dodd, C. F., *et al.*, "The Middle Ontario Iroquoian Stage," in *The Archaeology of Southern Ontario to AD 1650*, eds. C. J. Ellis and N. Ferris. London, ON: Ontario Archaeological Society, 1990.

Dragoo, D. W., and C. F. Wray, "Hopewell Figurine Rediscovered," *American Antiquity* 30 (1964):195–99.

Driskell, B. N., "Stratified Late Pleistocene and Early Holocene Deposits at Dust Cave, Northwestern Alabama," in *The Paleoindian and Early Archaic Southeast*, eds. D. G. Anderson and K. E. Sassaman. Tuscaloosa: University of Alabama Press, 1996.

Drooker, P. B., "Madisonville Metal and Glass Artifacts: Implications for Western Fort Ancient Chronology and Interaction Networks," *Midcontinental Journal of Archaeology* 21 (1996):145–90.
— *The View from Madisonville*. Ann Arbor: Museum of Anthropology, University of Michigan, 1997.
— "The Fabric of Power: Textiles in Mississippian Politics and Ritual," in *Forging Southeastern Identities: Social Archaeology, Ethnohistory, and Folklore of the Mississippian to Early Historic South*, eds. G. A. Waselkov and M. T. Smith. Tuscaloosa: University of Alabama Press, 2017.

Drooker, P. B., and C. W. Cowan, "Transformation of the Fort Ancient Cultures of the Central Ohio Valley," in *Societies in Eclipse*, eds. D. S. Brose, C. W. Cowan, and R. C. Mainfort Jr. Washington, DC: Smithsonian Institution Press, 2001.

Dunbar, J. S., "Paleoindian Archaeology," in *First Floridians and Last Mastodons: The Page-Ladson Site in the Aucilla River*, ed. S. D. Webb. Dordrecht: Springer, 2006.

Dunbar, J. S., and S. D. Webb, "Bone and Ivory Tools from Submerged Paleoindian Sites in Florida," in *The Paleoindian and Early Archaic Southeast*, eds. D. G. Anderson and K. E. Sassaman. Tuscaloosa: University of Alabama Press, 1996.

Dunford, F. J., "Paleoenvironmental Context for the Middle Archaic Occupation of Cape Cod, Massachusetts," in *The Archaeological Northeast*, eds. M. A. Levine, K. E. Sassaman, and M. S. Nassaney. Westport, CT: Bergin and Garvey, 1999.

Dunham, G. H., D. L. Gold, and J. L. Hantman, "Collective Burial in Late Prehistoric Virginia: Excavation an Analysis of the Rapidan Mound," *American Antiquity* 68 (2003):109–28.

Du Pratz, A. S. L. P., *The History of Louisiana*. Baton Rouge, LA: Claitor's Publishing, 1972 [1774].

Dye, D. H., "Riverine Adaptation in the Midsouth," in *Of Caves and Shell Mounds*, eds. K. C. Carstens and P. J. Watson. Tuscaloosa: University of Alabama Press, 1996.
— "Art, Ritual, and Chiefly Warfare in the Mississippian World," in *Hero, Hawk, and Open Hand*, eds. R. F. Townsend and R. V. Sharp. Chicago: Art Institute of Chicago, 2004.

Dye, D. H., and A. King, "Desecrating the Sacred Ancestor Temples: Chiefly Conflict and Violence in the American Southeast," in *North American Indigenous Warfare and Ritual Violence*, eds. R. J. Chacon and R. G. Mendoza. Tucson: University of Arizona Press, 2007.

Early, A. M., "Hardman and Caddoan Saltmaking," in *Caddoan Saltmakers in the Ouachita Valley*, ed. A. M. Early. Fayetteville: Arkansas Archeological Survey, 1993.
— "The Caddos of the Trans-Mississippi South," in *Indians of the Greater Southeast*, ed. B. G. McEwan. Gainesville: University Press of Florida, 2000.

Ellis, C., "Measuring Paleoindian Range Mobility and Land-Use in the Great Lakes/Northeast," *Journal of Anthropological Archaeology* 30 (2011):385–401.

Emerson, T. E., "Cahokian Elite Ideology and the Mississippian Cosmos," in *Cahokia: Domination and Ideology in the Mississippian World*, eds. T. R. Pauketat and T. E. Emerson. Lincoln: University of Nebraska Press, 1997.
— "The Langford Tradition and the Process of Tribalization on the Middle Mississippian Borders," *Midcontinental Journal of Archaeology* 24 (1999):3–56.
— "Greater Cahokia – Chiefdom, State, or City?" in *Revealing Greater Cahokia, North America's First Native City*, eds. T. E. Emerson, B. H. Koldehoff, and T. K. Brennan. Urbana: Illinois State Archaeological Survey, University of Illinois, 2018.

Emerson, T. E., and D. L. McElrath, "A Settlement-Subsistence Model of the Terminal Late Archaic Adaptation in the American Bottom, Illinois," in *Archaic Hunters and Gatherers in the American Midwest*, eds. J. L. Phillips and J. A. Brown. New York: Academic Press, 1983.

Emerson, T. E., K. M. Hedman, and M. L. Simon, "Marginal Horticulturalists or Maize Agriculturalists? Archaeobotanical, Paleopathological, and Isotopic Evidence Relating to Langford Tradition Maize Consumption," *Midcontinental Journal of Archaeology* 30 (2005):67–118.

Emerson, T. E., *et al.*, "The Allure of the Exotic: Reexamining the Use of Local and Distant Pipestone Quarries in Ohio Hopewell Pipe Caches," *American Antiquity* 78 (2013):48–67.

Emerson, T. E., *et al.*, "Paradigms Lost: Reconfiguring Cahokia's Mound 72 Beaded Burial," *American Antiquity* 81 (2016):405–25.

Esarey, D., "Red Ochre Mound Building and Marion Phase Associations: A Fulton County, Illinois Perspective," in *Early Woodland Archeology*, eds. K. B. Farnsworth and T. E. Emerson. Kampsville, IL: Center for American Archeology, 1986.
— "The Late Woodland Maples Mills and Mossville Phase Sequence in the Central Illinois River Valley," in *Late Woodland Societies: Tradition and Transformation Across the Midcontinent*, eds. T. E. Emerson, D. L. McElrath, and A. C. Fortier. Lincoln: University of Nebraska Press, 2000.

Esarey, D., and L. A. Conrad, "The Bold Counselor Phase of the Central Illinois River Valley: Oneota's Middle Mississippian Margin," *The Wisconsin Archeologist* 79 (1998):38–61.

Esarey, D., and S. K. Santure, "The Morton Site Oneota Component and the Bold Counselor Phase," in *Archaeological Investigations at the Morton Village and Norris Farms 36 Cemetery*, eds. S. K. Santure, A. D., Harn, and D. Esarey. Springfield: Illinois State Museum, 1990.

Essenpreis, P. S., and M. E. Moseley, "Fort Ancient: Citadel or Coliseum?," *Field Museum of Natural History Bulletin* 55 (1984):5–10, 20–26.

Essink, K., and A. P. Oost, "How did *Mya arenaria* (Mollusca; Bivalvia) Repopulate European Waters in Mediaeval Times?," *Marine Biodiversity* 49 (2019):1–10.

Ewen, C. R., and J. H. Hann, *Hernando De Soto Among the Apalachee*. Gainesville, University Press of Florida, 1998.

Fairbridge, R. W., "Holocene Marine Coastal Evolution of the United States," in *Quaternary Coasts of the United States: Marine and Lacustrine Systems*, eds. C. H. Fletcher III and J. F. Wehmiller. Tulsa, OK: Society of Sedimentary Geology, 1992.

Farnsworth, K. B., T. J. Martin, and A. R. Perri, *Modified Predator Mandible and Maxilla Artifacts and Predator Symbolism in Illinois Hopewell*. Urbana: Illinois State Archaeological Survey, University of Illinois, 2015.

Faulkner, C. H., "The Old Stone Fort Revisited: New Clues to an Old Mystery," in *Mounds, Embankments, and Ceremonialism in the Midsouth*, eds. R. C. Mainfort and R. Walling. Fayetteville: Arkansas Archeological Survey, 1996.

Fenton, J. P., and R. W. Jefferies, "The Camargo Mound and Earthworks: Preliminary Findings," in *The Human Landscape in Kentucky's Past: Site Structure and Settlement Patterns*, eds. C. Stout and C. K. Hensley. Frankfort: Kentucky Heritage Council, 1991.

Fenton, W. N., *The Great Law and the Longhouse*. Norman: University of Oklahoma Press, 1998.

Finlayson, W. D., *The 1975 and 1978 Rescue Excavations at the Draper Site: Introduction and Settlement Patterns*. Ottawa: National Museum of Man, 1985.

Fletcher, R. V., *et al.*, "Serpent Mound: A Fort Ancient Icon?," *Midcontinental Journal of Archaeology* 21 (1996):105–43.

Ford, J. A., *Hopewell Culture Burial Mounds Near Helena, Arkansas*. New York: American Museum of Natural History, 1963.

Ford, J. A., and G. R. Willey, *Crooks Site, A Marksville Period Burial Mound in La Salle Parish, Louisiana*. New Orleans: Louisiana Geological Survey, 1940.

Fortier, A. C., "Settlement and Subsistence at the Go-Kart North Site: A Late Archaic Titterington Occupation in the American Bottom, Illinois," in *Archaic Hunters and Gatherers in the American Midwest*, eds. J. L. Phillips and J. A. Brown. New York: Academic Press, 1983.
— "Community Plan and Feature Assemblage," in *The Holding Site: A Hopewell Community in the American Bottom*. Urbana: University of Illinois Press, 1989.

Fortier, A. C., and F. A. Finney, "Features," in *The Archaeology of the East St. Louis Mound Center, Part II: The Northside Excavations*. ed. A. C. Fortier. Urbana: Illinois Transportation Archaeological Research Program, University of Illinois, 2007.

Foster, J. W., *Pre-Historic Races of the United States of America*. Chicago: S. C. Griggs, 1873.

Foster, H. T. II, B. Black, and M. D. Abrams, "A Witness Tree Analysis of the Effects of Native American Indians on the Pre-European Settlement Forests in East-Central Alabama," *Human Ecology* 32 (2004):27–47.

Fowke, G., "Some Popular Errors in Regard to Mound Builders and Indians," *Ohio Archaeological and Historical Publications* 2 (1898):380–403.
— *Archaeological History of Ohio*. Columbus: Ohio State Archaeological and Historical Society, 1902.
— "Archeological Investigations II," in *44th Annual Report*. Washington, DC: Bureau of American Ethnology, Smithsonian Institution, 1928.

Fowler, M. L., *Summary Report of Modoc Rock Shelter 1952, 1953, 1955, 1956*. Springfield: Illinois State Museum, 1959.
— *The Cahokia Atlas: A Historical Atlas of Cahokia Archaeology*, rev. ed. Urbana: Illinois Transportation Archaeological Research Program, University of Illinois, 1997.

Fowler, M. L., *et al.*, *The Mound 72 Area: Dedicated and Sacred Space in Early Cahokia*. Springfield: Illinois State Museum, 1999.

Freeman, A. K. L., E. E. Smith Jr., and K. B. Tankersley, "A Stone's Throw from Kimmswick: Clovis Period Research in Kentucky," in *The Paleoindian and Early Archaic Southeast*, eds. D. G. Anderson and K. E. Sassaman. Tuscaloosa: University of Alabama Press, 1996.

Fritz, G. J., "Multiple Pathways to Farming in Precontact Eastern North America," *Journal of World Prehistory* 4 (1990):387–435.
— "New Dates and Data on Early Agriculture: The Legacy of Complex Hunter-Gatherers," *Annals of the Missouri Botanical Garden* 82 (1995):3–15.
— "Native Farming Systems and Ecosystems in the Mississippi River Valley," in *Imperfect Balance: Landscape Transformations in the Precolumbian Americas*, ed. D. L. Lentz. New York: Columbia University Press, 2000.

— *Feeding Cahokia: Early Agriculture in the North American Heartland.* Tuscaloosa: University of Alabama Press, 2019.

Futato, E. M., "A Synopsis of Paleoindian and Early Archaic Research in Alabama," in *The Paleoindian and Early Archaic Southeast*, eds. D. G. Anderson and K. E. Sassaman. Tuscaloosa: University of Alabama Press, 1996.

Gallagher, J. P., and R. F. Sasso, "Investigations into Oneota Ridged Field Agriculture on the Northern Margin of the Prairie Peninsula," *Plains Anthropologist* 32 (1987):141–51.

Gallivan, M. D., *James River Chiefdoms: The Rise of Social Inequality in the Chesapeake.* Lincoln: University of Nebraska Press, 2003.

Garland, E. B., and S. G. Beld, "The Early Woodland: Ceramics, Domesticated Plants, and Burial Mounds Foretell the Shape of the Future," in *Retrieving Michigan's Buried Past*, ed. J. R. Halsey. Bloomfield Hills, MI: Cranbrook Institute of Science, 1999.

Genheimer, R. A., "Stubbs Cluster: Hopewellian Site Dynamics at a Forgotten Little Miami River Valley Settlement," in *Ohio Hopewell Community Organization*, eds. W. S. Dancey and P. J. Pacheco. Kent, OH: Kent State University Press, 1997.

Gettys, M., "Historical Archaeology in Oklahoma," *Oklahoma Anthropological Society Bulletin* 44 (1995):1–84.

Gibson, J., "Poverty Point and Greater Southeastern Prehistory: The Culture That Did Not Fit," in *Archaeology of the Mid-Holocene Southeast*, eds. K. E. Sassaman and D. G. Anderson. Gainesville: University Press of Florida, 1996.
— *The Ancient Mounds of Poverty Point: Place of Rings.* Gainesville: University Press of Florida, 2000.

Gilmore, M. R., "Uses of Plants by the Indians of the Missouri River Region," in *33rd Annual Report*. Washington DC: Bureau of American Ethnology, Smithsonian Institution, 1919.

Goebel, T., M. R. Waters, and D. H. O'Rourke, "The Late Pleistocene Dispersal of Modern Humans in the Americas," *Science* 319 (2008):1497–1502.

Gold, D. L., "'Utmost Confusion' Reconsidered: Bioarchaeology and Secondary Burial in Late Prehistoric Interior Virginia," in *Biological Studies of Life in the Age of Agriculture: A View from the Southeast*, ed. P. M. Lambert. Tuscaloosa: University of Alabama Press, 2000.

Goldstein, L. G., *Mississippian Mortuary Practices: A Case Study of Two Cemeteries in the Lower Illinois Valley.* Evanston, IL: Archeological Program, Northwestern University, 1980.
— "Landscapes and Mortuary Practices: A Case for Regional Perspectives," in *Regional Approaches to Mortuary Analysis*, ed. L. A. Beck. New York: Plenum, 1995.
— "An Analysis of Plummets in the Lower Illinois River Valley," in *Aboriginal Ritual and Economy in the Eastern Woodlands*, eds. A. M. Cantwell, L. A. Conrad, and J. E. Reyman. Springfield: Illinois State Museum, 2004.

Gonzales, L. M., and E. C. Grimm, "Synchronization of Late-Glacial Vegetation Changes at Crystal Lake, Illinois, USA with the North Atlantic Event Stratigraphy," *Quaternary Research* 72 (2009):234–245.

Goodyear, A. C., "The Early Holocene Occupation of the Southeastern United States: A Geoarchaeological Summary," in *Ice Age People of North America: Environments, Origins, and Adaptations*, eds. R. Bonnichsen and K. L. Turnmire. Corvallis: Oregon State University Press, 1999.

Graham, R. W., "Plant-Animal Interactions and Pleistocene Extinctions," In *Dynamics of Extinction*, ed. D. K. Elliott. New York: John Wiley, 1986.

Graham, R. W., and E. L. Lundelius Jr., "Coevolutionary Disequilibrium and Pleistocene Extinctions," in *Quaternary Extinctions: A Prehistoric Revolution*, eds. P. S. Martin and R. G. Klein. Tucson: University of Arizona Press, 1984.

Graham, R. W., et al., "Kimmswick: A Clovis-Mastodon Association in Eastern Missouri," *Science* 213 (1981): 1115–17.

Graham, R. W., et al., "Spatial Response of Mammals to Late Quaternary Environmental Fluctuations," *Science* 272 (1996):1601–06.

Grayson, D. K., and D. J. Meltzer, "Revisiting Paleoindian Exploitation of Extinct North American Mammals," *Journal of Archaeological Science* 56 (2015):177–93.

Greber, N. B., "A Comparative Study of Site Morphology and Burial Patterns at Edwin Harness Mound and Seip Mounds 1 and 2," in *Hopewell Archaeology*, eds. D. S. Brose and N. B. Greber. Kent, OH: Kent State University Press, 1979.
— *Recent Excavations at the Edwin Harness Mound.* Kent, OH: Kent State University Press, 1983.

— "Two Geometric Enclosures in the Paint Creek Valley: An Estimate of Possible Changes in Community Patterns Through Time," in *Ohio Hopewell Community Organization*, eds. W. S. Dancey and P. J. Pacheco. Kent, OH: Kent State University Press, 1997.
— "Wooden structures and cultural symbolism in Ohio Hopewell," in *Building the Past: Prehistoric Wooden Post Architecture in the Ohio Valley – Great Lakes*, eds. B. G. Redmond and R. A. Genheimer. Gainesville: University Press of Florida, 2015.

Greber, N. B., and K. C. Ruhl, *The Hopewell Site: A Contemporary Analysis Based on the Work of Charles C. Willoughby.* Boulder , CO: Westview Press, 1989.

Greber N. B., and O. C. Shane III., "Field Studies of the Octagon and Great Circle, High Bank Earthworks, Ross County, Ohio," in *In the Footprints of Squier and Davis: Archeological Fieldwork in Ross County, Ohio*, ed. M. J. Lynott. Lincoln, NE: Midwest Archeological Center, National Park Service, 2009.

Green, W., "A Prehistoric Frontier in the Prairie Peninsula: Late Woodland Upland Settlement and Subsistence Patterns," *Illinois Archaeology* 5 (1993):201–14.

Greenman, E. F., "The Garden Beds Around Lake Michigan," *The Michigan Archaeologist* 3 (1957):12–27.

Gremillion, K. J., "Adoption of Old World Crops and Processes of Cultural Change in the Historic Southeast," *Southeastern Archaeology* 12 (1993):15–20.
— *Food Production in Native North America: An Archaeological Perspective.* Washington, DC: SAA Press, 2018.

Griffin, J. B., "The Spruce Run Earthworks: A Forgotten Adena Site in Delaware County, Ohio," *Ohio State Archaeological and Historical Society Quarterly* 56 (1947):188–200.
— *The Fort Ancient Aspect.* Ann Arbor: Museum of Anthropology, University of Michigan, 1966.
— "Eastern North American Archaeology: A Summary," *Science* 156 (1967):175–91.
— "Late Prehistory of the Ohio Valley," in *Handbook of North American Indians: Northeast*, vol. 15, ed. B. G. Trigger. Washington, DC: Smithsonian Institution Press, 1978.

Griffin, J. B., R. E. Flanders, and P. F. Titterington, *The Burial Complexes of the Knight and Norton Mounds in Illinois and Michigan.* Ann Arbor: Museum of Anthropology, University of Michigan, 1970.

Guccione, M. J., R. H. Lafferty III, and L. S. Cummings, "Environmental Constraints of Human Settlement in an Evolving Holocene Alluvial System, the Lower Mississippi Valley," *Geoarchaeology* 3 (1988):65–84.

Guthrie, R. D., "Origin and Causes of the Mammoth Steppe: A Story of Cloud Cover, Woolly Mammoth Tooth Pits, Buckles, and Inside-Out Beringia," *Quaternary Science Reviews* 20 (2001):549–74.

Hally, D. J., "The Territorial Size of Mississippian Chiefdoms," in *Archaeology of Eastern North America: Papers in Honor of Stephen Williams*, ed. J. B. Stoltman. Jackson: Mississippi Department of Archives and History, 1993.
— "Mississippian Shell Gorgets in Regional Perspective," in *Southeastern Ceremonial Complex: Chronology, Content, Context*, ed. A. King. Tuscaloosa: University of Alabama Press, 2007.
— *King: The Social Archaeology of a Late Mississippian Town in Northwestern Georgia.* Tuscaloosa: University of Alabama Press, 2008.

Hally, D. J., and J. F. Chamblee, "The Temporal Distribution and Duration of Mississippian Polities in Alabama, Georgia, Mississippi, and Tennessee," *American Antiquity* 83 (2019):420–37.

Hally, D. J., and H. Kelly, "The Nature of Mississippian Towns in Georgia: The King Site Example," in *Mississippian Towns and Sacred Spaces*, eds. R. B. Lewis and C. Stout. Tuscaloosa: University of Alabama Press, 1998.

Hally, D. J., and J. L. Rudolph, *Mississippi Period Archaeology of the Georgia Piedmont.* Athens: University of Georgia, 1986.

Halsey, J. R., "Late Woodland Burial Practices," in *Retrieving Michigan's Buried Past*, ed. J. R. Halsey. Bloomfield Hills, MI: Cranbrook Institute of Science, 1999.

Hammerstedt, S. W., "Mississippian Status in Western Kentucky: Evidence from the Annis Mound," *Southeastern Archaeology* 24 (2005):11–27.
— "New Deal Archaeology in West-Central Kentucky: Excavations at Annis Village," in *Shovel Ready: Archaeology and Roosevelt's New Deal for America*, ed. B. K. Means. Tuscaloosa: University of Alabama Press, 2013.

Hammerstedt, S. W., and E. R. Hughes, "Mill Creek Chert Hoes and Prairie Soils: Implications for Cahokian Production and Expansion," *Midcontinental Journal of Archaeology* 40 (2015):149–65.

Hammerstedt, S. W., *et al.*, "Multisensor Remote Sensing at Spiro: Discovering Intrasite Organization," in *Archaeological Remote Sensing in North America*, eds. D. P. McKinnon and B. S. Haley. Tuscaloosa: University of Alabama Press, 2017.

Hantman, J. L., "Between Powhatan and Quirank: Reconstructing Monacan Culture and History in the Context of Jamestown," *American Anthropologist* 92 (1990):676–90.

— "Monacan Archaeology of the Virginia Interior, AD 1400–1700," in *Societies in Eclipse*, eds. D. S. Brose, C. W. Cowan, and R. C. Mainfort Jr. Washington, DC: Smithsonian Institution Press, 2001.

Harn, A. D., *The Prehistory of Dickson Mounds: The Dickson Excavation*. Springfield: Illinois State Museum, 1980.

— *Variation in Mississippian Settlement Patterns: The Larson Settlement System in the Central Illinois River Valley*. Springfield: Illinois State Museum, 1994.

Harriot, T., *A Briefe and True Report of the New Found Land of Virginia*. New York: Dover, 1972 [1590].

Hart, J. P., "Monongahela Subsistence-Settlement Change: The Late Prehistoric Period in the Lower Upper Ohio River Valley," *Journal of World Prehistory* 7 (1993):71–120.

— "Dating Roundtop's Domesticates: Implications for Northeast Late Prehistory," in *Current Northeast Paleoethnobotany*, ed. J. P. Hart. Albany: New York State Museum, 1999.

Hart, J. P., and C. M. Scarry, "The Age of Common Beans (*Phaseolus vulgaris*) in the Northeastern United States," *American Antiquity* 64 (1999):653–58.

Hart, J. P., and N. A. Sidell, "Additional Evidence for Early Cucurbit Use in the Northern Eastern Woodlands East of the Allegheny Front," *American Antiquity* 62 (1997):523–37.

Higgins, M. J., *The Nochta Site: The Early, Middle, and Late Archaic Occupations* (11-Ms-128). Urbana: University of Illinois Press, 1990.

Hill, M. A., "Tracing Social Interaction: Perspectives on Archaic Copper Exchange from the Upper Great Lakes," *American Antiquity* 77 (2012):279–92.

Hill, M. A., *et al.*, "Elemental Analysis of Late Archaic Copper from the McQueen Shell Ring, St. Catherine's Island, Georgia," *Journal of Archaeological Science: Reports* 24 (2019):1083–94.

Hinsdale, W. B., "The Missaukee Preserve and Rifle River Forts," *Papers of the Michigan Academy of Science, Arts, and Letters* 4 (1924):1–14.

Hoffman, C. F., *A Winter in the West by a New Yorker*. 2nd edn. New York: Harper and Brothers, 1835.

Holliday, V. T., and D. J. Meltzer, "The 12.9-ka ET Impact Hypothesis and North American Paleoindians," *Current Anthropology* 51 (2010):575–607.

Hollinger, R. E., "Residence Patterns and Oneota Cultural Dynamics," in *Oneota Archaeology: Past, Present, and Future*, ed. W. Green. Iowa City: Office of the State Archaeologist, 1995.

House, J., "Powell Canal: Baytown Period Adaptation on Bayou Macon, Southeast Arkansas," in *The Mississippian Emergence*, ed. B. D. Smith. Washington, DC: Smithsonian Institution Press, 1990.

Howey, M. C. L., *Mound Builders and Monument Makers of the Northern Great Lakes, 1200–1600*. Norman: University of Oklahoma Press, 2012.

— "Dead Kettles and Indigenous Afterworlds in Early Colonial Encounters in the Maritimes," in *Relational Identities and Other-Than-Human Agency in Archaeology*, eds. E. Harrison-Buck and J. A. Hendon. Louisville: University Press of Colorado, 2018.

Howey, M. C. L., and M. Clark, "Analyzing landform patterns in the monumental landscape of the northern Great Lakes, 1200–1600 CE," *Journal of Archaeological Science: Reports* 19 (2018):886-893.

Howey, M. C. L., M. W. Palace, and C. H. McMichael, "Geospatial Modeling Approach to Monument Construction Using Michigan from A.D. 1000–1600 as a Case Study," *Proceedings of the National Academy of Sciences* 113 (2016):7443–48.

Hudson, C., *The Southeastern Indians*. Knoxville: University of Tennessee Press, 1976.

Hutchinson, D. L., "Brief Encounters: Tatham Mound and the Evidence for Spanish and Native American Confrontation," *International Journal of Osteoarchaeology* 6 (1996):51–65.

— *Bioarchaeology of the Florida Gulf Coast*. Gainesville: University Press of Florida, 2004.

Hutchinson, D. L. and J. M. Mitchem, "The Weeki Wachee Mound, An Early Contact Period Mortuary Locality in Hernando County, West-Central Florida," *Southeastern Archaeology* 15 (1996):47–65.

Hutchinson, D. L., *et al.*, "Agricultural Melodies and Alternative Harmonies in Florida and Georgia," in *Biological Studies of Life in the Age of Agriculture: A View from the Southeast*, ed. P. M. Lambert. Tuscaloosa: University of Alabama Press, 2000.

Hutchinson, D. L., *et al.*, "The Calusa and Prehistoric Subsistence in Central and South Gulf Coast Florida," *Journal of Anthropological Archaeology* 41 (2016):55–73.

Jackson, D. K., "Settlement on the Southern Frontier: Oneota Occupations in the American Bottom," *The Wisconsin Archeologist* 79 (1998):93–116.

Jackson, H. E., "Little Spanish Fort: An Early Middle Woodland Enclosure in the Lower Yazoo Basin, Mississippi," *Midcontinental Journal of Archaeology* 23 (1998):199–220.

Jackson, H. E., and S. L. Scott, "Mississippian Homestead and Village Subsistence Organization: Contrasts in Large-Mammal Remains from Two Sites in the Tombigbee Valley," in *Mississippian Communities and Households*, eds. J. D. Rogers and B. D. Smith. Tuscaloosa: University of Alabama Press, 1995.

— "Archaic Faunal Utilization in the Louisiana Bottomlands," *Southeastern Archaeology* 20 (2001):187–96.

— "Zooarchaeology of the Moundville Elite," in *Mound Excavations at Moundville*, ed. V. J. Knight Jr. Tuscaloosa: University of Alabama Press, 2010.

Jackson, S. T., *et al.*, "Vegetation and Environment in Eastern North America During the Last Glacial Maximum," *Quaternary Science Reviews* 19 (2000):489–508.

Jacobson, G. L. Jr., T. Webb III, and E. C. Grimm, "Patterns and Rates of Vegetation Change During the Deglaciation of Eastern North America," in *North America and Adjacent Oceans During the Last Deglaciation*, ed. W. F. Ruddiman. Boulder, CO: Geological Society of America, 1987.

Jantz, R. L., and M. K. Spradley, "Cranial Morphometric Evidence for Early Holocene Relationships and Population Structure," in *Kennewick Man: The Scientific Investigation of an Ancient American Skeleton*, eds. D. W. Ousley and R. L. Jantz. College Station: Texas A&M University Press, 2014.

Jefferies, R. W., *The Tunacunnhee Site: Evidence of Hopewell Interaction in Northwest Georgia*. Athens: Department of Anthropology, University of Georgia, 1976.

— "Middle Archaic – Late Archaic Transition in Southern Illinois: An Example from the Carrier Mills Archaeological District," *American Archeology* 3 (1983):199–206.

— "The Swift Creek Site and Woodland Platform Mounds in the Southeastern United States," in *Ocmulgee Archaeology 1936–1986*, ed. D. J. Hally. Athens: University of Georgia Press, 1994.

— "Preliminary Assessment of Mississippian Settlement at the Croley-Evans Site (15KX24), Knox County, Kentucky," in *Current Archaeological Research in Kentucky*, vol. 3, eds. J. F. Doershuk, C. A. Bergman, and D. Pollack. Frankfort: Kentucky Heritage Council, 1995a.

— "The Status of Archaic Period Research in the Midwestern United States," *Archaeology of Eastern North America* 23 (1995b):119–44.

— "Hunters and Gatherers after the Ice Age," in *Kentucky Archaeology*, ed. R.B. Lewis. Lexington: University of Kentucky Press, 1996a.

— "The Emergence of Long-Distance Exchange Networks in the Southeastern United States," in *Archaeology of the Mid-Holocene Southeast*, eds. K. E. Sassaman and D. G. Anderson. Gainesville: University Press of Florida, 1996b.

— "Middle Archaic Bone Pins: Evidence of Mid-Holocene Regional-Scale Social Groups in the Southern Midwest," *American Antiquity* 62 (1997):464–87.

— "Regional-Scale Interaction Networks and the Emergence of Cultural Complexity Along the Northern Margins of the Southeast," in *Signs of Power: The Rise of Cultural Complexity in the Southeast*, eds. J. L. Gibson and P. J. Carr. Tuscaloosa: University of Alabama Press, 2004.

— *Holocene Hunter-Gatherers of the Lower Ohio River Valley*. Tuscaloosa: University of Alabama Press, 2008.

— "Population Aggregation and the Emergence of Circular Villages in Southwest Virginia," in *The Archeology of*

Villages in Eastern North America, eds. J. Birch and V. D. Thompson. Gainesville: University of Florida Press, 2018.

Jefferies, R. W., and B. M. Lynch, "Dimensions of Middle Archaic Cultural Adaptation at the Black Earth Site, Saline County, Illinois," in *Archaic Hunters and Gatherers in the American Midwest*, eds. J. L. Phillips and J. A. Brown. New York: Academic Press, 1983.

Jefferies, R. W., G. R. Milner, and E. R. Henry, "Winchester Farm: A Small Adena Enclosure in Central Kentucky," in *Early and Middle Woodland Landscapes of the Southeast*, eds. A. P. Wright and E. R. Henry. Gainesville: University Press of Florida, 2013.

Jefferson, T., *Notes on the State of Virginia*. New York: W. W. Norton, 1954 [1787].

Jeske, J. A., *The Grand River Mound Group and Camp Site*. Milwaukee, WI: Milwaukee Public Museum, 1927.

Johannessen, S., "Paleoethnobotany," in *American Bottom Archaeology*, eds. C. J. Bareis and J. W. Porter. Urbana: University of Illinois Press, 1984.
— "Farmers of the Late Woodland," in *Foraging and Farming in the Eastern Woodlands*, ed. C. M. Scarry. Gainesville: University Press of Florida, 1993.

Johnson, J. K., "The Chickasaws," in *Indians of the Greater Southeast*, ed. B. G. McEwan. Gainesville: University Press of Florida, 2000.

Johnson, J. K., and S. O. Brookes, "Benton Points, Turkey Tails, and Cache Blades: Middle Archaic Exchange in the Midsouth," *Southeastern Archaeology* 8 (1989):134–45.

Johnson, J. K., and G. R. Lehmann, "Sociopolitical Devolution in Northeast Mississippi and the Timing of the De Soto Entrada," in *Bioarchaeology of Native American Adaptation in the Spanish Borderlands*, eds. B. J. Baker and L. Kealhofer. Gainesville: University Press of Florida, 1996.

Johnson, J. K., *et al.*, "Measuring Chickasaw Adaptation on the Western Frontier of the Colonial South: A Correlation of Documentary and Archaeological Data," *Southeastern Archaeology* 27 (2008):1–30.

Johnston, C. A., "Aging and sexing human remains from the Hopewell site," in *The Scioto Hopewell and Their Neighbors*, eds. D. T. Case and C. Carr. New York: Springer, 2008.

Jones, D., and C. Kuttruff, "Prehistoric Enclosures in Louisiana and the Marksville Site," in *Ancient Earthen Enclosures of the Eastern Woodlands*, eds. R. C. Mainfort Jr. and L. P. Sullivan. Gainesville, University Press of Florida, 1998.

Jones, E. E., "Population History of the Onondaga and Oneida Iroquois, A.D. 1500–1700," *American Antiquity* 75 (2010):387–407.

Jones, E. E., and J. W. Wood, "Using Event-History Analysis to Examine the Causes of Semi-Sedentism Among Shifting Cultivators: A Case Study of the Haudenosaunee, AD 1500–1700," *Journal of Archaeological Science* 39 (2012):2593–603.

Kane, L. M., J. D. Holmquist, and C. Gilman (eds.), *The Northern Expeditions of Stephen H. Long*. St. Paul: Minnesota Historical Society Press, 1978.

Karsten, J. K., *et al.*, "Assessing Subsistence and Its Relationship to Cultural Complexity in the Late Prehistoric Upper Midwest: A New Perspective Provide by Dental Health," *American Journal of Physical Anthropology* 168 (2019):750–63.

Katzenberg, M. A., *et al.*, "Stable Isotope Evidence for Maize Horticulture and Paleodiet in Southern Ontario, Canada," *American Antiquity* 60 (1995):335–50.

Kay, M., "The Ozark Highland Paleoarchaic," in *From the Pleistocene to the Holocene: Human Organization and Cultural Transformations in Prehistoric North America*, eds. C. B. Bousman and B. J. Vierra. College Station: Texas A&M University Press, 2012.

Kellar, J. H., "The Mann Site and "Hopewell" in the Lower Wabash-Ohio Valley," in *Hopewell Archaeology*, eds. D. S. Brose and N. Greber. Kent, OH: Kent State University Press, 1979.

Kelly, J. E., "Range Site Community Patterns and the Mississippian Emergence," in *The Mississippian Emergence*, ed. B. D. Smith. Washington, DC: Smithsonian Institution Press, 1990a.
— "The Emergence of Mississippian Culture in the American Bottom Region," in *The Mississippian Emergence*, ed. B. D.Smith. Washington, DC: Smithsonian Institution Press, 1990b.

Kelly, J. E., and J. A. Brown, "Cahokia: The Processes and Principals of the Creation of an Early Mississippian City," in *Making Ancient Cities: Space and Place in Early Urban Societies*, eds. A. T. Creekmore III and K. D. Fisher. Cambridge: Cambridge University Press, 2014.

Kelly, J. E., S. J. Ozuk, and J. A. Williams, *The Range Site 2: The Emergent Mississippian Dohack and Range Phase Occupations*. Urbana: University of Illinois Press, 1990.

Kelly, L. S., "Patrick Phase Faunal Remains," in *The Range Site: Archaic Through Late Woodland Occupations*. Urbana: University of Illinois Press, 1987.

Kent, B. C., *Susquehanna's Indians*. Harrisburg: Pennsylvania Historical and Museum Commission, 1984.

Kidder, T. R., "Coles Creek Period Social Organization and Evolution in Northeast Louisiana," in *Lords of the Southeast: Social Inequality and the Native Elites of Southeastern North America*, eds. A. W. Barker and T. R. Pauketat. American Anthropological Association, 1992.
— "Mississippi Period Mound Groups and Communities in the Lower Mississippi Valley," in *Mississippian Towns and Sacred Spaces*, eds. R. B. Lewis and C. Stout. Tuscaloosa: University of Alabama Press, 1998.
— "Mapping Poverty Point," *American Antiquity* 67 (2002):89–101.

Kidder, T. R., and K. M. Ervin, "Hunter-Gatherer Surplus Accumulation and Monumental Construction at Poverty Point, Mississippi," in *Surplus Without the State – Political Forms in Prehistory*, eds. H. H. Meller, D. Gronenborn, and R. Risch. Halle: Landesmuseums für Vorgeschichte, 2018.

Kimball, L. R., "Early Archaic Settlement and Technology: Lessons from Tellico," in *The Paleoindian and Early Archaic Southeast*, eds. D. G. Anderson and K. E. Sassaman. Tuscaloosa: University of Alabama Press, 1996.

King, A., *Etowah: The Political History of a Chiefdom Capital*. Tuscaloosa: University of Alabama Press, 2003.

Kistler, L., *et al.*, "Transoceanic Drift and the Domestication of African Bottle Gourds in the Americas," *Proceedings of the National Academy of Sciences* 111 (2014):2937–41.

Klepinger, L., and D. R. Henning, "The Hatten Mound: A Two-Component Burial Site in Northeast Missouri," *The Missouri Archaeologist* 37 (1976):92–170.

Knight, V. J. Jr., *Excavation of the Truncated Mound at the Walling Site: Middle Woodland Culture and Copena in the Tennessee Valley*. Tuscaloosa: Alabama State Museum of Natural History, 1990.
— "Moundville as a Diagrammatic Ceremonial Center," in *Archaeology of the Moundville Chiefdom*, eds. V. J. Knight Jr. and V. P. Steponaitis. Washington, DC: Smithsonian Institution Press, 1998.
— "Farewell to the Southeastern Ceremonial Complex," *Southeastern Archaeology* 25 (2006):1–5.
— *Mound Excavations at Moundville*. Tuscaloosa: University of Alabama Press, 2010.
— "Social Archaeology of Monumental Spaces at Moundville," in *Rethinking Moundville and Its Hinterland*, eds. V. P. Steponaitis and C. M. Scarry. Gainesville: University Press of Florida, 2016.

Knight, V. J. Jr., and V. P. Steponaitis, "A New History of Moundville," in *Archaeology of the Moundville Chiefdom*, eds. V. J. Knight Jr. and V. P. Steponaitis. Tuscaloosa: University of Alabama Press, 1998.

Knight, V. J. Jr., J. A. Brown, and G. E. Lankford, "On the Subject Matter of Southeastern Ceremonial Complex Art," *Southeastern Archaeology* 20 (2001):129–41.

Konisberg, L. W., "Demography and Mortuary Practice at Seip Mound One," *Midcontinental Journal of Archaeology* 10 (1985):123–48.

Kowalewski, S. A., and J. W. Hatch, "The Sixteenth-Century Expansion of Settlement in the Upper Oconee Watershed, Georgia," *Southeastern Archaeology* 10 (1991):1–17.

Krause, R. A., "The Death of the Sacred: Lessons from a Mississippian Mound in the Tennessee River Valley," *Journal of Alabama Archaeology* 36 (1990):63–98.
— "Federal Archaeology in the Southeast," in *Dam Projects and the Growth of American Archaeology*, eds. K. M. Banks and J. S. Czaplicki. Walnut Creek, CA: Left Coast Press, 2014.

Krech, S., *The Ecological Indian: Myth and History*. New York: W. W. Norton, 1999.

Kreisa, P. P., "Oneota Burial Patterns in Eastern Wisconsin," *Midcontinental Journal of Archaeology* 18 (1993):35–60.

Krogman, W. M., "The Archaeology of the Chicago Area," *Transactions of the Illinois State Academy of Science* 23 (1931):413–20.

Kuhn, R. D. and M. L. Sempowski, "A New Approach to Dating the League of the Iroquois," *American Antiquity* 66 (2001):301–14.

Kullen, D., "The Comstock Trace: A Huber Phase Earthwork and Habitation Site Near Joliet, Will County, Illinois," *Midcontinental Journal of Archaeology* 19 (1994):3–38.

Lacquement, C. H., "The Energetics of Earthen Landscape Modification: An Assessment of an Emerging Mississippian Polity," in *Architectural Energetics in Archaeology: Analytical Expansions and Global Explorations*, eds. L. McCurdy and E. M. Abrams. Abingdon, Oxon: Routledge, 2019.

Laliberte, A. S., and W. J. Ripple, "Wildlife Encounters by Lewis and Clark: A Spatial Analysis of Interactions Between Native Americans and Wildlife," *BioScience* 53 (2003):994–1003.

Langford, G., "The Fisher Mound and Village Site," *Transactions of the Illinois State Academy of Science* 24 (1930):79–92.

Lankford, G. E., "World on a String," in *Hero, Hawk, and Open Hand*, eds. R. F. Townsend and R. V. Sharp. Chicago: Art Institute of Chicago, 2004.

Larsen, C. S., *The Anthropology of St. Catherines Island 3. Prehistoric Human Biological Adaptation*. New York: American Museum of Natural History, 1982.
— "Bioarchaeology of Spanish Florida," in *Bioarchaeology of Spanish Florida: The Impact of Colonialism*, ed. C. S. Larsen. Gainesville: University Press of Florida, 2001.
— *Bioarchaeology: Interpreting Behavior from the Human Skeleton*, 2nd edn. Cambridge: Cambridge University Press, 2015.

Larsen, C. S., R. Shavit, and M. C. Griffin, "Dental Caries Evidence for Dietary Change: An Archaeological Context," in *Advances in Dental Anthropology*, eds. M. A. Kelley and C. S. Larsen. New York: Wiley-Liss, 1991.

Larsen, C. S., *et al.*, "Population Decline and Extinction in La Florida," in *Disease and Demography in the Americas*, eds. J. W. Verano and D. H. Ubelaker. Washington, DC: Smithsonian Institution Press, 1992.

Larson, L. H. Jr., "Archaeological Implications of Social Stratification at the Etowah Site, Georgia', *American Antiquity Memoir* 25 (1971):58–67.

Latham, I. A., *The Antiquities of Wisconsin*. Washington, DC: Smithsonian Institution, 1855.

Latta, M. A., "Iroquoian Stemware," *American Antiquity* 52 (1987):717–24.

La Vere, D., *Looting Spiro Mounds*. Norman: University of Oklahoma Press, 2007.

Lawson, J., *A New Voyage to Carolina*. New York: Readex Microprint, 1966 [1709].

Leathlobhair, M. N., *et al.*, "The Evolutionary History of Dogs in the Americas," *Science* 361 (2018):81–85.

Leigh, S. R., "Comparative Analysis of the Elizabeth Middle Woodland Artifact Assemblage," in *The Archaic and Woodland Cemeteries at the Elizabeth Site in the Lower Illinois Valley*, eds. D. K. Charles, S. R. Leigh, and J. E. Buikstra. Kampsville, IL: Center for American Archeology, 1988.

Leigh, S. R., D. K. Charles, and D. G. Albertson, "Middle Woodland Component," in *The Archaic and Woodland Cemeteries at the Elizabeth Site in the Lower Illinois Valley*, eds. D. K. Charles, S. R. Leigh, and J. E Buikstra. Kampsville, IL: Center for American Archeology, 1988.

Leonard, J. A., *et al.*, "Ancient DNA Evidence for Old World Origin of New World Dogs," *Science* 298 (2002):1613–16.

Lepper, B. T., "The Newark Earthworks and the Geometric Enclosures of the Scioto Valley: Connections and Conjectures," in *A View from the Core: A Synthesis of Ohio Hopewell Archaeology*, ed. P. J. Pacheco. Columbus: Ohio Archaeological Council, 1996.
— "The Archaeology of the Newark Earthworks," in *Ancient Earthen Enclosures of the Eastern Woodlands*, eds. R. C. Mainfort Jr. and L. P. Sullivan. Gainesville, University Press of Florida, 1998.
— "On the Age of Serpent Mound: A Reply to Romain and Colleagues," *Midcontinental Journal of Archaeology* 43 (2018):62–75.

Lepper, B. T. and R. Yerkes, "Hopewellian Occupations at the Northern Periphery of the Newark Earthworks," in *Ohio Hopewell Community Organization*, eds. W. S. Dancey and P. J. Pacheco. Kent, OH: Kent State University Press, 1997.

Limp, W. F., and V. A. Reidhead, "An Economic Evaluation of the Potential of Fish Utilization in Riverine Environments," *American Antiquity* 44 (1979):70–78.

Little, E. A., "Kautantouwit's Legacy: Calibrated Dates on Prehistoric Maize in New England," *American Antiquity* 67 (2002):109–18.

Llamas, B., *et al.*, "Ancient Mitochondrial DNA Provides High-Resolution Time Scale of the Peopling of the Americas," *Science Advances* 2 (2016):e1501385.

Loewen, B., and V. Delmas, "The Basques in the Gulf of St. Lawrence and Adjacent Shores," *Canadian Journal of Archaeology* 36 (2012):213–66.

Lopinot, N. H., "Archaeobotanical Remains," in *The Archaeology of the Cahokia Mounds ICT-II: Biological Remains*. Springfield: Illinois Historic Preservation Agency, 1991.

Lovis, W. A., *et al.*, "Wetlands and Emergent Horticultural Economies in the Upper Great Lakes: A New Perspective from the Schultz Site." *American Antiquity* 66 (2001):615–32.

Lynott, M. J., *Hopewell Ceremonial Landscapes of Ohio*. Oxford: Oxbow, 2014.

Lyon, E. A., *A New Deal for Southeastern Archaeology*. Tuscaloosa: University of Alabama Press, 1996.

Mainfort, R. C. Jr., *Pinson Mounds: A Middle Woodland Ceremonial Center*. Nashville: Division of Archaeology, Tennessee Department of Conservation, 1986.
— "The Late Prehistoric and Protohistoric Periods in the Central Mississippi Valley,'" in *Societies in Eclipse*, eds. D. S. Brose, C. W. Cowan, and R. C. Mainfort Jr. Washington, DC: Smithsonian Institution Press, 2001.

Mainfort, R. C., and K. C. Carstens, "A Middle Woodland Embankment and Mound Complex in Western Kentucky," *Southeastern Archaeology* 6 (1987):57–61.

Mallam, R. C., *The Iowa Effigy Mound Manifestation: An Interpretive Model*. Iowa City: Office of the State Archaeologist, 1976.

Mandryk, C. A. S., *et al.*, "Late Quaternary Paleoenvironments of Northwestern North America: Implications for Inland Versus Coastal Migration Routes," *Quaternary Science Reviews* 20 (2001):301–14.

Mann, D. H., and T. D. Hamilton, "Late Pleistocene and Holocene Paleoenvironments of the North Pacific Coast," *Quaternary Science Reviews* 14 (1995):449–71.

Mann, M. E., *et al.*, "Global Signatures and Dynamical Origins of the Little Ice Age and Medieval Climate Anomaly," *Science* 326 (2009):1256–60.

Marcoux, J. B., *Pox, Empire, Shackles, and Hides*. Tuscaloosa: University of Alabama Press, 2010a.
— "The Materialization of Status and Social Structure at Koger's Island Cemetery, Alabama," in *Mississippian Mortuary Practices: Beyond Hierarchy and the Representationist Perspective*, eds. L. P. Sullivan and R. C. Mainfort Jr. Gainesville: University Press of Florida, 2010b.

Markman, C. W., *Chicago Before History: The Prehistoric Archaeology of a Modern Metropolitan Area*. Springfield: Illinois Historic Preservation Agency, 1991.

Marquardt, W. H., "Complexity and Scale in the Study of Fisher-Gatherer-Hunters: An Example from the Eastern United States," in *Prehistoric Hunter-Gatherers: The Emergence of Cultural Complexity*, eds. T. D. Price and J. A. Brown. Orlando, FL: Academic Press, 1985.
— "The Emergence and Demise of the Calusa," in *Societies in Eclipse*, eds. D. S. Brose, C. W. Cowan, and R. C. Mainfort Jr. Washington, DC: Smithsonian Institution Press, 2001.
— "Lithic Artifacts in the Middle Green River Region," in *Archaeology of the Middle Green River Region, Kentucky*, eds. W. H. Marquardt and P. J. Watson. Gainesville: Florida Museum of Natural History, 2005.
— "Shell Mounds in the Southeast: Middens, Monuments, Temple Mounds, Rings, or Works?," *American Antiquity* 75 (2010):551–70.

Marquardt, W. H., and K. J. Walker, "Southwest Florida During the Mississippian Period," in *Late Prehistoric Florida: Archaeology at the Edge of the Mississippian World*, eds. K. Ashley and N. M. White. Gainesville: University Press of Florida, 2012.

Marquardt, W. H., and P. J. Watson, "The Shell Mound Archaic of Western Kentucky," in *Archaic Hunters and Gatherers in the American Midwest*, eds. J. L. Phillips and J. A. Brown. New York: Academic Press, 1983.
— "The Green River Shell Mound Archaic: Conclusions," in *Archaeology of the Middle Green River Region, Kentucky*, eds. W. H. Marquardt and P. J. Watson. Gainesville: Florida Museum of Natural History, 2005.

Martin, P. S., "The Discovery of America," *Science* 179 (1973):969–74.

Martin, P. S., and C. R. Szuter, "War Zones and Game Sinks in Lewis and Clark's West," *Conservation Biology* 13 (1999):36–45.

Mazrim, R. F., "The Seventeenth Century Samples and Affiliations at Grid A," in *Protohistory at the Grand Village of the Kaskaskia*, ed. R. F. Mazrim. Urbana: Illinois State Archaeological Survey, University of Illinois, 2015.

McElrath, D. L., and A. C. Fortier, "The Early Late Woodland Occupation of the American Bottom," in *Late Woodland Societies: Tradition and Transformation Across the Midcontinent*, eds. T. E. Emerson, D. L. McElrath, and A. C. Fortier. Lincoln: University of Nebraska Press, 2000.

McGahey, S. O., "Paleoindian and Early Archaic Data from Mississippi," in *The Paleoindian and Early Archaic Southeast*, eds. D. G. Anderson and K. E. Sassaman. Tuscaloosa: University of Alabama Press, 1996.

McGimsey, C. R., and M. D. Wiant, "The Woodland Occupations: Summary and Conclusion," in *Woodland Period Occupations of the Napoleon Hollow Site in the Lower Illinois Valley*, eds. M. D. Wiant and C. R. McGimsey. Kampsville, IL: Center for American Archaeology, 1986.

McKern, W. C., *A Wisconsin Variant of the Hopewell Culture*. Milwaukee: Milwaukee Public Museum, 1931.

McKusick, M., *The Grant Oneota Village*. Iowa City: Office of the State Archaeologist, 1973.

McManamon, F. P., "From RBS to CRM: Late Twentieth-Century Developments in American Archaeology," in *Dam Projects and the Growth of American Archaeology*, eds. K. M. Banks and J. S. Czaplicki. Walnut Creek, CA: Left Coast Press, 2014.

McManamon, F. P., J. W. Bradley, and A. L. Magennis, *The Indian Neck Ossuary*. Boston: North Atlantic Regional Office, National Park Service, 1986.

McMillan, R. B., "Early Canid Burial from the Western Ozark Highland," *Science* 167 (1970):1246–47.

Means, B. K., *Circular Villages of the Monongahela Tradition*. Tuscaloosa: University of Alabama Press, 2007.

Meltzer, D. J., "Late Pleistocene Human Adaptations in Eastern North America," *Journal of World Prehistory* 2 (1988):1–51.
— "Was Stone Exchanged Among Eastern North American Paleoindians?," in *Eastern Paleoindian Lithic Resource Use*, eds. C. J. Ellis and J. C. Lothrop. Boulder, CO: Westview Press, 1989.
— *Search for the First Americans*. Washington, DC: Smithsonian Books, 1993.
— "Monte Verde and the Pleistocene Peopling of the Americas," *Science* 276 (1997):754–55.
— "The Human Colonization of the Americas: Archaeology," in *The Encyclopedia of Global Human Migration*, ed. I. Ness. Hoboken, NJ: Wiley-Blackwell, 2013. doi:10.1002/9781444351071.wbeghm808
— "Pleistocene Overkill and North American Mammalian Extinctions," *Annual Review of Anthropology* 44 (2015):33–53.

Meltzer, D. J., and B. D. Smith, "Paleoindian and Early Archaic Subsistence Strategies in Eastern North America," in *Foraging, Collecting, and Harvesting: Archaic Period Subsistence and Settlement in the Eastern Woodlands*, ed. S. W. Neusius. Carbondale: Center for Archaeological Investigations, Southern Illinois University, 1986.

Meltzer, D. J., *et al.*, "On the Pleistocene Antiquity of Monte Verde, Southern Chile," *American Antiquity* 62 (1997):659–63.

Mensforth, R. P., "Paleodemography of the Carlston Annis (Bt-5) Late Archaic Skeletal Population," *American Journal of Physical Anthropology* 82 (1990):81–99.
— "Human Trophy Taking in Eastern North America During the Archaic Period: The Relationship to Warfare and Social Complexity," in *The Taking and Displaying of Human Body Parts as Trophies by Amerindians*, eds. R. J. Chacon and D. H. Dye. New York: Springer, 2007.

Meyers, M. S., "Leadership at the Edge," in *Leadership and Polity in Mississippian Society*, eds. B. M. Butler and P. D. Welch. Carbondale: Center for Archaeological Investigations, Southern Illinois University, 2006.

Milanich, J. T., *Archaeology of Precolumbian Florida*. Gainesville: University Press of Florida, 1994.

Miller, D. S., V. T. Holliday, and J. Bright, "Clovis Across the Continent," in *Paleoamerican Odyssey*, eds. K. E. Graf, C. V. Ketron, and M. R. Waters. College Station: Texas A&M University Press, 2014.

Mills, W. C., "Explorations of the Edwin Harness Mound, Ohio," *Archaeological and Historical Quarterly* 16 (1907):5–85.

— "Exploration of the Mound City Group," *Certain Mounds and Village Sites in Ohio* 3 (1922):245–408.

Milner, C. M., and J. M. O'Shea, "The Socioeconomic Role of Late Woodland Enclosures in Northern Lower Michigan," in *Ancient Earthen Enclosures of the Eastern Woodlands*, eds. R. C. Mainfort Jr. and L. P. Sullivan. Gainesville, University Press of Florida, 1998.

Milner, G. R., *The East St. Louis Stone Quarry Site Cemetery*. Urbana: University of Illinois Press, 1983.
— "Mississippian Sand Prairie Phase Mortuary Complex," in *The Florence Street Site*. Urbana: University of Illinois Press, 1984a.
— *The Julien Site*. Urbana: University of Illinois Press, 1984b.
— *The Cahokia Chiefdom: The Archaeology of a Mississippian Society*. Washington, DC: Smithsonian Institution Press, 1998.
— "Warfare in Prehistoric and Early Historic Eastern North America," *Journal of Archaeological Research* 7 (1999):105–51.

Milner, G. R., and G. Chaplin, "Eastern North American Population at ca. A.D. 1500," *American Antiquity* 75 (2010):707–26.

Milner, G. R., and R. J. Ferrell, "Conflict and Death in a Late Prehistoric Community in the American Midwest," *Anthropologischer Anzeiger* 68 (2011):415–36.

Milner, G. R., and R. W. Jefferies, "A Reevaluation of the WPA Excavation of the Robbins Mound in Boone County, Kentucky," in *Current Archaeological Research in Kentucky: Volume 1*, ed. D. Pollack. Frankfort: Kentucky Heritage Council, 1987.
— "The Read Archaic Shell Midden in Kentucky," *Southeastern Archaeology* 17 (1998):119–32.

Milner, G. R., and S. Schroeder, "The Guy Smith Site and Stone-Box Graves: New Perspectives from Old Collections," *Illinois Archaeology* 4 (1992):49–73.

Milner, G. R., and V. G. Smith, *New Deal Archaeology in Kentucky: Excavations, Collections, and Research*. Lexington: Program for Cultural Resource Assessment, University of Kentucky, 1986.

Milner, G. R., D. G. Anderson, and M. T. Smith, "The Distribution of Eastern Woodlands Peoples at the Prehistoric and Historic Interface," in *Societies in Eclipse*, eds. D. S. Brose, C. W. Cowan, and R. C. Mainfort Jr. Washington, DC: Smithsonian Institution Press, 2001.

Milner, G. R., E. Anderson, and V. G. Smith, "Warfare in Late Prehistoric West-Central Illinois," *American Antiquity* 56 (1991):581–603.

Milner, G. R., J. E. Buikstra, and M. D. Wiant, "Archaic Burial Sites in the American Midcontinent," in *Archaic Societies: Diversity and Complexity Across the Midcontinent*, eds. T. E. Emerson, D. L. McElrath, and A. C. Fortier. Albany: State University of New York Press, 2009.

Milner, G. R., G. Chaplin, and E. Zavodny, "Conflict and Societal Change in Late Prehistoric Eastern North America," *Evolutionary Anthropology* 22 (2013):96–102.

Milner, G. R., S. W. Hammerstedt, and K. D. French, "Chert Hoes as Digging Tools," *Antiquity* 84 (2010):103–13.

Milner, G. R., D. H. Humpf, and H. C. Harpending, "Pattern Matching of Age-at-Death Distributions in Paleodemographic Analysis," *American Journal of Physical Anthropology* 80 (1989):49–58.

Milner, G. R., J. W. Wood, and J. L. Boldsen, "Paleodemography: Problems, Progress, and Potential," in *Biological Anthropology of the Human Skeleton*, 3rd edn, eds. M. A. Katzenberg, and A. L. Grauer. Hoboken, NJ: Wiley-Blackwell, 2018.

Mitchie, J. L., "The Taylor Site: An Early Occupation in Central South Carolina," in *The Paleoindian and Early Archaic Southeast*, eds. D. G. Anderson and K. E. Sassaman. Tuscaloosa: University of Alabama Press, 1996.

Mitchem, J. M., "Artifacts of Exploration: Archaeological Evidence from Florida," in *First Encounters: Spanish Explorations in the Caribbean and the United States, 1492–1570*, eds. J. T. Milanich and S. Milbrath, Gainesville: University of Florida Press, 1989.

Monaghan, G. W., and C. S. Peebles, "The Construction, Use, and Abandonment of Angel Site Mound A: Tracing the History of a Middle Mississippian Town Through Its Earthworks," *American Antiquity* 75 (2010):935–53.

Monaghan, G. W., T. M. Schilling, and K. E. Parker, "The Age and Distribution of Domesticated Beans (*Phaseolus vulgaris*) in Eastern North America: Implications for Agricultural

Practices and Group Interactions," in *Reassessing the Timing, Rate, and Adoption Trajectories of Domesticate Use in the Midwest and Great Lakes*, ed. M. E. Raviele and W. A. Lovis. Midwest Archaeological Conference, 2014.

Moore, C. R., and V. D. Thompson, "Animism and Green River Persistent Places: A Dwelling Perspective of the Shell Mound Archaic," *Journal of Social Archaeology* 12 (2012):264–84.

Moore, D. G., C. B. Rodning, and R. A. Beck, "Joara, Cuenca, and Fort San Juan: The Construction of Colonial Identities at the Berry Site," in *Forging Southeastern Identities: Social Archaeology, Ethnohistory, and Folklore of the Mississippian to Early Historic South*, eds. G. A. Waselkov, and M. T. Smith. Tuscaloosa: University of Alabama Press, 2017.

Moreno-Mayar, J. V., *et al.*, "Terminal Pleistocene Alaskan Genome Reveals First Founding Population of Native Americans," *Nature* 553 (2018):203–8.

Morey, D. F., and M. D. Wiant, "Early Holocene Domestic Dog Burials from the North American Midwest," *Current Anthropology* 33 (1992):224–29.

Morgan, R. G., "Outline of Cultures in the Ohio Region," in *Archeology of Eastern United States*, ed. J. B. Griffin. Chicago: University of Chicago Press, 1952.

Morse, D. F., "The Hazel Site: Archeological Salvage During the Construction of Route 308," *Arkansas Archeologist* 14 (1973):36–77.
— "The Nodena Phase," in *Towns and Temples Along the Mississippi*, eds. D. H. Dye and C. A. Cox. Tuscaloosa: University of Alabama Press, 1990.

Morse, D. F., and P. A. Morse, *Archaeology of the Central Mississippi Valley*. New York: Academic Press, 1983.
— (eds.) *The Lower Mississippi Valley Expeditions of Clarence Bloomfield Moore*. Tuscaloosa: University of Alabama Press, 1998.

Morse, P. A., "The Parkin Site and the Parkin Phase," in *Towns and Temples Along the Mississippi*, eds. D. H. Dye and C. A. Cox. Tuscaloosa: University of Alabama Press, 1990.

Mosimann, J. E., and P. S. Martin, "Simulating Overkill by Paleoindians," *American Scientist* 63 (1975):304–13.

Moulton, G. E. (ed.), *The Journals of the Lewis & Clark Expedition*, vol. 2. Lincoln: University of Nebraska Press, 1986.
— (ed.) *The Journals of the Lewis & Clark Expedition*, vol. 6. Lincoln: University of Nebraska Press, 1990.

Mueller, N. G., "The Earliest Occurrence of a Newly Described Domesticate in Eastern North America: Adena/Hopewell Communities and Agricultural Innovation," *Journal of Anthropological Archaeology* 49 (2018):39–50.
— "Documenting the Evolution of Agrobiodiversity in the Archaeological Record: Landraces of a Newly Described Domesticate (*Polygonum erectum*) in North America," *Journal of Archaeological Method and Theory* 26 (2019):313–43.

Muller, J., *Archaeology of the Lower Ohio River Valley*. Orlando, FL: Academic Press, 1986.
— *Mississippian Political Economy*. New York: Plenum, 1997a.
— Native Eastern American Population Continuity and Stability," in *Integrating Archaeological Demography: Multidisciplinary Approaches to Prehistoric Population*, ed. R. R. Paine. Carbondale: Center for Archaeological Investigations, Southern Illinois University, 1997b.
— "Prolegomena for the Analysis of the Southeastern Ceremonial Complex," in *Southeastern Ceremonial Complex: Chronology, Content, Context*, ed. A. King. Tuscaloosa: University of Alabama Press, 2007.

Munoz, S. E., *et al.*, "Defining the Spatial Patterns of Historical Land Use Associated with the Indigenous Societies of Eastern North America," *Journal of Biogeography* 41 (2014):2195–210.

Nass, J. P. Jr., and J. P. Hart, "Subsistence-Settlement Change During the Late Prehistoric Period in the Upper Ohio River Valley: New Models and Old Constructs" in *Cultures Before Contact: The Late Prehistory of Ohio and Surrounding Regions*, ed. R. A. Genheimer. Columbus: Ohio Archaeological Council, 2000.

Nass, J. P. Jr., and R. W. Yerkes, "Social Differentiation in Mississippian and Fort Ancient Societies," in *Mississippian Communities and Households*, eds. J. D. Rogers and B. D. Smith. Tuscaloosa: University of Alabama Press, 1995.

Nassaney, M. S., "The Late Woodland Southeast," in *Late Woodland Societies: Tradition and Transformation Across the Midcontinent*, eds. T.E. Emerson, D. L. McElrath, and

A. C. Fortier. Lincoln: University of Nebraska Press, 2000.

Neel, J. V., and F. M. Salzano, "Further Studies on the Xavante Indians. X. Some Hypotheses-Generalizations Resulting from those Studies," *American Journal of Human Genetics* 19 (1967):554–74.

Neumann, G. K., "Types of Artificial Cranial Deformation in the Eastern United States," *American Antiquity* 7 (1942):306–10.

Neumann, G. K., and M. L. Fowler, *Hopewellian Sites in the Lower Wabash Valley*. Springfield: Illinois State Museum, 1952.

Neusius, S. W., *et al.*, "Fortified Village or Mortuary Site? Exploring the Use of the Ripley Site," in *Ancient Earthen Enclosures of the Eastern Woodlands*, eds. R. C. Mainfort Jr. and L. P. Sullivan. Gainesville: University Press of Florida, 1998.

Newsom, L. A., "The Paleoethnobotany of the Archaic Mortuary Pond," in *Windover: Multidisciplinary Investigations of an Early Archaic Florida Cemetery*, ed. G. H. Doran. Gainesville: University Press of Florida, 2002.

Newsom, L. A., and D. A. Trieu Gahr, "Fusion Gardens: Native North America and the Columbian Exchange," in *The Subsistence Economies of Indigenous North American Societies: A Handbook*, ed. B. D. Smith. Washington, DC: Smithsonian Institution Scholarly Press, 2011.

O'Brien, M. J., *Mississippian Community Organization: The Powers Phase in Southeastern Missouri*. New York: Plenum, 2001.

O'Gorman, J. A., "Exploring the Longhouse and Community in Tribal Society," *American Antiquity* 75 (2010):571–97.

O'Gorman, J. A., and W. A. Lovis, "Before Removal: An Archaeological Perspective on the Southern Lake Michigan Basin," *Midcontinental Journal of Archaeology* 31 (2006):21–56.

Ortmann, A. L., "Placing the Poverty Point Mounds in Their Temporal Context," *American Antiquity* 75 (2010):657–78.

Ortmann, A. L., and T. R. Kidder, "Building Mound A at Poverty Point, Louisiana: Monumental Public Architecture, Ritual Practice, and Implications for Hunter-Gatherer Complexity," *Geoarchaeology* 28 (2013):66–86.

O'Shea, J. M., "Social Organization and Mortuary Behavior in the Late Woodland Period in Michigan," in *Interpretations of Culture Change in the Eastern Woodlands During the Late Woodland Period*, ed. R. W. Yerkes. Columbus: Department of Anthropology, Ohio State University, 1988.

O'Steen, L. D., "Paleoindian and Early Archaic Settlement Along the Oconee Drainage," in *The Paleoindian and Early Archaic Southeast*, eds. D. G. Anderson and K. E. Sassaman. Tuscaloosa: University of Alabama Press, 1996.

Overstreet, D. F., "Oneota Prehistory and History," *Wisconsin Archeologist* 78 (1997):250–96.

Pacheco, P. J., "Ohio Hopewell Regional Settlement Patterns," in *A View from the Core: A Synthesis of Ohio Hopewell Archaeology*, ed. P. J. Pacheco. Columbus: Ohio Archaeological Council, 1996.

Pacheco, P. J., and W. S. Dancey, "Integrating Mortuary and Settlement Data on Ohio Hopewell Society," in *Recreating Hopewell*, eds. D. K. Charles and J. E. Buikstra. Gainesville: University Press of Florida, 2006.

Pauketat, T. R., *The Ascent of Chiefs: Cahokia and Mississippian Politics in Native North America*. Tuscaloosa: University of Alabama Press, 1994.
— *The Archaeology of Downtown Cahokia: The Tract 15A and Dunham Tract Excavations*. Urbana: Illinois Transportation Archaeological Research Program, University of Illinois, 1998.
— *Ancient Cahokia and the Mississippians*. Cambridge: Cambridge University, 2004.

Pauketat, T. R., and N. H. Lopinot, "Cahokian Population Dynamics," in *Cahokia: Domination and Ideology in the Mississippian World*, eds. T. R. Pauketat and T. E. Emerson, Lincoln: University of Nebraska Press, 1997.

Pauketat, T. R., *et al.*, "The Residues of Feasting and Public Ritual at Early Cahokia," *American Antiquity* 67 (2002):257–79.

Pavao-Zuckerman, B., and E. J. Reitz, "Eurasian Domesticated Livestock in Native American Economies," in *The Subsistence Economies of Indigenous North American Societies: A Handbook*, ed. B. D. Smith. Washington, DC: Smithsonian Institution Scholarly Press, 2011.

Payne, C., and J. F. Scarry, "Town Structure at the Edge of the Mississippian World," in *Mississippian Towns and Sacred Spaces*, eds. R. B. Lewis and C. Stout. Tuscaloosa: University of Alabama Press, 1998.

Peebles, C. S., "Moundville and Surrounding Sites: Some Structural Considerations of Mortuary Practices II," *American Antiquity Memoir* 25 (1971):68–91.

— "Moundville: Late Prehistoric Sociopolitical Organization in the Southeastern United States," in *The Development of Political Organization in Native North America*, ed. E. Tooker. Washington, DC: American Ethnological Society, 1983.

Penney, D. W., "The Late Archaic Period," in *Ancient Art of the American Woodland Indians*. New York: Harry N. Abrams, 1985.

Perino, G. H., "The Mississippian Component at the Schild Site (No. 4), Greene County, Illinois," in *Mississippian Site Archaeology in Illinois*. Urbana: Illinois Archaeological Survey, 1971a.

— "The Yokem Site, Pike County, Illinois," in *Mississippian Site Archaeology in Illinois*. Urbana: Illinois Archaeological Survey, 1971b.

Perri, A., *et al.*, "New Evidence of the Earliest Domestic Dogs in the Americas," *American Antiquity* 84 (2019):68–87.

Perttula, T. K., *et al.*, "A Revolution in Caddo Archaeology: The Remote Sensing and Archaeological View from the Hill Farm Site (41BW169) in Bowie County, Texas," *Southeastern Archaeology* 27 (2008):93–107.

Petersen, K. S., *et al.*, "Clams before Columbus?," *Nature* 359 (1992):679.

Petersen, J. B., and N. A. Sidell, "Mid-Holocene Evidence of *Cucurbita* sp. from Central Maine," *American Antiquity* 61 (1996):685–98.

Petersen, J. B., M. Blustain, and J. W. Bradley, "'Mawooshen' Revisited: Two Native American Contact Period Sites on the Central Maine Coast," *Archaeology of Eastern North America* 32 (2004):1–71.

Phillips, P., *Archaeological Survey in the Lower Yazoo Basin, Mississippi, 1949–1955*. Cambridge, MA: Peabody Museum, Harvard University, 1970.

Phillips, P., and J. A. Brown, *Pre-Columbian Shell Engravings From the Craig Mound at Spiro, Oklahoma*, Part 1. Cambridge, MA: Peabody Museum Press, 1978.

Phillips, P., J. A. Ford, and J. B. Griffin, *Archaeological Survey in the Lower Mississippi Alluvial Valley, 1940–1947*. Cambridge, MA: Peabody Museum, Harvard University, 1951.

Pickard, W. H., "1990 Excavations at Capitolium Mound (33WN13), Marietta, Washington County, Ohio: A Working Evaluation," in *A View from the Core: A Synthesis of Ohio Hopewell Archaeology*, ed. P. J. Pacheco. Columbus: Ohio Archaeological Council, 1996.

Pleger, T. C., and J. B. Stoltman, "The Archaic Tradition in Wisconsin," in *Archaic Societies: Diversity and Complexity Across the Midcontinent*, eds. T. E. Emerson, D. L. McElrath, and A. C. Fortier. Albany: State University of New York Press, 2009.

Pluckhahn, T. J., *Kolomoki: Settlement, Ceremony, and Status in the Deep South, A.D. 350–750*. Tuscaloosa: University of Alabama Press, 2003.

Pluckhahn, T. J., and V. D. Thompson, "Woodland-Period Mound Building as Historical Tradition: Dating the Mounds and Monuments at Crystal River (8Ci1)," *Journal of Archaeological Science: Reports* 15 (2017):73–94.

Pluckhahn, T. J., *et al.*, "A New History of Community Formation and Change at Kolomoki (9ER1)," *American Antiquity* 83 (2018):320–44.

Pollack, D., "Late Mississippian Caborn-Welborn Social and Political Relationships," in *Leadership and Polity in Mississippian Society*, eds. B. M. Butler and P. D. Welch. Carbondale: Center for Archaeological Investigations, Southern Illinois University, 2006.

Pollack, D., and A. G. Henderson, "Insights into Fort Ancient Culture Change: A View from South of the Ohio River," in *Cultures Before Contact: The Late Prehistory of Ohio and Surrounding Regions*, ed. R. A. Genheimer. Columbus: Ohio Archaeological Council, 2000a.

— "Late Woodland Cultures in Kentucky," in *Late Woodland Societies: Tradition and Transformation Across the Midcontinent*, eds. T. E. Emerson, D. L. McElrath, and A. C. Fortier. Lincoln: University of Nebraska Press, 2000b.

— "Fort Ancient public structures," in *Building the Past: Prehistoric Wooden Post Architecture in the Ohio Valley – Great Lakes*, eds. B. G. Redmond and R. A. Genheimer. Gainesville: University Press of Florida, 2015.

Porter, J. W., *Cahokia Archaeology as Viewed from the Mitchell Site: A Satellite Community at AD 1150–1200*.

PhD dissertation. Madison: Department of Anthropology, University of Wisconsin, 1974.

Potter, B. A., *et al.*, "Early Colonization of Beringia and Northern North America: Chronology, Routes, and Adaptive Strategies," *Quaternary International* 444 (2017):36–55.

Potter, S. R., *Commoners, Tribute, and Chiefs: The Development of Algonquian Culture in the Potomac Valley*. Charlottesville: University Press of Virginia, 1993.

Powell, M. L., "The Analysis of Dental Wear and Caries for Dietary Reconstruction," in *The Analysis of Prehistoric Diets*, eds. R. I Gilbert Jr. and J. H. Mielke. Orlando: Academic Press, 1985.

— "Endemic Treponematosis and Tuberculosis in the Prehistoric Southeastern United States: Biological Costs of Chronic Endemic Disease," in *Human Paleopathology: Current Syntheses and Future Options*, eds. D. J. Ortner and A. C. Aufderheide, Washington, DC: Smithsonian Institution Press, 1991.

— "Health and Disease in the Green River Archaic," in *Of Caves and Shell Mounds*, eds. K. C. Carstens and P. J. Watson. Tuscaloosa: University of Alabama Press, 1996.

— "Of Time and the River: Perspectives on Health During the Moundville Chiefdom," in *Archaeology of the Moundville Chiefdom*, eds. V. J. Knight Jr. and V. P. Steponaitis. Tuscaloosa: University of Alabama Press, 1998.

Price, J. E. and G. L. Fox, "Recent Investigations at Towosahgy State Historic Site," *The Missouri Archaeologist* 51 (1990):1–71.

Price, J. E. and J. B. Griffin, *The Snodgrass Site of the Powers Phase of Southeast Missouri*. Ann Arbor: Museum of Anthropology, University of Michigan, 1979.

Prufer, O. H., "Fort Hill 1964: New Data and Reflections on Hopewell Hilltop Enclosures in Southern Ohio," in *Ohio Hopewell Community Organization*, eds. W. S. Dancey and P. J. Pacheco. Kent, OH: Kent State University Press, 1997.

Putnam, F. W., The Serpent Mound Saved. *Ohio Archaeological and Historical Quarterly* 1 (1887):187–90.

Railey, J. A., *The Pyles Site (15MS228): A Newtown Village in Mason County, Kentucky*. Lexington, KY: W. S. Webb Archaeological Society, 1984.

Ramsden, P. G., "The Hurons: Archaeology and Culture History," in *The Archaeology of Southern Ontario to AD 1650*, eds. C. J. Ellis and N. Ferris. London, ON: London Chapter, Ontario Archaeological Society, 1990.

Rasmussen, S. O., *et al.*, "A Stratigraphic Framework for Abrupt Climatic Changes During the Last Glacial Period Based on Three Synchronized Greenland Ice-Core Records: Refining and Extending the INTIMATE Event Stratigraphy," *Quaternary Science Reviews* 106 (2014):14–28.

Read, M. C., "Ancient Mound Near Chattanooga, Tennessee," in *Annual Report, 1867*. Washington DC: Smithsonian Institution, 1872.

Reeder, R. L., "The Maramec Spring Phase," in *Late Woodland Societies: Tradition and Transformation Across the Midcontinent*, eds. T. E. Emerson, D. L. McElrath, and A. C. Fortier. Lincoln: University of Nebraska Press, 2000.

Regnier, A. L., S. W. Hammerstedt, and S. Bobalik Savage, *The Ritual Landscape of Late Precontact Eastern Oklahoma*. Tuscaloosa: University of Alabama Press, 2019.

Rindos, D., and S. Johannessen, "Human–Plant Interactions and Cultural Change in the American Bottom," in *Cahokia and the Hinterlands: Middle Mississippian Cultures of the Midwest*, eds. T. E. Emerson and R. B. Lewis. Urbana: University of Illinois Press, 1991.

Riordan, R. V., "The Enclosed Hilltops of Southern Ohio," in *A View from the Core: A Synthesis of Ohio Hopewell Archaeology*, ed. P. J. Pacheco. Columbus: Ohio Archaeological Council, 1996.

— "Boundaries, Resistance, and Control: Enclosing the Hilltops in Middle Woodland Ohio," in *Ancient Earthen Enclosures of the Eastern Woodlands*, eds. R. C. Mainfort Jr. and L. P. Sullivan. Gainesville, University Press of Florida, 1998.

— "The end," in *Building the Past: Prehistoric Wooden Post Architecture in the Ohio Valley – Great Lakes*, eds. B. G. Redmond and R. A. Genheimer. Gainesville: University Press of Florida, 2015.

Ritchie, W. A., *The Archaeology of New York State*. rev. edn. Harrison, NY: Harbor Hill Books, 1980.

Robinson, B. S., *et al.*, "Paleoindian Aggregation and Social Context at Bull Brook," *American Antiquity* 74 (2009):423–47.

Rodell, R. L., "Patterns of Oneota Settlement Within the Middle Portion of the Upper Mississippi Valley," in *Mounds, Modoc, and Mesoamerica: Papers in Honor of Melvin L. Fowler*, ed. S. R. Ahler. Springfield: Illinois State Museum, 2000.

Rodning, C. B., "European Trade Goods at Cherokee Settlements in Southwestern North Carolina," *North Carolina Archaeology* 59 (2010):1–84.

Rodning, C. B. and D. G. Moore, "South Appalachian Mississippian and Protohistoric Mortuary Practices in Southwestern North Carolina," *Southeastern Archaeology* 29 (2010):80–100.

Rodning, C. B., R. A. Beck, and D. G. Moore, "Conflict, Violence, and Warfare in La Florida," in *Native and Spanish New Worlds: Sixteenth-Century Entradas in the American Southwest and Southeast*, eds. C. Mathers, J. M. Mitchem, and C. M. Haecker. Tucson: University of Arizona Press, 2013.

Rodning, C. B., *et al.*, "Spanish Material Culture from the Berry Site," in *Fort San Juan and the Limits of Empire*, eds. R. A. Beck, C. B. Rodning, and D. G. Moore. Gainesville: University Press of Florida, 2016.

Rogers, J. D., "Dispersed Communities and Integrated Households: A Perspective from Spiro and the Arkansas Basin," in *Mississippian Communities and Households*, eds. J. D. Rogers and B. D. Smith. Tuscaloosa: University of Alabama Press, 1995.

Rolingson, M. A., "Excavations of Mound S at the Toltec Mounds Site: Preliminary Report," *The Arkansas Archeologist* 31 (1990):1–29.
— *Toltec Mounds and Plum Bayou Culture: Mound D Excavations*. Fayetteville: Arkansas Archeological Survey, 1998.

Romain, W. F., *et al.*, "Radiocarbon Dates Reveal Serpent Mound is More than Two Thousand Years Old," *Midcontinental Journal of Archaeology* 42 (2017):201–22.

Rountree, H. C., and E. R. Turner III, "The Evolution of the Powhatan Paramount Chiefdom in Virginia," in *Chiefdoms and Chieftaincy in the Americas*, ed. E. M. Redmond. Gainesville: University Press of Florida, 1998.

Ruby, B. J., "Spruce Hill Earthworks: The 1995–1996 National Park Service Investigations," in *In the Footprints of Squier and Davis: Archeological Fieldwork in Ross County, Ohio*, ed. M. J. Lynott. Lincoln, NE: Midwest Archeological Center, National Park Service, 2009.

Ruby, B. J., C. Carr, and D. K. Charles, "Community Organizations in the Scioto, Mann, and Havana Hopewellian Regions: A Comparative Perspective," in *Gathering Hopewell: Society, Ritual, and Ritual Interaction*, eds. C. Carr and D. T. Case. New York: Kluwer Academic, 2005.

Rudolph, J. L., "Earthlodges and Platform Mounds: Changing Public Architecture in the Southeastern United States," *Southeastern Archaeology* 3 (1984):33–45.

Ruff, C. B., "Skeletal Structure and Behavioral Patterns of Prehistoric Great Basin Populations," in *Prehistoric Lifeways in the Great Basin Wetlands: Bioarchaeological Reconstruction and Interpretation*, eds. B. E. Hemphill and C. S. Larsen. Salt Lake City: University of Utah Press, 1999.

Russo, M., "Southeastern Archaic Mounds," in *Archaeology of the Mid-Holocene Southeast*, eds. K. E. Sassaman and D. G. Anderson. Gainesville: University Press of Florida, 1996a.
— "Southeastern Mid-Holocene Coastal Settlements," in *Archaeology of the Mid-Holocene Southeast*, eds. K. E. Sassaman and D. G. Anderson. Gainesville: University Press of Florida, 1996b.
— "Shell Rings and Other Settlement Features as Indicators of Cultural Continuity Between the Late Archaic and Woodland Periods of Coastal Florida," in *Trend, Tradition, and Turmoil: What Happened to the Southeastern Archaic?*, eds. D. H. Thomas and M. C. Sanger. New York: American Museum of Natural History, 2010.

Salkin, P. H., "The Horicon and Kekoskee Phases: Cultural Complexity in the Late Woodland Stage in Southeastern Wisconsin," in *Late Woodland Societies: Tradition and Transformation Across the Midcontinent*, eds. T. E. Emerson, D. L. McElrath, and A. C. Fortier. Lincoln: University of Nebraska Press, 2000.

Samuelsen, J. R., "Geophysical Investigations of Late Fourche Maline and Early Caddo Settlement Patterning at the Crenshaw Site (3MI6)," *Southeastern Archaeology* 29 (2010):261–78.

Sanger, M. C. and D. H. Thomas, "The Two Rings of St. Catherines Island: Some Preliminary Results from the St. Catherines and McQueen Shell Rings," in *Trend, Tradition, and Turmoil: What Happened to the Southeastern Archaic?*, eds. D. H. Thomas and M. C. Sanger. New York: American Museum of Natural History, 2010.

Sanger, M. C., *et al.*, "Early Metal Use and Crematory Practices in the American Southeast," *Proceedings of the National Academy of Sciences* 115 (2018):E7672–E7679.

Santure, S. K., "Norris Farms 36: A Bold Counselor Phase Oneota Cemetery," in *Archaeological Investigations at the Morton Village and Norris Farms 36 Cemetery*, eds. S. K. Santure, A. D. Harn, and D. Esarey. Springfield: Illinois State Museum, 1990.

Santure, S. K., and D. Esarey, "Analysis of Artifacts from the Oneota Mortuary Component," in *Archaeological Investigations at the Morton Village and Norris Farms 36 Cemetery*, eds. S. K. Santure, A. D. Harn, and D. Esarey. Springfield: Illinois State Museum, 1990.

Sassaman, K. E., *Early Pottery in the Southeast: Tradition and Innovation in Cooking Technology*. Tuscaloosa: University of Alabama Press, 1993.
— "Technological Innovations in Economic and Social Contexts," in *Archaeology of the Mid-Holocene Southeast*, eds. K. E. Sassaman and D. G. Anderson. Gainesville: University Press of Florida, 1996.
— "A Southeastern Perspective on Soapstone Vessel Technology in the Northeast," in *The Archaeological Northeast*, eds. M. A. Levine, K. E. Sassaman, and M. S Nassaney. Westport, CT: Bergin and Garvey, 1999.

Sassaman, K. E., and R. J. Ledbetter, "Middle and Late Archaic Architecture," in *Archaeology of the Mid-Holocene Southeast*, eds. K. E. Sassaman and D. G. Anderson. Gainesville: University Press of Florida, 1996.

Sasso, R. F., "Vestiges of Ancient Cultivation: The Antiquity of Garden Beds and Corn Hills in Wisconsin," *Midcontinental Journal of Archaeology* 28 (2003):195–231.

Saunders, J. W., "Are We Fixing To Make the Same Mistake Again?," in *Signs of Power: The Rise of Cultural Complexity in the Southeast*, eds. J. L. Gibson and P. J. Carr. Tuscaloosa: University of Alabama Press, 2004.

Saunders, J. W., *et al.*, "A Mound Complex in Louisiana at 5400–5000 Years Before the Present," *Science* 277 (1997):1796–99.

Saunders, J. W., *et al.*, "An Assessment of the Antiquity of the Lower Jackson Mound," *Southeastern Archaeology* 20 (2001):67–77.

Saunders, J. W., *et al.*, "Watson Brake, a Middle Archaic Mound Complex in Northeast Louisiana," *American Antiquity* 70 (2005):631–68.

Schoeninger, M. J., and M. R. Schurr, "Human Subsistence at Moundville: The Stable-Isotope Data," in *Archaeology of the Moundville Chiefdom*, eds. V. J. Knight Jr. and V. P. Steponaitis. Tuscaloosa: University of Alabama Press, 1998.

Schroeder, S., "Power and Place: Agency, Ecology, and History in the American Bottom, Illinois," *Antiquity* 78 (2004):812–27.
— "Walls as Symbols of Political, Economic, and Military Might," in *Leadership and Polity in Mississippian Society*, eds. B. M. Butler and P. D. Welch. Carbondale: Center for Archaeological Investigations, Southern Illinois University, 2006.

Schroedl, G. F., "Mississippian Towns in the Eastern Tennessee Valley," in *Mississippian Towns and Sacred Spaces*, eds. R. B. Lewis and C. Stout. Tuscaloosa: University of Alabama Press, 1998.

Schroedl, G. F., C. C. Boyd Jr., and R. P. S. Davis Jr., "Explaining Mississippian Origins in East Tennessee," in *The Mississippian Emergence*, ed. B. D. Smith. Washington, DC: Smithsonian Institution Press, 1990.

Schuldenrein, J., "Geoarchaeology and the Mid-Holocene Landscape History of the Greater Southeast," in *Archaeology of the Mid-Holocene Southeast*, eds. K. E. Sassaman and D. G. Anderson. Gainesville: University Press of Florida, 1996.

Schurr, M. R., "Archaeological Indices of Resistance: Diversity in the Removal Period Potawatomi of the Western Great Lakes," *American Antiquity* 75 (2010):44–60.

Seeman, M. F., "The Bow and Arrow, the Intrusive Mound Complex, and a Late Woodland Jack's Reef Horizon in the Mid-Ohio Valley," in *Cultural Variability in Context: Woodland Settlements of the Mid-Ohio Valley*, ed. M. F. Seeman. Kent, OH: Kent State University Press, 1992.
— "When Words are Not Enough: Hopewell Interregionalism and the Use of Material Symbols at the GE Mound," in *Native American Interactions: Multiscalar*

Analyses and Interpretations in the Eastern Woodlands,
eds. M. S. Nassaney and K. E. Sassaman. Knoxville:
University of Tennessee Press, 1995.

Seeman, M. F., and W. S. Dancey, "The Late Woodland Period
in Southern Ohio: Basic Issues and Prospects," in *Late
Woodland Societies: Tradition and Transformation Across
the Midcontinent*, eds. T. E. Emerson, D. L. McElrath, and
A. C. Fortier. Lincoln: University of Nebraska Press, 2000.

Semken, H. A. Jr., R. W. Graham, and T. W. Stafford Jr., "AMS
¹⁴C Analysis of Late Pleistocene Non-Analog Faunal
Components from 21 Cave Deposits in Southeastern North
America," *Quaternary International* 217 (2010):240–55.

Sharp, W. E., "Fort Ancient Farmers," in *Kentucky Archaeology*,
ed. R. B. Lewis. Lexington: University of Kentucky Press, 1996.

Sherwood, S. C., "A Geoarchaeological Study of the Mound A
Stratigraphy," in *Archeological Investigations at Shiloh Indian
Mounds National Historic Landmark (40HR7) 1999–2004*,
eds. D. G. Anderson, J. E. Cornelison Jr., and S. C. Sherwood.
Tallahassee, FL: Southeast Archeological Center, National
Park Service, 2013.

Sherwood, S. C., and T. R. Kidder, "The DaVincis of Dirt:
Geoarchaeological Perspectives on Native American
Mound Building in the Mississippi River Basin," *Journal of
Anthropological Archaeology* 30 (2011):69–87.

Shetrone, H. C., "Exploration of the Wright Group of
Prehistoric Earthworks," *Certain Mounds and Village Sites in
Ohio* 4 (1925):41–58.
— "Explorations of the Hopewell Group of Prehistoric
Earthworks," *Ohio Archaeological and Historical
Publications* 35 (1926):5–227.
— *Primer of Ohio Archaeology: The Mound Builders and
the Indians*. Columbus: Ohio State Archaeological and
Historical Society, 1951.

Shott, M. J., "Technological Organization in Great Lakes
Paleoindian Assemblages," in *Eastern Paleoindian Lithic
Resource Use*, eds. C. J. Ellis and J. C. Lothrop. Boulder, CO:
Westview Press, 1989.
— "Innovation and Selection in Prehistory: A Case Study
from the American Bottom," in *Stone Tools: Theoretical
Insights into Human Prehistory*, ed. G. H. Odell. New York:
Plenum Press, 1996.

Simon, M. L., "Regional Variations in Plant Use Strategies
in the Midwest During the Late Woodland," in *Late
Woodland Societies: Tradition and Transformation Across
the Midcontinent*, eds. T. E. Emerson, D. L. McElrath, and
A. C. Fortier. Lincoln: University of Nebraska Press, 2000.
— "Reevaluating the Introduction of Maize into the
American Bottom and Western Illinois," in *Reassessing the
Timing, Rate, and Adoption Trajectories of Domesticate Use
in the Midwest and Great Lakes*, eds. M. E. Raviele and
W. A. Lovis. Midwest Archaeological Conference, 2014.

Smith, B. D., "Variation in Mississippian Settlement Patterns,"
in *Mississippian Settlement Patterns*, ed. B. D. Smith.
New York: Academic Press, 1978.
— "The Archaeology of the Southeastern United States:
From Dalton to de Soto 10,500–500 B. P.," *Advances in
World Archaeology* 5 (1986):1–92.
— "The Economic Potential of *Chenopodium Berlandieri*
in Prehistoric Eastern North America," *Journal of
Ethnobiology* 7 (1987):29–54.
— "Origins of Agriculture in Eastern North America," *Science*
246 (1989):1566–71.
— *The Emergence of Agriculture*. New York: Scientific
American Library, 1995.
— "Resource Resilience, Human Niche Construction, and the
Long-Term Sustainability of Pre-Columbian Subsistence
Economies in the Mississippi River Valley Corridor,"
Journal of Ethnobiology 29 (2009):167–83.
— "The Cultural Context of Plant Domestication in
Eastern North America," *Current Anthropology* 52
(2011):S471–S484.
— "The Domestication of *Helianthus annuus* L. (sunflower),"
Vegetation History and Archaeobotany 23 (2014):57–74.

Smith, B. D., and R. A. Yarnell, "Initial Formation of an
Indigenous Crop Complex in Eastern North America at 3800
B.P.," *Proceedings of the National Academy of Sciences* 106
(2009):6561–66.

Smith, B. (trans.), *Narratives of De Soto in the Conquest of
Florida*. Gainesville, FL: Palmetto Books, 1968.

Smith, H. M., "The Murdock Mound, Cahokia," in *Explorations
into Cahokia Archaeology*, ed. M. L. Fowler. Urbana: Illinois
Archaeological Survey, 1969.

Smith, J., "The Generall Historie of Virginia, New-England, and
the Summer Isles," in *Captain John Smith: Writings with
Other Narratives of Roanoke, Jamestown, and the First English
Settlement of America*. New York: Library of America, 2007
[1624].

Smith, M. O., "Osteological Indications of Warfare in the
Archaic Period of the Western Tennessee Valley," in *Troubled
Times: Violence and Warfare in the Past*, eds. D. L. Martin and
D. W. Frayer. Amsterdam: Gordon and Breach, 1997.

Smith, M. T., *Archaeology of Aboriginal Culture Change in the
Interior Southeast*. Gainesville: University Press of Florida,
1987.
— *Coosa: The Rise and Fall of a Southeastern Mississippian
Chiefdom*. Gainesville: University Press of Florida, 2000.
— "The Rise and Fall of Coosa, AD 1350–1700," in *Societies in
Eclipse*, eds. D. S. Brose, C. W. Cowan, and R. C. Mainfort Jr.
Washington, DC: Smithsonian Institution Press, 2001.

Snow, D. R., *The Iroquois*. Oxford: Blackwell, 1994.
— "Microchronology and Demographic Evidence Relating
to the Size of Pre-Columbian North American Indian
Populations," *Science* 268 (1995):1601–4.
— "Mohawk Demography and the Effects of Exogenous
Epidemics on American Indian Populations," *Journal of
Anthropological Archaeology* 15 (1996):160–82.
— "Evolution of the Mohawk Iroquois," in *Societies in
Eclipse*, eds. D. S. Brose, C. W. Cowan, and R. C. Mainfort Jr.
Washington, DC: Smithsonian Institution Press, 2001.

Snyder, J. F., "A Group of Illinois Mounds," in *John Francis
Snyder: Selected Writings*, ed. C. C. Walton. Springfield:
Illinois State Historical Society, 1962 [1909].

Song, C. A., K. A. Jakes, and R. W. Yerkes, "Seip Hopewell Textile
Analysis and Cultural Implications," *Midcontinental Journal
of Archaeology* 21 (1996):247–65.

Speth, J. D., *et al.*, "Early Paleoindian Big-Game Hunting in
North America: Provisioning or Politics?," *Quaternary
International* 285 (2013):111–39.

Squier, E. G., and E. H. Davis, *Ancient Monuments of the
Mississippi Valley*. Washington, DC: Smithsonian Institution,
1848.

Stahle, D. W., *et al.*, "The Lost Colony and Jamestown
Droughts," *Science* 280 (1998):564–67.

Stafford, B. D., "Summary," in *Smiling Dan: Structure and
Function at a Middle Woodland Settlement in the Illinois
Valley*, eds. B. D. Stafford and M. B. Sant. Kampsville, IL:
Center for American Archeology, 1985.

Steadman, D. W., "Mississippians in Motion? A Population
Genetic Analysis of Interregional Gene Flow in West-Central
Illinois," *American Journal of Physical Anthropology* 114
(2001):61–73.
— "Warfare Related Trauma at Orendorf, A Middle
Mississippian Site in West-Central Illinois," *American
Journal of Physical Anthropology* 136 (2008):51–64.

Steponaitis, V. P., "Population Trends at Moundville," in
Archaeology of the Moundville Chiefdom, eds. V. J. Knight
Jr. and V. P. Steponaitis. Tuscaloosa: University of Alabama
Press, 1998.
— "Moundville Palattes – Prestige Goods or Inalienable
Possessions?," in *Rethinking Moundville and Its
Hinterland*, eds. V. P. Steponaitis and C. M. Scarry.
Gainesville: University Press of Florida, 2016.

Steponaitis, V. P., and V. J. Knight Jr., "Moundville Art in
Historical and Social Context," in *Hero, Hawk, and Open
Hand*, eds. R. F. Townsend and R. V. Sharp. Chicago: Art
Institute of Chicago, 2004.

Stewart, R. M., "The Status of Woodland Prehistory in the
Middle Atlantic Region," *Archaeology of Eastern North
America* 23 (1995):177–206.

Stoltman, J. B., "Middle Woodland Stage Communities of
Southwestern Wisconsin," in *Hopewell Archaeology*, eds.
D. S. Brose and N. B. Greber. Kent, OH: Kent State University
Press, 1979.

Stoltman, J. B., and G. W. Christiansen, "The Late Woodland
Stage in the Driftless Area of the Upper Mississippi Valley,"
in *Late Woodland Societies: Tradition and Transformation
Across the Midcontinent*, eds. T. E. Emerson, D. L. McElrath,
and A. C. Fortier. Lincoln: University of Nebraska Press,
2000.

Storck, P. L., and A. E. Spiess, "The Significance of New Faunal
Identifications Attributed to an Early Paleoindian (Gainey
Complex) Occupation at the Udora Site, Ontario, Canada,"
American Antiquity 59 (1994):121–42.

Stout, C., and R. B. Lewis, "Mississippian Towns in Kentucky," in *Mississippian Towns and Sacred Spaces*, eds. R. B. Lewis and C. Stout. Tuscaloosa: University of Alabama Press, 1998.

Stright, M. J., "Archaeological Sites on the North American Continental Shelf," in *Archaeological Geology of North America*, eds. N. P. Lasca and J. Donahue. Boulder, CO: Geological Society of America, 1990.

Styles, B. W., "The Value of Archaeological Faunal Remains for Paleodietary Reconstruction: A Case Study for the Midwestern United States," in *Paleonutrition: The Diet and Health of Prehistoric Americans*, ed. K. D. Sobolik. Carbondale: Center for Archaeological Investigations, Southern Illinois University, 1994.
 — "Late Woodland Faunal Exploitation in the Midwestern United States," in *Late Woodland Societies: Tradition and Transformation Across the Midcontinent*, eds. T. E. Emerson, D. L. McElrath, and A. C. Fortier. Lincoln: University of Nebraska Press, 2000.
 — "Animal Use by Holocene Aboriginal Societies of the Northeast," in *The Subsistence Economies of Indigenous North American Societies: A Handbook*, ed. B. D. Smith. Washington, DC: Smithsonian Institution Scholarly Press, 2011.

Styles, B. W., and W. E. Klippel, "Mid-Holocene Faunal Exploitation in the Southeastern United States," in *Archaeology of the Mid-Holocene Southeast*, eds. K. E. Sassaman and D. G. Anderson. Gainesville: University Press of Florida, 1996.

Styles, B. W., J. R. Purdue, and M. L. Colburn, "Faunal Exploitation at the Smiling Dan Site," in *Smiling Dan: Structure and Function at a Middle Woodland Settlement in the Illinois Valley*, eds. B. D. Stafford and M. B. Sant. Kampsville, IL: Center for American Archeology, 1985.

Sullivan, L. P., "The Mouse Creek Phase Household," *Southeastern Archaeology* 6 (1987):16–29.

Swanton, J. R., *Indian Tribes of the Lower Mississippi Valley and Adjacent Coast of the Gulf of Mexico*. Washington, DC: Bureau of American Ethnology, Smithsonian Institution, 1911.
 — *The Indians of the Southeastern United States*. Washington, DC: Bureau of American Ethnology, Smithsonian Institution, 1946.

Tankersley, K. B., "Late Pleistocene Lithic Exploitation in the Midwest and Midsouth: Indiana, Ohio, and Kentucky," in *Early Paleoindian Economies of Eastern North America*, eds. K. B. Tankersley and B. L. Isaac. Greenwich, CN: JAI Press, 1990.

Tankersley, K. B., and J. E. Morrow, "Clovis Procurement and Land-Use Patterns in the Confluence Region of the Mississippi, Missouri, and Illinois Rivers," *Illinois Archaeology* 5 (1993):119–29.

Tanner, H. H., *Atlas of Great Lakes Indian History*. Norman: University of Oklahoma Press, 1987.

Thomas, C., *Report on the Mound Explorations of the Bureau of Ethnology*. Washington, DC: Bureau of Ethnology, Smithsonian Institution, 1894.

Thomas, D. H., "Why Did Ascribed Social Inequality Develop on St. Catherines Island?," in *Native American Landscapes of St. Catherines Island, Georgia*, ed. D. H. Thomas. New York: American Museum of Natural History, 2008.

Thompson, V. D., "The Rhythms of Space-Time and the Making of Monuments and Places During the Archaic," in *Trend, Tradition, and Turmoil: What Happened to the Southeastern Archaic?*, eds. D. H. Thomas and M. C. Sanger. New York: American Museum of Natural History, 2010.

Thompson, V. D., and J. E. Worth, "Dwellers by the Sea: Native American Adaptations Along the Southern Coasts of Eastern North America," *Journal of Archaeological Research* 19 (2011):51–101.

Thompson, V. D., J. A. Turck, and C. B. DePratter, "Cumulative Actions and the Historical Ecology of Islands along the Georgia Coast," in *The Archaeology and Historical Ecology of Small Scale Economies*, eds. V. D. Thompson and J. C. Waggoner Jr. Gainesville: University Press of Florida, 2013.

Thompson, V. D., *et al.*, "Collective Action, State Building, and the Rise of the Calusa, Southwest Florida, USA," *Journal of Anthropological Archaeology* 51 (2018):28–44.

Thornton, R., *American Indian Holocaust and Survival: A Population History Since 1492*. Norman: University of Oklahoma Press, 1987.
 — "Trends Among American Indians in the United States," in *American Becoming: Racial Trends and their Consequences*, vol. 1, eds. N. J. Smelser, W. J. Wilson and F. Mitchell. Washington, DC: National Academy Press, 2001.

Thwaites, R. G., *The Jesuit Relations and Allied Documents: Travels and Explorations of the Jesuit Missionaries in New France 1610–1791*. 73 vols. Cleveland, OH: Burrows Brothers, 1896–1901.

Toth, A., *Archaeology and Ceramics at the Marksville Site*. Ann Arbor: Museum of Anthropology, University of Michigan, 1974.

Truncer, J., "Steatite Vessel Age and Occurrence in Temperate Eastern North America," *American Antiquity* 69 (2004):487–513.

Ubelaker, D. H., *Reconstruction of Demographic Profiles from Ossuary Skeletal Samples*. Washington, DC: Smithsonian Institution Press, 1974.
 — "North American Indian Population Size, AD 1500 to 1985," *American Journal of Physical Anthropology* 77 (1988):289–94.
 — "Ossuary III from the Juhle Site, Nanjemoy, Maryland: Bioarchaeological Features," in *The Dead Tell Tales: Essays in Honor of Jane E. Buikstra*, eds. M. C. Lozada and B. O'Donnabhain. Los Angeles: Cotsen Institute of Archaeology Press, 2013.

VanDerwarker, A. M., and G. D. Wilson, "War, Food, and Structural Violence in the Mississippian Central Illinois Valley," in *The Archaeology of Food and Warfare*, eds. A. M. VanDerwarker and G. D. Wilson. Cham: Springer, 2016.

VanDerwarker, A. M., C. M. Scarry, and J. M. Eastman, "Menus for Families and Feasts: Household and Community Consumption of Plants at Upper Saratown, North Carolina," in *The Archaeology of Food and Identity*, ed. K. C. Twiss. Carbondale: Center for Archaeological Investigations, Southern Illinois University, 2006.

Van Nest, J., *et al.*, "Sod Blocks in Illinois Hopewell Mounds," *American Antiquity* 66 (2001):633–50.

Varner, J. G., and J. J. Varner (trans. and eds.), *The Florida of the Inca*. Austin: University of Texas Press, 1951.

Vickery, K. D., ""Reluctant" or "Avant-garde" Hopewell?: Suggestions of Middle Woodland Culture Change in East-Central Indiana and South-Central Ohio," in *Hopewell Archaeology*, eds. D. S. Brose and N. Greber. Kent, OH: Kent State University Press, 1979.

Voss, J. A., and J. H. Blitz, "Archaeological Investigations in the Choctaw Homeland," *American Antiquity* 53 (1988):125–45.

Wagner, M. J., *The Windrose Site: An Early Nineteenth-Century Potawatomi Settlement in the Kankakee River Valley of Northeastern Illinois*. Springfield: Illinois State Museum, 2001.
 — *The Rhoads Site: A Historic Kickapoo Village on the Illinois Prairie*. Urbana: Illinois State Archaeological Survey, University of Illinois, 2011.

Walker, R. B., D. F. Morey, and J. H. Relethford, "Early and Mid-Holocene Dogs in Southeastern North America: Examples from Dust Cave," *Southeastern Archaeology* 24 (2005):83–92.

Walthall, J. A., "Hopewell and the Southern Heartland," in *Hopewell Archaeology*, eds. D. S. Brose and N. B. Greber. Kent, OH: Kent State University Press, 1979.

Ward, H. T., and R. P. S. Davis Jr., *Indian Communities on the North Carolina Piedmont AD 1000–1700*. Chapel Hill: Research Laboratories of Anthropology, University of North Carolina, 1993.
 — *Time Before History*. Chapel Hill: University of North Carolina Press, 1999.
 — "Tribes and Traders on the North Carolina Piedmont, AD 1000–1710," in *Societies in Eclipse*, eds. D. S. Brose, C. W. Cowan, and R. C. Mainfort Jr. Washington, DC: Smithsonian Institution Press, 2001.

Warrick, G. A., *Reconstructing Ontario Iroquoian Village Organization*. Ottawa: National Museum of Man, 1984.
 — "The Precontact Iroquoian Occupation of Southern Ontario," *Journal of World Prehistory* 14 (2000):415–46.
 — *A Population History of the Huron-Petun, A.D. 500–1650*. Cambridge: Cambridge University Press, 2008.

Waselkov, G. A., and K. E. H. Braund (eds.), *William Bartram on the Southeastern Indians*. Lincoln: University of Nebraska Press, 1995.

Waters. M. R., "Late Pleistocene Exploration and Settlement of the Americas by Modern Humans," *Science* 365 (2019):eaat5447.

Waters, M. R., *et al.*, "Pre-Clovis projectile points at the Debra L. Friedkin site, Texas – Implications for the late Pleistocene peopling of the Americas," *Science Advances* 3 (2018):eaat4505.

Watson, P. J., "Early Plant Cultivation in the Eastern Woodlands of North America," in *Foraging and Farming: The Evolution of Plant Exploitation*, eds. D. R. Harris and G. C. Hillman. London: Unwin Hyman, 1989.

Weaver, S. A., *et al.*, "Middle Woodland Domestic Architecture and the Issue of Sedentism: Evidence from the Patton Site (33AT990), Hocking Valley, Ohio," *Journal of Ohio Archaeology* 1 (2011):22–37.

Webb, C. H., *The Poverty Point Culture*. Baton Rouge: School of Geoscience, Louisiana State University, 1977.

Webb, S. D., *et al.*, "A *Bison Antiquus* Kill Site, Wacissa River, Jefferson County, Florida," *American Antiquity* 49 (1984):384–92.

Webb, W. S., *An Archaeological Survey of the Wheeler Basin on the Tennessee River in Northern Alabama*. Washington, DC: Bureau of American Ethnology, Smithsonian Institution, 1939.

— *The Wright Mounds*. Lexington: Department of Anthropology, University of Kentucky, 1940.

— *Mt. Horeb Earthworks and the Drake Mound*. Lexington: Department of Anthropology, University of Kentucky, 1941a.

— *The Morgan Stone Mound*. Lexington: Department of Anthropology, University of Kentucky, 1941b.

— *The C. and O. Mounds at Paintsville*. Lexington: Department of Anthropology, University of Kentucky, 1942a.

— *The Robbins Mounds*. Lexington: Department of Anthropology, University of Kentucky, 1942b.

— *The Crigler Mounds and the Hartman Mound*. Lexington: Department of Anthropology, University of Kentucky, 1943a.

— *The Riley Mound and the Landing Mound*. Lexington: Department of Anthropology, University of Kentucky, 1943b.

— *Indian Knoll*. Lexington: Department of Anthropology, University of Kentucky, 1946.

— *The Read Shell Midden*. Lexington: Department of Anthropology, University of Kentucky, 1950.

Webb, W. S., and R. S. Baby, *The Adena People No. 2*. Columbus: Ohio Historical Society, 1957.

Webb, W. S., and D. L. DeJarnette, *An Archeological Survey of Pickwick Basin in the Adjacent Portions of the States of Alabama, Mississippi and Tennessee*. Washington, DC: Bureau of American Ethnology, Smithsonian Institution, 1942.

— *The Flint River Site, Ma°48*. University: Alabama Museum of Natural History, 1948.

Webb, W. S., and W. G. Haag, *Cypress Creek Villages*. Lexington: Department of Anthropology, University of Kentucky, 1940.

Webb, W. S., and C. E. Snow, *The Adena People*. Lexington: Department of Anthropology, University of Kentucky, 1945.

Webster, D., "Late Pleistocene Extinction and Human Predation: A Critical Review," in *Omnivorous Primates*, eds. R. S. O. Harding and G. Teleki. New York: Columbia University Press, 1981.

Welch, P. D., "Outlying Sites Within the Moundville Chiefdom," in *Archaeology of the Moundville Chiefdom*, eds. V. J. Knight Jr. and V. P. Steponaitis. Tuscaloosa: University of Alabama Press, 1998.

Wesler, K. W., *Excavations at Wickliffe Mounds*. Tuscaloosa: University of Alabama Press, 2001.

White, A. J., *et al.*, "An Evaluation of Fecal Stanols as Indicators of Population Change at Cahokia, Illinois," *Journal of Archaeological Science* 93 (2018):19–134.

Wiant, M. D., "Exploring Paleoindian Site Distribution in Illinois," *Illinois Archaeology* 5 (1993):108–18.

Wiant, M. D., K. B. Farnsworth, and E. R. Hajic, "The Archaic Period in the Lower Illinois River Basin," in *Archaic Societies: Diversity and Complexity Across the Midcontinent*, eds. T. E. Emerson, D. L. McElrath, and A. C. Fortier. Albany: State University of New York Press, 2009.

Widmer, R. J., *The Evolution of the Calusa: A Nonagricultural Chiefdom on the Southwest Florida Coast*. Tuscaloosa: University of Alabama Press, 1988.

Williams, S., "Armorel: A Very Late Phase in the Lower Mississippi Valley," *Southeastern Archaeological Conference Bulletin* 22 (1980):105–10.

Williams, S., and J. P. Brain, *Excavations at the Lake George Site, Yazoo County, Mississippi, 1958–1960*. Cambridge, MA: Peabody Museum, Harvard University, 1983.

Williams, T. J., *et al.*, "Evidence of an early projectile point technology in North America at the Gault site, Texas, USA," *Science Advances* 4 (2018):eaar5954.

Williamson, R. F., and D. A. Steiss, "A History of Ontario Iroquoian Multiple Burial Practice," in *Bones of the Ancestors: The Archaeology and Osteobiography of the Moatfield Ossuary*, eds. R. F. Williamson and S. Pfeiffer. Gatineau, QC: Canadian Museum of Civilization, 2003.

Williamson, R. F., *et al.*, "The Archaeology of the Moatfield Ossuary," in *Bones of the Ancestors: The Archaeology and Osteobiography of the Moatfield Ossuary*, eds. R. F. Williamson and S. Pfeiffer. Gatineau, QC: Canadian Museum of Civilization, 2003.

Willoughby, C. C., "The Serpent Mound of Adams County, Ohio," *American Anthropologist* 21 (1919):153–63.

Wilson, G. D., and A. M. VanDerwarker, "The Functional Dimensions of Earth Oven Cooking: An Analysis of an Accidentally Burned Maize Roast at the C. W. Cooper Site in West-Central Illinois," *Journal of Field Archaeology* 40 (2015):166–75.

Wilson, J. J., "Paradox and Promise: Research on the Role of Recent Advances in Paleodemography and Paleoepidemiology to the Study of "Health" in Precolumbian Societies," *American Journal of Physical Anthropology* 155 (2014):268–80.

Winters, H. D., "Some Unusual Grave Goods from a Mississippian Burial Mound," *Indian Notes* 10 (1974):34–46.

Winthrop, J., "The Description, Culture, and Use of Maize," *Royal Society of London Philosophical Transactions*, vol. 12. New York: Johnson and Kraus Reprint Corporations, 1963 [1678].

Worne, H., *et al.*, "The Space of War: Connecting Geophysical Landscapes with Skeletal Evidence of Warfare-Related Trauma," in *The Bioarchaeology of Violence*, eds. D. L. Martin, R. P. Ryan, and V. R. Pérez. Gainesville: University Press of Florida, 2012.

Wright, H. E. Jr., "Patterns of Holocene Climatic Change in the Midwestern United States," *Quaternary Research* 38 (1992):129–34.

Wymer, D. A., "Paleoethnobotany in the Licking River Valley, Ohio: Implications for Understanding Ohio Hopewell," in *Ohio Hopewell Community Organization*, eds. W. S. Dancey and P. J. Pacheco. Kent, OH: Kent State University Press, 1997.

Yu, Z., "Ecosystem Response to Late Glacial and Early Holocene Climate Oscillations in the Great Lakes Region of North America," *Quaternary Science Reviews* 19 (2000):1723–47.

Zurell, R. L., "Earthwork Enclosure Sites in Michigan," in *Retrieving Michigan's Buried Past*, ed. J. R. Halsey. Bloomfield Hills, MI: Cranbrook Institute of Science, 1999.

Sources of Illustrations

1   Out of copyright
2   Drawing T. Murtha
3   Photo G. Milner
4   Courtesy of the Library of Congress
5   Courtesy of the Alabama Museum of Natural History (3Mb5)
6   Photo G. Milner
7   Courtesy of the Ohio History Connection (P396, B1, F4, E8)
8   W. S. Webb Museum of Anthropology, University of Kentucky
9   Photo T. M. Easterly, courtesy of the Missouri Historical Society, St. Louis
10 Courtesy of the Alabama Museum of Natural History (14Je14)
11 Photo G. Milner
12 Photo G. Milner
13 Drawing T. Murtha
14 Courtesy Illinois State Museum, Illinois Legacy Collection, painting: R. Larson
15 Drawing G. Milner after Goodyear 1999: Figure 2b
16 Courtesy of the Illinois State Museum, Illinois Legacy Collection, photograph: R. Graham
17 Drawing G. Milner
18 Courtesy Frank H. McClung Museum, University of Tennessee
19 Courtesy Illinois State Museum, Illinois Legacy Collection (AR985)
20 Out of copyright
21 Drawing M. Lorenz
22 Drawing G. Milner after neg. 3667, W. S. Webb Museum of Anthropology, University of Kentucky
23 Photo John Bigelow Taylor ©/Gilcrease Museum, Tulsa, Oklahoma
24 Drawing G. Milner after Wiant et al. 2009: Figures 9.31, 9.40
25 Pennsylvania Historical & Museum Commission
26 William S. Webb Museum of Anthropology, University of Kentucky (4467)
27 Photo G. Milner
28 Courtesy of the Center for Archaeological Investigations, Southern Illinois University, and R. Jefferies
29 Drawing J. Cooper after photo by R. Jefferies
30 Drawing G. Milner
31 ML Design, after Saunders, J. W. et al. "Watson Brake, A Middle Archaic Mound Complex in Northeast Louisiana," *American Antiquity* 70 (2005), pp. 631–68, fig. 2
32 Photo G. Milner
33 Drawing G. Milner after Penney 1985: Plate 24
34 Louisiana Ancient Mounds Heritage Area and Trails Advisory Commission
35 Louisiana Division of Archaeology
36 Photo M. Schwadron, courtesy of M. Russo and the U.S. National Park Service
37 Courtesy Illinois State Museum, Illinois Legacy Collection
38 Drawing T. Murtha
39 Courtesy of the Ohio History Connection (P396, B1, F1, E3)
40 Out of copyright
41 Drawing S. Hammerstedt after Webb 1942a: Figure 14
42 William S. Webb Museum of Anthropology, University of Kentucky (5622)
43 William S. Webb Museum of Anthropology, University of Kentucky (4699)
44 Drawing J. Cooper
45 Photo G. Milner
46 Photo W. Clarke, courtesy of the Cleveland Museum of Natural History and N. Greber
47 Photo C. Carr and A. Lydecker, courtesy of C. Carr and the Ohio Historical Society
48 Courtesy of the Ohio History Connection (P396, B3, F6, E4)
49 Drawing S. Hammerstedt after Buikstra 1976: Figure 2
50 Photo D. Baston, courtesy the Center for American Archeology
51 Courtesy of the Alabama Museum of Natural History (1Ma49)

52 Courtesy of R. Jefferies and D. Hally
53 Photo G. Milner
54 Courtesy of the Ohio History Connection (P396, B4, F2, E6)
55 Drawing S. Hammerstedt after Webb 1941a: Figures 5 and 11
56 Out of copyright
57 William S. Webb Museum of Anthropology at the University of Kentucky (3190)
58 Out of copyright
59 Photo G. Milner (Field Museum of Natural History, Illinois, 56784, 56797)
60 Field Museum of Natural History, Illinois
61 Photo © The Field Museum of Natural History, Illinois neg. CSA39671
62 Courtesy of the Ohio History Connection (P129, B1, F28)
63 Drawing G. Milner
64 Drawing J. Cooper after Brose 1985: Plate 48
65 Photo G. Milner
66 Drawing J. Cooper after the Ohio History Connection (P396, B6, F1, E7)
67 Photo Dirk Bakker © 1985 The Detroit Institute of Arts/ Permission of the University of Michigan Museum of Anthropology
68 Courtesy of the William S. Webb Museum of Anthropology, University of Kentucky (2092)
69 Courtesy of the Illinois State Archaeological Survey, University of Illinois
70 Wisconsin Historical Society (WHi-2385)
71 Wisconsin Historical Society (WHi-2389)
72 Drawing S. Hammerstedt after Birmingham and Eisenberg 2000: Figure 5.9
73 Drawing S. Hammerstedt after Rolingson 1998: Figure 1
74 With the permission of the Arkansas Archeological Survey (TOL C440/19)
75 Courtesy of the Illinois State Archaeological Survey, University of Illinois
76 Drawing G. Milner after Kelly 1987: Plate 40
77 Drawing T. Murtha
78 Courtesy of the Alabama Museum of Natural History (25Ja180)
79 Photo G. Milner
80 Drawing S. Hammerstedt after Blitz 1993: Figures 11 and 13
81 Courtesy Illinois State Museum, computer image E. Schroeder
82 Photo G. Milner
83 Courtesy of the Library of Congress
84 Drawing S. Hammerstedt after National Museum of Natural History field notes
85 Courtesy of the Oklahoma Archaeological Survey
86 Photo John Bigelow Taylor ©/From the Collections of the National Museum of the American Indian
87 Drawing G. Milner after Lankford 2004: Figure 2
88 Drawing G. Milner after Perino 1971b: Figure 73c
89 Drawing J. Cooper after Brown 1985b: Figure 19
90 Photo G. Milner (Field Museum of Natural History, Illinois, 55500)
91 Photo Dirk Bakker © 1985 The Detroit Institute of Arts/ Courtesy of the University of Alabama Museums
92 Drawing J. Cooper after an Illinois State Archaeological Survey photo
93 Photo G. Milner
94 Photo Dirk Bakker © 1985 The Detroit Institute of Arts/ From the Collections of the Saint Louis Science Center
95 Photo John Bigelow Taylor ©/From the Collections of the Saint Louis Science Center
96 Courtesy of the W. S. Webb Museum of Anthropology, University of Kentucky (7109)
97 Photo G. Milner
98 Drawing G. Milner after an Illinois State Archaeological Survey photo
99 Courtesy of the Center for Archaeological Investigations, Southern Illinois University, and J. Porter
100 Courtesy of the Alabama Museum of Natural History (3896)
101 Courtesy of R. Diehl

102 With the permission of the Arkansas Archeological Survey
103 © Scott W. Hammerstedt
104 © Scott W. Hammerstedt
105 Drawing S. Hammerstedt after O'Brien 2001: Figure 5.8, and Price and Griffin 1979: Figure 12
106 Courtesy of the Illinois State Archaeological Survey, University of Illinois
107 Drawing M. Lorenz after Swanton 1946: Plate 73.1
108 Courtesy Illinois State Museum, Illinois Legacy Collection, photographer: M. Fowler
109 Photo G. Milner
110 Courtesy of the Illinois State Archaeological Survey, University of Illinois
111 Drawing G. Milner (Illinois State Museum specimens)
112 Photo G. Milner (Field Museum of Natural History, Illinois, 50717)
113 Photo G. Milner (Illinois State Museum specimens)
114 © Scott W. Hammerstedt
115 Courtesy of Penn State Field School
116 Courtesy of the W. S. Webb Museum of Anthropology, University of Kentucky (7285)
117 Painting Martin Pate, Newnan, GA, courtesy of the artist and the Southeast Archeological Center, National Park Service
118 Photo G. Milner (Illinois State Archaeological Survey specimen)
119 Photo G. Milner (Matson Museum of Anthropology, Pennsylvania State University, specimen)
120 Drawing G. Milner after Brown 1967: Figure 13c,f
121 Drawing G. Milner after photo courtesy of the Illinois State Museum
122 Wisconsin Historical Society
123 Drawing G. Milner after Santure and Esarey 1990: Figure 10.4
124 Photo D. Snow
125 © Robert Cook
126 Photo D. Snow
127 Drawing G. Milner after N. Meister photograph, courtesy of Logan Museum of Anthropology, Beloit College, Wisconsin, 16725
128 © The Trustees of the British Museum. All rights reserved
129 Drawing G. McKay, courtesy of D. Snow
130 Courtesy of the Arkansas Archeological Survey (PAR-93 946060)
131 Courtesy of Claitor's Publishing Division: Du Pratz, 1972 [1790]: 338
132 Drawing G. Milner after Smith 2000: Plate 2d
133 Drawing G. Milner after D. Snow photograph
134 Pennsylvania Historical & Museum Commission
135 Warren Wilson College Archaeology
136 Warren Wilson College Archaeology
137 Courtesy Illinois State Museum, Illinois Legacy Collection
138 Painting R. Lindeaux, courtesy of the Woolaroc Museum, Bartlesville, Oklahoma

Plate 1   Out of copyright
Plate 2   Photo G. Milner
Plate 3   Photo G. Milner
Plate 4   Out of copyright
Plate 5   Photo © Richard Alexander Cooke III
Plate 6   Photo Dirk Bakker © 1985 The Detroit Institute of Arts/Ohio Historical Society
Plate 7   Photo Dirk Bakker © 1985 The Detroit Institute of Arts/Courtesy of the U.S. National Park Service, Hopewell Culture National Historical Park
Plate 8   From the Collection of the Milwaukee Public Museum, #A50673d. Photograph by John Bigelow Taylor
Plate 9   © The Trustees of the British Museum
Plate 10 Photo G. Milner
Plate 11 Photo John Bigelow Taylor ©/Gilcrease Museum, Tulsa, Oklahoma
Plate 12 Photo G. Milner
Plate 13 National Park Service
Plate 14 Photo Melvin L. Fowler
Plate 15 Photo John Bigelow Taylor ©/From the Collections of the National Museum of the American Indian, Smithsonian Institution
Plate 16 Photo Dirk Bakker © The Detroit Institute of Arts/Catalogue No. 448892, National Museum of the American Indian, Smithsonian Institution
Plate 17 Photo G. Milner
Plate 18 Photo G. Milner
Plate 19 Photo Dirk Bakker © The Detroit Institute of Arts/Georgia Department of Natural Resources, Etowah Indian Mounds State Historic Site
Plate 20 Photo Dirk Bakker © The Detroit Institute of Arts/Ohio Historical Society

Index